Qualitative Nursing Research

To our students

who keep asking questions
until our answers make sense.

Revised Edition

Qualitative Nursing Research

A
Contemporary Dialogue

edited by
Janice M. Morse

SAGE PUBLICATIONS
The International Professional Publishers
Newbury Park   London   New Delhi

For information address:

SAGE Publications, Inc.
2455 Teller Road
Newbury Park, California 91320

SAGE Publications Ltd.
6 Bonhill Street
London EC2A 4PU
United Kingdom

SAGE Publications India Pvt. Ltd.
M-32 Market
Greater Kailash I
New Delhi 110 048 India

Printed in the United States of America

Library of Congress Cataloging-in-Publication Data

Main entry under title:
Qualitative nursing research : a contemporary dialogue / edited by
  Janice M. Morse. — Rev. ed.
    p. cm.
  Newly revised versions of papers from a symposium held in Chicago,
Nov. 16-17, 1987.
  Includes bibliographical references and indexes.
  ISBN 0-8039-4078-5 (c). — ISBN 0-8039-4079-3 (p)
  1. Nursing—Research—Methodology—Congresses. I. Morse, Janice M.
  [DNLM: 1. Nursing Research—methods—congresses. WY 20.5 Q14]
RT81.5.Q34 1991
610.73'072—dc20
DNLM/DLC   90-9165
for Library of Congress   CIP

92 93 94 15 14 13 12 11 10 9 8 7 6 5 4

Sage Production Editor: Diane S. Foster

Contents

Preface

Q: Who's the audience for this book?
A: You and me, for pity's sake.

This book is different. This book was planned as an edited volume in which some of the sticky issues in qualitative research could be "placed on the table," addressed as best the author could (given the stage of development of qualitative methods), argued, and, given a long shot, resolved. In order to achieve this end, leading qualitative methodologists selected their favorite "sticky issue" and prepared a paper on that topic. The papers were circulated, and the group met for a two-day symposium in Chicago, November 16-17, 1987, to discuss these issues. The papers were subsequently revised and appear in this volume. As a consequence, every chapter is a composite of the group's thinking and has passed the test of a rigorous "no holds barred" peer review. Even if the chapters do not provide a solution, at least they contribute to the present debate by clearly delineating many of the problems surrounding qualitative research.

However, this volume in no way attempts to list all the problems that may be encountered in qualitative methods. We recognize that some of the problems (such as the difficulties with getting funded) are very much problems of today, problems that hopefully will be very short-lived. Consequently, this volume does not offer solutions in all cases. We did the best we could, and if popular demand is insistent and loud, we will do it again.

Those who attended the symposium were: phenomenologists Joan Anderson (University of British Columbia), Vangie Bergum (University of Alberta), Sally Hutchinson (University of Florida), and Patricia Munhall (Hunter College); grounded theorists Kathy Knafl

(University of Illinois), Katharyn May (Vanderbilt University), and Phyllis Stern (Dalhousie University); and ethnographers Agnes Aamodt (University of Arizona), Evelyn Barbee (University of Michigan), Joyceen Boyle (Medical College of Georgia), Pam Brink (University of Alberta), Sandra Faux (University of Western Ontario), Juliene Lipson (University of California at San Francisco), Jan Morse (University of Alberta), Judith Strasser (University of Maryland), and Toni Tripp-Reimer (University of Iowa). Jan Morse organized and chaired the sessions. Papers and/or thoughts were contributed by Janet Deatrick (Northwestern University), Peggy Anne Field (University of Alberta), and Marilyn Ray (University of Colorado).

Examples of discussions that took place at the meeting are included as Dialogues between chapters. These dialogues are perhaps the most revealing statements about the evolving nature of qualitative methods. Sometimes there was disagreement, sometimes commiseration, sometimes agreement, and always laughter. The title of the book was suggested by Sally Hutchinson and Patricia Munhall, and when it became clear that our discussions must be considered within the contemporary context, the decision was made to include dialogues from the taped sessions. Being qualitative researchers, we felt our taped transcripts were, unfortunately, more revealing than our scholarly analysis.

This book is not intended for the beginning qualitative researcher but for the advanced graduate student who is beginning to worry about gaps in the basic qualitative books. It is for the qualitative researcher who is struggling daily with these issues, and it is for the reviewer who is unfamiliar with qualitative methods, but who has some very real and important questions to ask. Although the book is written by nurses, the issues discussed in this volume are also important for other disciplines that use qualitative methods, and I hope that we will receive some response from "outside."

                                        Janice M. Morse
                                        University of Alberta

Preface to the Revised Edition

I used to wonder when qualitative research would make it in nursing. I no longer worry about that—qualitative research has made its mark; it's here to stay.

(Agnes Aamodt, personal communication, June, 1990)

The development of qualitative research is accelerating at a breathtaking speed, and we stand in awe and admiration at the quality, the quantity, and the caliber of qualitative researchers in the 1990s. Agnes Aamodt is right: Qualitative research is beginning to make a strong impression on nursing science. Nursing as a science is beginning to appreciate the role, function, and significance of theory. Nursing as a profession has begun to realize that without solid theory, *nursing* theory, the research process is expensive, cumbersome, and often lacking legitimacy for clinicians—the very population for whom the research is intended to serve. And granting agencies are now funding qualitative research, appreciating the power of qualitative research as a different kind of power, as a necessary step in the development of a discipline. The group of enthusiastic contributors to this book who struggled in a symposium to come to terms with—as one reviewer called it—"vexing" problems with difficult concepts, have increased in confidence and developed into investigators with strong research programs. This is not to say that minds have been changed or that we now have newer and better answers to the thorny issues; it is merely that we are getting better at responding to queries now that we have a legitimate place in the world. There is still a lot of work to be done in the development and the refinement of qualitative methods; there is still only a small group of nurse researchers qualified in this area, and there are still mighty problems to be solved using qualitative methods.

However, the work becomes easier when there is funding available to support the research. And as more qualitative research is
published, as more qualitative books are published, the demand for
qualitative research grows. I am delighted that SAGE has supported
and published a second edition of this book. I am indebted to all the
contributors who revised their chapters so willing and quickly and
to Don Wells for his careful editing.

Janice M. Morse
University of Alberta

Dialogue

Is Qualitative Research an End in Itself or the Beginning of a Process?

BRINK: For me, this raises the following question: Do we really want to do the groundwork, the problem-identification level of study, or is the qualitative study the beginning of a research program?

LIPSON: Oh, but it's so much fun to break new ground. To be where no man has dared to tread before!

MORSE: Right! And some one else can take it from there! It's the most important part! The rest is common sense and research technique. Real creativity is so crucial in the first part—it's the part that not everyone can do.

BARBEE: I do believe that. Why can't we have the same privileges as theorists?

MORSE: Yes! And no one expects them to test their own theory!

AAMODT: Well, I have a program, but it stays at the same level. Who said a program could not be a topic, or a method?

BRINK: That's right, by golly!—this is what our introductory chapter should say: This is what we are about, and why shouldn't other people take it from there!

1

Qualitative Nursing Research:
A Free-For-All?

JANICE M. MORSE

The burgeoning interest in qualitative research methods delineates a most exciting and significant period for nursing research, but not one without growing pains. The rapid increase in the use of qualitative methods began at a time when minimal reference materials written for nursing were available, and even at this time, there is still a great need for written guidelines. In 1985, the first three qualitative books were published (Field & Morse, 1985; Leininger, 1985a; Parse, Coyne, & Smith, 1985), and in 1986, another qualitative book appeared (Munhall & Oiler, 1986) as well as a book on grounded theory (Chenitz & Swanson, 1986). Discussions on particular aspects of qualitative methods are becoming increasingly commonplace in nursing journals (see for example, the *Western Journal of Nursing Research, 10* (2), 1988). Nevertheless, qualitative research methods are suffering from a lack of protocols and are becoming increasingly unstructured.

Qualitative methods came into nursing through nurses who, while participating in the Nurse Scientist Program, obtained their doctorate in other fields, such as, anthropology. When these scientists returned to nursing, they continued to conduct research using the methods of their adopted discipline. For example, nurse-anthropologists continued to use anthropological methods, such as, ethnography, and they incorporated these research methods into their teaching. Grounded theory was developed at the University of California at San Francisco, and nurses who were students of or collaborators with Glaser and Strauss continue to use this method. Phenomenological methods were also introduced as nurses took courses in other departments with such leaders in phenomenology as Giorgi (University of Pittsburgh) and van Manen (University of Alberta).

The first issue that arises from this interdisciplinary transfer of qualitative methods in the application of these methods for examining nursing phenomena. As these research methods were designed for use in other situations, with other disciplinary assumptions, paradigms, and goals, could these methods be used in nursing without modification?

The second important question relates to the methods themselves. One must consider if these methods are simply techniques of data collection and analysis—that is, the tools of researchers—or if they must be used within the context of their discipline's theoretical assumptions and perspectives.

An increasing number of researchers are "self-taught" in qualitative methods, learning from texts or by trial and error. As a result, qualitative methods have become increasingly diverse as they are adapted to meet the needs of a particular situation or, perhaps, the personal style of the investigator. Such adaption and mixing of methods was described in an article by Swanson Kauffman (1986):

> The methodology evolved as I and my study progressed. It is a somewhat unique blending of phenomenological, grounded theory, and ethnographic methodologies. The combined qualitative strategy described is offered as a nurse-appropriate methodology that fits our unique phenomena of discernment, namely, persons, environments, health and nursing. (p. 59)

Such mixing, while certainly "do-able," violates the assumption of data collection techniques and methods of analysis of all the methods used. The product is not good science; the product is a sloppy mishmash. If the goal of a study is phenomenological, then clearly, phenomenological methods must be used if the goal is to be attained. As ethnoscience methods of data collection have been developed to elicit a particular kind of structured data, and grounded theory methods of analysis have been developed to answer yet another type of question, any mixing or adapting of these methods runs the risk of producing other than the desired results. If methods are developed, changed, or blended, this should be done by the experienced researcher and not the neophyte.

This conceptual confusion extends beyond the methods to the nomenclature used when describing methods. For example, phenomenology may be used to refer to a philosophical stance or to the research method. However, some authors are using phenomenology as an equivalent term for qualitative research.

Another serious problem is the quantification of qualitative data. Stern (this volume) addresses this problem using a recent example from an article published in *Nursing Research*. This article details a study in which Bliss-Holtz (1988) measures the length of text in transcribed interviews to calculate the interviewees' "desire to learn infant care." Such measurement is absurd. Apart from the technical threats to validity (e.g., justification of the right margin artificially alters spacing between the characters, especially if hyphenation is not used in the transcript, and one may ask if the same font or type-style was used in all transcriptions), the author did not identify a linguistic or psychological theory to give credence to the assumption that the number of phrases a subject uses to express interest is indicative of "a desire to learn" a particular topic. The tendency to quantify qualitative data is becoming one of the major threats to qualitative methods as such techniques do not make qualitative methods more rigorous.

The last area of concern is the use of qualitative methods to test theory. This area is less clear-cut than the previous criticisms as the confirmation stage for testing emerging hypotheses and seeking negative cases is inherent in the process of grounded theory. This concern is focused on the use of qualitative data to test theory (for example, see Parse, Coyne, & Smith, 1985). Parse tested her own theory of man-living-health by conducting content analysis of 400 participants' statements defining health. These statements were not derived according to the phenomenological method of using in-depth conversations, but were written definitions. The process of writing itself would have decreased the amount of descriptive material available compared with that obtained orally. Nevertheless, the major problem is that Parse's results are presented on four tables, each with descriptive expressions pertaining to common elements of her theory, each with three columns, and each column with 10 lines (pp. 31-33). These results are surprisingly neat—much tidier than one would expect to be derived from the natural world. The strength of qualitative methods is in the process of induction; the data "emerge" to provide the theory, not the reverse. Qualitative data cannot be categorized to fit into a framework. A more appropriate way for Parse to test her theory (given she knew all the components a priori and was seeking confirmation) would be to use a quantitative technique, such as a Likert scale, correlating the resulting attitude scores of the respondents with reported age.

From these five major methodological concerns, new questions arise. If nursing phenomena are different from phenomena or questions in other disciplines in which the qualitative methods originated *and* the methods must be adapted for use in nursing, who is responsible for this task, and is the process of modification a matter of trial and error, debated in the literature? Or is it a planned risk? Should qualitative methods be rigorously prescriptive, as are quantitative methods, or loosely described in order to give the investigators the freedom to develop their own style?

These questions were loudly debated during the symposium on qualitative research methods held in Chicago, November 16-17, 1987, and there was both agreement and disagreement among participants. There was agreement that nursing problems and situations for which nurses use qualitative methods generally differ from the situations and contexts found in the disciplines in which they were developed. For example, in traditional ethnography, the unit of analysis may be a village, and the anthropologist would move into the village and live among the people to collect data. Generally, in nursing, the unit of ethnography is a health care unit, a hospital unit or ward (e.g., Germain, 1979), or a support group of patients with a particular problem (e.g., Lipson, 1980, 1982). Even if a village unit is used, nurse-ethnographers tend to focus on topics of interest to nursing, such as, Aamodt's (1981) work on neighboring, Boyle's (this volume) study on adolescent mothering, or Strasser's (this volume) focus on health. Although some research in applied anthropology, such as the work by McClain (1987), is more focused and resembles the methods being used in nursing, anthropologists would traditionally describe the culture as a *whole*. Consequently, the question is: Do these types of ethnography need to be differentiated?

Although Leininger (1985b, pp. 34-36) has suggested the terms "maxi" ethnography and "mini" ethnography, there was some dissatisfaction expressed with these terms at the symposium. The participants felt that "mini" has a connotation of "meager" or "less than," giving the false impression that the mini ethnography is less significant than a traditional anthropological ethnography. It was suggested that the holistic, anthropological ethnography be referred to as *traditional ethnography* and the nursing, topic-oriented ethnography be referred to as *focused ethnography,* but this issue is not yet resolved.

Another difficulty identified is that qualitative researchers do legitimate qualitative research for which, as yet, there is no name. For example, many researchers are conducting unstructured, open-ended interviews (or semi structured interviews) with patients who share a common experience or problem, such as, patients following a heart attack. The interviews may be conducted with patients at various stages of recovery (i.e., cross-sectionally) or over time (i.e., longitudinally). Data are analyzed using content analysis. There is no label for this type of research, except to clumsily refer to it as "unstructured, open-ended interviews and content analysis" or "semi structured interviews." *Interactive interview* was suggested as a term to describe the interviewing process or dialogue in which the researcher uses probes and explores concepts, tape records the interview, and then transcribes the tape verbatim. It was noted that participant observation was not a part of this method, and as this is an essential component of ethnography, this research approach could not be considered ethnography.

Even among the experts, there appear to be contradictions. In this volume, Brink promotes procedures for enhancing reliability and validity, such as, training interviewers in order to achieve consistency, using multiple coders, and establishing inter-rater reliability; Stern and May argue for diversity, stating that the variation enhances the richness of the data. Questions must still be resolved about the appropriateness of various approaches to rigor. I am suggesting that the methods of establishing reliability and validity are closely associated with the research purpose. If the purpose is descriptive, then ethnography is the appropriate method, and within limits, replicability is an issue. Therefore, consistency and methods to obtain reliability and validity as described by Brink are appropriate and essential. However, if the purpose of the research is interpretative, as in phenomenology or grounded theory, the aim for consistency of interviewers or the establishment of inter-rater reliability is antithetical to the purpose of a study that is dependent upon the creative insights of the investigator (see Stern, this volume). In this case other methods are used to ensure that the data are valid; in phenomenology, the analysis is given back to the participants (Bergum, this volume); in grounded theory, the researcher uses another sample to "check out" hunches or seeks exceptions (i.e., negative cases) to elicit variation and to expand the developing theory. Another technique is to examine the "fit" of the findings to the results of other studies—the "emergent fit"—and if there are commonalities with the other theory, then credence is added to the present investigations. Although discussion at the symposium about theoretical generalizability and the stability of theory over time added insights into the power of knowledge gained from qualitative research, more work needs to be done in this area.

Levels of Qualitative Research

There is a common assumption that qualitative nursing research is the foundation of a research project, the first stage in a series of projects. It is the step in which the validity of subsequent studies rests—and is, therefore, crucial. With the validity issue, there was consensus; however, considerable concern was expressed about the assumption that qualitative methods must always be followed by quantitative methods before the research is "finished." Two aspects of this approach were criticized.

First, a qualitative research project should be considered as a study complete in itself. This is rarely recognized by granting agencies, who consider that the value of the qualitative study is to identify variables or the theoretical framework on which a quantitative study will then be based. This attitude devalues the contribution of the qualitative component to a pilot project (Brink, this volume), for which funding is difficult to obtain and for which the amount of work contributed by the investigator and the value of the scientific insights gained remain unrecognized. Perhaps this is one of the reasons why qualitative studies are more difficult to get published.

The second aspect is the desirability for investigators to develop a research program in which investigation of a particular topic builds from inductive to deductive theory-testing and that the projects be continued by the same investigator. This attitude assumes that all researchers are experts with all types of designs, can readily flip from inductive to deductive modes of conceptualizing, and are not "specialists" in particular types of research methods. The result is that investigators who are trained in quantitative inquiry may abuse qualitative methods (see May, this volume), using sloppy techniques or violating assumptions under the misconception that qualitative methods do not require special training. The most important quality for researchers in qualitative research is their creative ability, the ability to be perceptive and to think abstractly. Albert Szent-Gyorgy is attributed with saying, if one accepts that "research is to see what everybody has seen and to think what nobody has thought," then it may be that the ability to do qualitative research is a gift, something that cannot be taught, and something that may be learned without instruction. I feel rather uncomfortable when I read excellent ethnographical analyses of cultural rules written by non researchers. One such example is Garrison Keillor's (1985, pp. 131-132) description (which he attributes to Gaylord Gibbon) of porch behavior in the Midwest—where did he receive his qualitative training? Nevertheless, it was the consensus of this group that researchers should not be pressured into using research methods or continuing investigation beyond the level of their expertise, interest, or the point where they feel their contribution is the greatest. The development of theory using qualitative methods must be considered as legitimate a role for nurse-researchers as is the role of nurse-theorists or those engaging in philosophical inquiry, and it must be supported, nurtured, and applauded. Qualitative researchers must be left to "do their own thing," however marginal that may initially appear, for this is one area in nursing where the true breakthrough will be made and new directions identified. This is what we are about.

The Potential Contribution of Qualitative Inquiry

The impression given that the results of qualitative inquiry are not fully utilized is intentional. Thus far, some of the advantages have been listed: The results of qualitative inquiry may provide the theoretical framework or identify variables, hypotheses, or theory to be tested in subsequent research. But this is only the beginning.

Another significant purpose of qualitative research is that qualitative inquiry may challenge the status quo and may identify new paradigms or directions of inquiry. Used alone, qualitative research may provide answers or insights into difficult questions so obvious that subsequent research—the testing—is not necessary. Qualitative research in this category may be clinically applicable, that is, the findings may be immediately incorporated into practice. Such an example is Hutchinson's (1984) investigation of the turnover rate of staff in a neonatal ICU. The ability of the nurses to cope with the everyday work—the horror of infants dying—determined the nurses' "satisfaction with the work." Coping was the ability of the nurses to "make meaning" of the situation. Another example is a study on the "social coercion for weaning" (Morse & Harrison, 1987), in which it is argued that the duration of breastfeeding is not the mother's choice. In prolonged breastfeeding, significant others coerce the mother to wean by withdrawing their support and then actually encouraging weaning "when the infant is perceived to be old enough to be weaned." Thus the role of a *doula* (i.e., the primary support person for the breastfeeding mother) includes facilitating weaning or the assisting with the severance of the breastfeeding relationship. If the goal of health professionals is to increase the duration of breastfeeding, then the clinical "solution" to this problem is to provide information on breastfeeding to the mother's entire social support group rather than teaching just the mother.

Finally, qualitative methods provide rich descriptions of what it is like to be sick or, for example, suffering with cancer, pain, or altered body image; what it is like to be a patient; and what it is like to have a baby or to breastfeed. When teaching nursing to young students, we are presently teaching psychosocial skills out of context. That is, we are teaching appropriate responses to sadness, anger, uncertainty, and how to have an empathetic attitude in a stimulus-response mode. Perhaps that is necessary, for the nurse who feels too much for her patient may burn out quickly. But it appears that there is a need to provide some context as some nursing programs have added fictitious (or semi-fictitious?) literature, such as, Lear's *Heartsounds* (1980), to their reading lists. This reading could and should be replaced with solid qualitative studies. For instance, consider how much more a nurse, new to pediatric oncology, would understand about her patients if she were required to read "Discovering the child's view of alopecia" (Aamodt, 1986), or a nurse in her maternity rotation, if she could read "Ear on the belly" (Kelpin, 1985). Qualitative nursing research will have come of age when it is required reading for students in undergraduate clinical courses.

It is an exciting time to be involved with and using qualitative research methods. Qualitative research is going through the changes of adolescence—profound changes that are sometimes painful but never boring. Qualitative research is reaching maturity rapidly, and perhaps, in a few years, it will have "come of age." This book is certainly a step in that direction.

References

Aamodt, A. M. (1981). Neighboring: Discovering support systems among Norwegian-American women. In D. A. Messerschmidt (Ed.). *Anthropologists at home in North America: Methods and issues in the study of one's own society* (pp. 133-149). New York: Cambridge University Press.

Aamodt, A. M. (1986). Discovering the child's view of alopecia: Doing ethnography. In P. Munhall & C. Oiler (Eds.). *Nursing research: A qualitative perspective* (pp. 163-171). Norwalk, CT: Appleton-Century-Crofts.

Bliss-Holtz, V. J. (1988). Primiparas' prenatal concern for learning infant care. *Nursing Research, 37* (1), 20-24.

Chenitz, W. C., & Swanson, J. M. (1986). *From practice to grounded theory: Qualitative research in nursing.* Menlo Park, CA: Addison-Wesley.

Field, P. A., & Morse, J. M. (1985). *Nursing research: The application of qualitative approaches.* London: Croom Helm.

Germain, C. (1979). *The cancer unit: An ethnography.* Wakefield, MA: Nursing Resources.

Hutchinson, S. (1984). Creating meaning out of horror. *Nursing Outlook, 32* (2), 86-90.

Keillor, G. (1985). *Lake Wobegon days.* New York: Viking.

Kelpin, V. (1985). *Ear on the belly: A question of fetal monitors.* Edmonton, Alta: Department of Secondary Education, Faculty of Education.

Lear, M. W. (1980). *Heartsounds.* New York: Simon & Schuster.

Leininger, M. (Ed.). (1985a). *Qualitative research methods in nursing.* Orlando, FL: Grune & Stratton.

Leininger, M. (1985b). Ethnography and ethnonursing: Models and modes of qualitative data analysis. In M. Leininger (Ed.). *Qualitative research methods in nursing* (pp. 33-71). Orlando, FL: Grune & Stratton.

Lipson, J. G. (1980). Consumer activism in two women's self-help groups. *Western Journal of Nursing Research, 2* (1), 393-405.

Lipson, J. G. (1982). Effects of a support group on the emotional impact of caesarean childbirth. *Prevention in Human Services, 1* (3), 17-29.

McClain, C. S. (1987). Some social network differences between women choosing home and hospital birth. *Human Organizations, 46* (2), 146-152.

Morse, J. M., & Harrison, M. J. (1987). Social coercion for weaning. *Journal of Nurse-Midwifery, 32* (4), 205-210.

Munhall, P. L., & Oiler, C. J. (1986). *Nursing research: A qualitative perspective.* Norwalk, CT: Appleton-Century-Crofts.

Parse, R. , Coyne, A. B., & Smith, M. J. (1985). *Nursing research: Qualitative methods.* Bowie, MD: Brady Communications Company.

Swanson-Kauffman, K. M. (1986). A combined qualitative methodology for nursing research. *Advances in Nursing Science, 8* (3), 58-69.

Dialogue

On Bracketing

BERGUM: I was talking to a phenomenologist friend and told him I was writing a paper on the "use of self," and he said, "Well, that's interesting. Heidigger has just written on 'use' and 'utilization'." And he said, "You should think about that in terms of 'self' What is the difference between utilization and use, and how do you see that!"

My understanding of self is not an instrumental one but, just to give a frame for my understanding, is that we come, in phenomenology, as who we are. One of the problems I have with phenomenology and self is the use of bracketing.

BOYLE: How does one discriminate and know when to use self and when to bracket?

BERGUM: I think it is the thoughtfulness and the awareness that one enters setting with—a sense of questioning—so there is a self-questioning about the nature of one's involvement.

STERN: That's not unique to phenomenology. I think all of these methods are very important to nursing as we don't separate ourselves from whom we are working with.

MUNHALL: Then what is the difference? Is it the level of intimacy? Is it the one-to-one? I think phenomenology is more intimate.

HUTCHINSON: I think there is always an identification that is more fundamental and more ego-focused. More focused on empathy in phenomenology, where it can, but may not be, in the other methods.

LIPSON: That's right! It can be in the other methods, but not in the same amount of intensity, to the same amount of time, or depth, or anything else. . . .

BERGUM: Is it valid to use self?

MUNHALL: Is it valid *not* to use self? When Joan said that those people would have reacted to her differently if she had been in a tweed suit, it's almost as though our subjects need to bracket—because they may have given her different information. They had presuppositions that they may not have given up.

LIPSON: And it is up to the self to sort that out!

MORSE: Can you do phenomenology without the "self"?

OTHERS: No.

TRIPP-REIMER: I think you can if you take a non-Western position. All of Western science is ego-focused, even when we are doing qualitative, or when we are doing quantitative. Qualitative analysis has very little difference from quantitative from this perspective, because as soon as you start looking for themes and categories in qualitative research, you have objectified the subjects, and that's no different than looking for statistical means. You take two similar experiences, and you "average" them, and that's your description or interpretation!

BERGUM: The question is whether or not personal experience helps or hinders one's being in the situation.

KNAFL: I have a real hard time getting a handle on it. On one hand, one is bracketing, and on the other, one is using the self.

LIPSON: Aha! That's the trick! We're grappling with where you do this! Do you do this in the data-gathering? You do this in the analysis? You do this in the write-up? Where do you do it? But you do it everywhere, from the very beginning to the very end! And I enjoyed your paper, Vangie, because I could see that struggle going on. I have been trying to express that struggle, but in different kinds of ways. It's a paradoxical struggle—to both keep yourself in there and out at the same time. I don't know if it's a back-and-forth or a dual concept, but it goes on all the time. And I'm still struggling with it.

MAY: Someone said that bracketing means rendering the known biases problematic, but that assumes considerable self-knowledge.

ANDERSON: How then do you go about preparing yourself for an interview? Students talk a lot about that. One told me that she actually meditates before, that cleanses her mind, puts everything aside so that she is more receptive and open to what is going on.

TRIPP-REIMER: I think the tough question is that if we go into it "ego-less," can we do any more than transcribe their autobiography? I mean, that's one end of the spectrum.

2

The Phenomenological Perspective

JOAN M. ANDERSON

In a paper, entitled "What is phenomenology?", Merleau-Ponty (1967) notes, "It may seem strange that this question has still to be asked half a century after the first works of Husserl. The fact remains that it has by no means been answered" (p. 356). The question raised by Merleau-Ponty in 1967 is as relevant now as it was then. Not only are we still grappling with the question, "What is phenomenology?", but we also are still examining basic issues that pertain to the use of phenomenology as a method of inquiry. Omery (1983) notes that phenomenology as a method for research has grown "out of a philosophical movement that is still in the process of being clarified. As a result, one can find multiple interpretations and modifications of phenomenological philosophy" (p. 50).

The last few decades have seen a proliferation of perspectives, especially in the field of sociology, which all come under the rubric of "phenomenological research." John O'Neill (1985) suggests that phenomenological sociology may be seen as "a covering description for several theory groups which at their own level differ with respect to particular theoretical issues and empirical research strategies but nevertheless share a respect for philosophical, i.e., phenomenological reflection upon the practice of sociology" (p. 748). Anthony Giddens (1976) points out that "to speak of 'phenomenology' is not to speak of a single, unified body of thought" (p. 24). The issue, however, is that while there might be tensions and conflicts in the varying perspectives, there are also commonalities, which will be discussed later in this chapter.

Phenomenology and Nursing Research

"Qualitative" research methodologies made their appearance in nursing in the 1960s, but it was not until the 1970s that the phenomenological approach started to gain cautious acceptance (see, for example, Davis, 1973, 1978). Some nurse researchers saw the scientific method as constraining and, therefore, looked to phenomenology as a way of investigating questions concerned with the lived experience of patients and their families. Davis (1978) argues that "phenomenology provides a more perfect fit conceptually with the functions of clinical nursing and with many of the research questions that evolve from clinical practice" (p. 187).

The 1980s have seen an upsurge in the use of the phenomenological approach in nursing research (e.g., Anderson 1981a, 1981b; Munhall & Oiler 1986; Oiler, 1982; Omery 1983; Watson 1985). The need to clarify issues pertaining to phenomenology's philosophical underpinnings and methodological directives has become more acute as nurse-researchers have started to examine phenomenology as a method and have begun to discuss ways of combining different paradigms in nursing research (see, for example, Goodwin & Goodwin, 1984; Jick, 1979; Mitchell, 1986; Tinkle & Beaton, 1983). The movement to combine different methodological approaches represents a vigorous attempt to build a science of nursing, but it can be argued that in some instances discussions revolve around "qualitative" versus "quantitative" methods and seem solely related to issues of method, without clarifying the epistemological issues that are at the very heart of the matter. Although the phenomenological tradition is a diversified one, phenomenology is nonetheless a distinctive philosophy, theory, and method for studying the world of everyday life. As such, it should be differentiated from what has come to be known more generally as "qualitative" or "descriptive"research. From the standpoint of phenomenology, we are forced to examine certain questions about the social production of knowledge which may not be germane to other "qualitative methods."

In this chapter, I will argue that phenomenology represents a drastic shift from the intellectual perspective of the positivist tradition, as exemplified in the empirical natural science approach, and will contrast the epistemological underpinnings of phenomenology with empirical natural science. Also, I will argue that the issues

being raised in research at the present time must ask how knowledge is constructed and must examine the epistemic claims nurse-
researchers make. From this examination, a question emerges: "Given
the epistemological issues, should we attempt to blend different
methods in one study?" I will attempt to make explicit the underlying
assumptions of both the natural science and the phenomenological
perspective in order to examine this question.

Some of the methodological issues associated with phenomenological research will also be examined, bringing to light the nagging
questions that remain unanswered. The attempt to wed "qualitative
methods" to "quantitative methods" appears to be a current trend in
nursing research, but before such a marriage can take place, nurse-
researchers must come to terms with some basic philosophical and
methodological issues in phenomenological research. What seems
to be needed at this time is greater conceptual clarity and a commitment to develop a more rigorous method for doing phenomenology.
In the long run, this might yield a rigorous science of nursing.

Natural Science Perspective

Much of social science and nursing research has been influenced
by the basic premises of the natural sciences. In fact, the development of mainstream sociology closely adhered to the premises of
empirical natural science. In *The Rules of Sociological Method* (1964),
for example, Durkheim proposed that the methods of natural science
(as these were understood in the late nineteenth and early twentieth
centuries) were also applicable in the social field.

Some key assumptions about the social world underscore the
perspective derived from the natural sciences. It is held that there
are "objective social facts," which are logically separate from the
values of the researcher and are capable of being described and
investigated in a wholly neutral way. From the standpoint of empirical theory, social reality exists in the fact of the social structure and
is independent of the experiences of individual members of society.
The "facts," so to speak, are "out there" in the "real world" and can
be studied objectively (Skinner, 1978; Smith, 1983).

Skinner notes that another central feature of the mainstream outlook is an account of the logic of explanation. All explanations are

held to be deductive. It is also assumed that the real business of science, as Bernstein (1976) points out, is:

> the collection of data and the advancing of empirical generalizations based on it . . . It is also frequently believed that when and if we collect enough data and discover correlations that hold among these data, then we will be in a position to arrive at those higher empirical generalizations that constitute genuine science. (p. 10)

A key notion that has dominated social science research is that the observer is separate from the observed. What we "see" and how we describe phenomena should be untainted by our own subjective interpretations. The objective of the researcher should be to discover the facts as they really are. This same set of assumptions about research has been very much a part of the development of nursing research, and it was not until the 1960s that these assumptions were challenged. The restructuring of social theory in the 1960s had an impact on the restructuring of nursing research. In tracing the historical development of phenomenology, it becomes apparent that this perspective was a response to the objectivism that determined the study of social phenomena.

The Phenomenological Approach

The name of Edmund Husserl has been most frequently associated with phenomenology. Phenomenology has become known to English-speaking scholars through the writings of people like Alfred Schutz (1964, 1967, 1973), Merleau-Ponty (1962, 1964), Paul Ricoeur (1973), and Richard Zaner (1970). Of these writers, it is Alfred Schutz who has become most noted for using phenomenology to understand sociological problems.

Central assumptions rooted in philosophical soil underlie the phenomenological approach. These assumptions have important implications for the way we view the production of knowledge. Schutz (1973, pp. 3-66) lays special emphasis on the ways in which the social world is a domain of typifications. In any situation, individuals bring a "stock of knowledge" that allows them to typify one another and to sustain communication.

Natanson (1970) points out that we see the conception of typification at work in the example of *intersubjectivity*. He argues that all of us have an anatomy of rules and relationships, which any given individual must follow: "For the individual to find his way in the social world he must come to appreciate the order of its typical procedures and the typified manner in which those procedures are to be followed" (p. 4).

The problem of *intersubjectivity* is at the heart of phenomenological theory and methodology. As Natanson points out, "[the] 'raw givenness' [of everyday life] and [the] subjective interpretation are . . . inevitable partners in philosophical analysis; to deny either and cut it off from consideration is to commit an epistemic atrocity" (p. 6).

Making sense of the world and creating "meaning" are socially constructed and must be understood within typificatory schemes embedded within the social context and the system of relevances rooted in the biographical context that each person brings to the situation. "Meaning" is constructed in ongoing relations between people; it is constructed through a dialectical process in everyday interaction. As Schutz (1967) notes, "Every act of mine through which I endow the world with meaning refers back to some meaning-endowing act . . . of yours with respect to the same world. *Meaning is thus constituted as an intersubjective phenomenon*" [italics added] (p. 32).

This perspective is in contrast with the empirical natural science perspective, which sees social facts as *located in the social structure,* independent of the interpretive schemes of societal members. From the perspective of phenomenology, the world is not just waiting to be discovered; the "facts" cannot be taken for granted; it is the task of the social scientist to explicate how meanings in everyday life are constituted and maintained. Giddens (1976) observes that:

> the difference between society and nature is that nature is not man-made, is not produced *by* man. Human beings, of course, transform nature, and such transformation is both the condition of social existence and a driving force of cultural development. But nature is not a human

production; society is. While not made by any single person, society is created and recreated afresh, if not *ex nihilo*, by the participants in every social encounter. *The production of society* is a skilled performance, sustained and "made to happen" by human beings. (p. 15)

This quotation from Giddens raises important issues about the nature of human actors in society and posits a particular "image of person" embedded in phenomenological theory, which is in contrast with the image of person espoused by the empiricists. The phenomenological/interpretative perspectives have in common a view of the human individual as a skilled actor. This is referred to as the "existential view" or the manifest image of person. The manifest image is concerned with the human individual who acts intentionally in the world and who can guide his or her actions with reference to principles and actions. This view of man/woman implies an indispensable core of conceptual equipment. Man/woman has conscious feelings, ideas, and impulses (Berstein, 1976; Giddens, 1976; Mehan & Wood, 1975).

This perspective orients to the "gestalt"—it addresses human subjectivity and intersubjectivity. Those who subscribe to the manifest image argue that science has taken the world of everyday life as a given and has not explicated the fundamental structures that underlie scientific reasoning. They argue that there is more to human beings than even the complete scientific account represents.

Some scholars argue that competing images of man/woman in the world have important implications for the sciences of human life. If we are convinced that man/woman is nothing but a complex physical system, then we look to science as the only proper means for explaining how the system works. But if we are not convinced about the scientific view, and if we see the human individual as more than a complex system, then we must explore other approaches to help us understand what human beings are (Berstein, 1976; Mehan & Wood, 1975). We could argue, as Clifford Geertz (1973) has argued, that the study of man/woman in the world and the analysis of them can "be therefore not an experimental science in search of law but an interpretive one in search of meaning" (p. 5). This debate raises primary questions about the nature of human beings, what constitutes knowledge, how this knowledge is produced, and what is and what ought to be the relation of theory to practice (Berstein, 1976).

Epistemological Issues:
Differences Between the Natural Science
and Phenomenological Perspectives

The main point that has been made in the discussion thus far is that phenomenology is not just another method for collecting data but that it represents a shift from empirical natural science. Given the epistemological foundations of this methodology, fundamental questions about the social production of knowledge cannot be sidestepped. I will, therefore, attempt to highlight the conceptual issues that have to be resolved if one wishes to combine methodologies underpinned by different epistemologies.

Nurse-researchers must recognize that each perspective has a different view of man/woman in the world. While this might seem like a philosophical issue, it has major implications for the research enterprise as, from the outset, the researcher is faced with reconciling a reductionist approach with a holistic orientation to the study of the individual. That is, the empirical tradition orients us to the investigation of predetermined "variables" that relate to human experience. Mehan and Wood (1975) point out that "the determinist tradition maintains that meanings are dictated to people by the world. Empirical social scientists within the determinist tradition treat meanings as 'facts'. . . . These researchs deny that interpretations constantly alter the world" (p. 370).

The phenomenological tradition, on the other hand, maintains that meaning is contextually constructed as an intersubjective phenomenon. Human beings create meaning in interaction with one another. Given the different views of man/woman in the world, it stands to reason that different questions will be asked, which will require the use of different methodological approaches.

Not only do these two perspectives reflect different images of the human individual, they also have different notions about the relationship of the investigator to what is being investigated (Smith, 1983). From the natural science perspective, reality exists independent of us. Smith notes that this idea stands behind subject-object dualism:

According to the realist perspective, [synonymous with the natural science perspective] knowledge and truth are questions of correspondence—what is true is what corresponds to reality . . . the activity of investigation does not affect what is being investigated. Idealism, in contrast, [synonymous with phenomenology] argues that what exists is mind-dependent. The subject and the object, perceived by realists as two elements, become one to idealists, who perceive no reality inde- pendent of the shaping or creating efforts of the mind. To idealists the relationship of investigation to subject can be more accurately de- scribed as subject-subject rather than subject-object; *what is investi- gated is not independent of the process of investigation. . . what is to count as knowledge or to be considered true is a matter of agreement within a socially and historically bound context* [italics added]. (p.8)

This quotation points to the fundamental difference in the way knowledge is seen to be constructed. Smith (1983) argues that "whether one takes an idealist position or a realist position will influence how the research process is conceived and actually con- ducted. . . . Accordingly, in the realist view an investigation is di- rected toward an external referent; whereas in the idealist view the process must be internal, a part of the investigator's active participa- tion in shaping the world" (p.9). He goes on to argue that the basic feature of the realist epistemology is that it espouses a correspon- dence theory of truth; truth has its source in reality. From the idealist position, the concept of correspondence is unacceptable. No exter- nal referent exists against which various claims to truth can be weighed. Contradictory notions of truth are seen as different ways of constituting reality based on different social and historical condi- tions. Agreement is reached not through an external referent but through a process of justification that is inescapably bound up with values and interests (pp. 9-11).

Given that the natural science and the phenomenological perspec- tives are grounded in competing epistemologies, one wonders if these perspectives can be reconciled. Or do they give researchers different ways for viewing the world, which in turn will determine the kinds of questions that are asked? It is not a simple matter of picking a method once one has stated a research question; the questions asked are enmeshed within a web of the researcher's own personal meanings and reflect the ways in which the researcher views the world. It would seem that, at the present time, instead of trying to find ways to combine different paradigms in nursing re- search, the energies of nurse-researchers could be more profitably spent on addressing some of the nagging questions about the actual doing of phenomenological research.

Issues in Doing Phenomenological Research

Several versions of phenomenological research have been documented in the literature. In fact, O'Neill (1985) associates areas like reflexive sociology, ethnomethodology, and conversational analysis with phenomenology. While the inclusion of these varied perspectives under the umbrella of phenomenology might appear problematic for those who seek a unified approach, this is not the issue to be addressed here. Instead, more fundamental matters are critical to nursing research and, therefore, warrant discussion and clarification.

Throughout Schutz's writings the researcher is reminded that the task of the social scientist qua scientist is to bring to explicit clarity the structures of the life-world. While this may seem a straightforward programmatic instruction for doing research, several questions arise. For example, Bernstein (1976) asks:

> What precisely are the nature and status of these structures? This question becomes acute when our chief concern is not the solitary ego but the social world. . . . More serious, there is a failure to distinguish clearly those structures which are presumably fixed, permanent, and a priori from those which have specific historical roots and causes. In understanding social reality we want to understand not only the permanent a priori structures, if there are any, but also those changing features and structures that characterize different societies and periods. (p. 159)

Bernstein's comments merit consideration as they bring to the foreground issues that plague the actual conduct of research. How, in fact, does one identify a structure when one is confronted with actual data? Are there given structures? Although the literature is replete with how to do phenomenology, several philosophical and methodological questions need to be examined, especially the question of how knowledge is constructed.

It might be argued that the question is not "What precisely are the nature and status of structures?", but given that meaning is intersubjectively constructed, the question might be "*Whose* structures are being described?" It is not as if the researcher is describing structures that are *out there and are independent of the researcher and informant*. To assume this would be contradictory to the basic assumptions underlying the phenomenological approach. In fact, what needs to be made explicit is that the structures described are those that one creates and imposes on the world—these structures are embedded in the system of relevances to the researcher; what gets *produced* as knowledge results from the dialectical process between researcher and informant. In other words, the researcher is not describing an objective state of affairs. In response to Bernstein's question, it could be argued that at any point in time and in any given context society is interpreted through the researcher's cognitive structures. Yet the researcher has to come to terms with the duality of self and world. The critical task of the phenomenologist, as Natanson notes, is to reconcile the "raw givenness" with subjective interpretation.

Further to this, there is another point that needs to be commented on. Schutz (1973) notes that:

> The thought objects constructed by the social scientists refer to and are founded upon the thought objects constructed by the common-sense thought of man living his everyday life among his fellow-men. Thus, the constructs used by the social scientist are, so to speak, constructs of the second degree, namely constructs of the constructs made by the actors on the social scene, whose behavior the scientist observes and tries to explain in accordance with the procedural rules of his science. (p. 6)

This quotation implies that, while on the one hand *meaning is intersubjectively constructed,* the constructs of the social scientist are *second order constructs.* This position embodies a fundamental contradiction. Does this mean that social scientists transform the structures of everyday life into the language of their scientific discipline? If this is the case, then there is a tendency toward reification and objectification.

In fact, this problem of objectification and reification seems to plague phenomenological description. A convincing argument might be made that intersubjective construction of meaning could be seen only to take place in those instances when both informant and researcher are involved in documenting an event. Perhaps the problem is not that researchers, of necessity, must impose a structure on the data, but that it is often unclear to the reader *that these are the researcher's structures.*

One should bear in mind that the purpose of phenomenology is to describe the lived experience of people. Methods of data analysis that fragment the lived experience may distort that which it seeks to describe. Furthermore, the documentation of that experience should be done in such a way that it is true to the lives of the people described.

Pointing to these difficulties does not mean that contemporary practicing phenomenologists have not grappled with them. Instead, they are presented to serve as a reminder that, within the phenomenological tradition, methodological issues and contradictions still need to be worked out. Many practicing phenomenologists have come to grips with the fact that life has indefiniteness, which is problematic for researcher and informant alike. The science that is produced, if it is to be reflective of everyday experiences, must, in fact, take into account this indefiniteness. This will always mean that any given phenomenon can be viewed in different ways—the issue is always the *relevance scheme* that one takes to the situation. There are always alternate explanations, and all explanations can be challenged. In other words, there is no knowledge that offers a full explanation of the world. However, the onus is always on researchers to make explicit their interpretative schemes.

One further criticism has been leveled at phenomenology. It has been argued that phenomenology fails to take into account the historical and macro social structures that shape human experience and, in fact, focuses solely on the micro processes of interaction. Although Bernstein (1976), like other critics, sees the need for this kind of analysis, it should be noted that practicing phenomenologists are not oblivious to the historical and sociopolitical contexts and the ways in which an individual's experiences are located within these structures. In fact, many phenomenologists are trying to reconcile the micro and macro levels of analysis. Smith's writings (1975, 1977, 1979, 1981) have exemplified how phenomenological analysis can be combined with a Marxist analysis. My own writings (Anderson, 1985, 1986, 1987; Anderson & Lynam, 1987), attempt to show how individual experiences of illness must be understood within the sociopolitical and historical context.

Several issues still have to be addressed if the researcher is to achieve the most rigorous phenomenology that is possible. The most pressing issues do not pertain to the reconciliation of different epistemologies. They are based in the actual doing of phenomenology.

Conclusion

In this chapter, the central tenets that underlie both the natural science and phenomenological perspectives have been discussed, and the issues that need to be taken into account if the researcher is to consider reconciling these approaches have been pointed out. However, before making further attempts to develop a paradigm for nursing research that would accommodate divergent epistemologies, nurse-researchers should consider the purpose for doing phenomenological research. It should be recognized that the intent of this method is not to build grand theories of nursing but to understand the lived experience of people (e.g., what it means to be a patient or to be a nurse). Thus it may be dangerous to reconcile epistemological differences that, at their very foundations, cannot be reconciled. Perhaps the key issue here is that nursing needs to value the merits of different perspectives and recognize what each has to offer.

References

Anderson, J. M. (1981a). The exploration of two distinctive research paradigms and the implications for research training. *Proceedings of the International Conference. "Research—A Base for the Future?* (pp. 127-134). Edinburgh: University of Edinburgh Press.

Anderson, J. M. (1981b). An interpretive approach to clinical nursing research. *Nursing Papers, 13,*(4), 6-12.

Anderson, J. M. (1985). Perspectives on the health of immigrant women: A feminist analysis. *Advances in Nursing Science, 8*(1), 61-76.

Anderson, J. M. (1986). Ethnicity and illness experience: Ideological structures and the health care delivery system. *Social Science and Medicine, 22*(11), 1277-1283.

Anderson, J. M. (1987). Migration and health: Perspectives on immigrant women. *Sociology of Health and Illness: A Journal of Medical Sociology, 9*(4), 410-438.

Anderson, J. M., & Lynam, M. J. (1987). The meaning of work for immigrant women in the lower echelons of the Canadian labour force. *Canadian Ethnic Studies, 19*(2), 67-90.

Bernstein, R. J. (1976). *The restructuring of social and political theory.* Philadelphia: University of Pennsylvania Press.

Davis, A. (1973). The phenomenological approach in nursing research. In E. Garrison (Ed.). *Doctoral preparation for nurses*. San Francisco: University of California.

Davis, A. (1978). The phenomenological approach in nursing research. In N. Chaska (Ed.). *The nursing profession: Views through the mist* (pp. 186-197). New York: McGraw Hill.

Durkheim, E. (1964). *The rules of sociological method* (8th ed.). New York: Free Press.

Geertz, C. (1973). *The interpretation of cultures*. New York: Basic Books.

Giddens, A. (1976). *New rules of sociological method: A positive critique of interpretative sociologies*. London: Hutchinson.

Goodwin, L. D., & Goodwin, W. L. (1984). Qualitative vs. quantitative research or qualitative and quantitative research? *Nursing Research, 33*(6), 378-380.

Jick, T. D. (1979). Mixing qualitative and quantitative methods: Triangulation in action. *Administrative Science Quarterly, 24*, 602-611.

Mehan, H., & Wood, H. (1975). An image of man for ethnomethodology. *Philosophy of the Social Sciences, 5*, 365-376.

Merleau-Ponty, M. (1962). *Phenomenology of perception*. London: Routledge & Kegan Paul.

Merleau-Ponty, M. (1964). *The primacy of perception, and other essays on phenomenological psychology*. Evanston, IL: Northwestern University Press.

Merleau-Ponty, M. (1967). What is phenomenology? In J. J. Kockelmans (Ed.). *Phenomenology: The philosophy of Edmund Husserl and its interpretation* (pp. 356-374). New York: Doubleday.

Mitchell, E. S. (1986). Multiple triangulation: A methodology for nursing science. *Advances in Nursing Science, 8*(3), 18-26.

Munhall, P., & Oiler, C. J. (Eds.). (1986). *Nursing research: A qualitative perspective*. Norwalk, CT: Appleton-Century-Crofts.

Natanson, M. (1970). Phenomenology and typification: A study in the philosophy of Alfred Schutz. *Social Research, 37*(1), 1-22.

Oiler, C. (1982). The phenomenological approach in nursing research. *Nursing Research, 31*(3), 178-181.

Omery, A. (1983). Phenomenology: A method for nursing research. *Advances in Nursing Science, 5*(2), 49-63.

O'Neill, J. (1985). Phenomenological sociology. *The Canadian Review of Sociology and Anthropology, 22*(5), 748-770.

Ricoeur, P. (1973). Hermeneutic method and reflective philosophy. In R. Zaner & D. Ihde (Eds.). *Phenomenology and existentialism* (pp. 333-349). New York: Capricorn Books.

Schutz, A. (1964). *Collected papers II: Studies in social theory*. The Hague: Martinus Nijhoff.

Schutz, A. (1967). *The phenomenology of the social world*. Northwestern University Press.

Schutz, A. (1973). *Collected papers I: The problem of social reality*. The Hague: Martinus Nijhoff.

Skinner, Q. (1978). The flight from positivism. *New York Review of Books, 25*(10), 26-28.

Smith, D. (1975). An analysis of ideological structures and how women are excluded: Considerations for academic women. *Canadian Review of Sociology and Anthropology, 12*(4), 353-369.

Smith, D. (1977). *Feminism and marxism: A place to begin, a way to go.* Vancouver: New Stars Books.

Smith, D. (1979). A sociology for women. In J. A. Sherman & E. T. Beck (Eds.). *The prism of sex: Essays in the sociology of knowledge* (pp. 135-187). Madison: The University of Wisconsin Press.

Smith, D. (1981, January). *The experienced world as problematic: A feminist method.* The Twelfth Annual Sorokin Lecture, University of Saskatchewan.

Smith, J. K. (1983). Quantitative versus qualitative research: An attempt to clarify the issue. *Educational Researcher, 12*(3), 6-13.

Tinkle, M., & Beaton, J. L. (1983). Toward a new view of science: Implications for nursing research. *Advances in Nursing Science, 5*(2), 27-36.

Watson, J. (1985). *Nursing: Human science and human care. A theory of nursing.* Norwalk, CT: Appleton-Century-Crofts.

Zaner, R. (1970). *The way of phenomenology: Criticism as a philosophical discipline.* New York: Pegasus.

Dialogue

On Developing Theory Inductively

KNAFL: Agnes, I am really intrigued about your comment of incorporating results of ethnographic studies like this into nursing theory. What are your fantasies along that line?

AAMODT: From my point of view, some of the existing theories have never come into a systematic form that students can use. The care concept is the one that I think of most of the time, and more of that needs to be incorporated into nursing theories, more of the client's view needs to come in. I do the culture of childhood stuff, and it is clear that kids have something different to say about care and caretaking, or about the world in general, that we really have ignored.

HUTCHINSON: But you know what might be interesting in response to Kathy's question is Chenitz and Swanson's (1986, pp. 24-38) concept of "surfacing nursing process," where they talk about taking grounded theory and making practice theories. Do you think you could take ethnography and use it to guide practice?

AAMODT: Yes, sure.

KNAFL: That's right. Most of what we do should be incorporated into the major conceptual frameworks.

AAMODT: But it won't be me that does it. Someone in the future, maybe 20, 40 years from now.

3

Ethnography and Epistemology: Generating Nursing Knowledge

AGNES M. AAMODT

> The stream of consciousness which we all experience has its
> foundations in abstract conceptual models of the world.
>
> (D'Andrade, 1976, p. 155)

The conceptual models of the world held by human beings can be discovered by observing patterns of meanings in communication used during individual reflection on and social interaction with the objects and events in one's environment. How can knowledge for nursing be generated from the patterns of meanings associated with objects and events in health care experiences? Such is the frame of human inquiry used by clinical nurse-researchers who seek to understand variations in the human condition, at times of birth, health, illness, and death. Science assumes that human meaning-making powers are intrinsic to any research focusing on human society. Science also assumes that by analyzing observed social behavior, using formal and informal interviews and conversations when humans feel lousy, when they hurt, when they do not feel, or when they seek a quality human experience, labels for human meanings and patterns can be created that provide culturally relevant domains of language. Clinical nurse-researchers use this ethnographic paradigm to uncover such culturally relevant domains of meaning. Such labels then can be used in the generation of nursing theory to understand and explain the meanings of quality experience during illness and health.

This chapter addresses questions of method and substance in ethnographic research useful in the generation of nursing knowledge by discussing: (a) What is the essence and sense of ethnography? (b) What kinds of ethnographic data can be useful in nursing research? (c) What characterizes the science of knowing, that is, the epistemology of ethnography in clinical nursing research? (d) Of what value is ethnography for practice theory in nursing? Seven years ago I published a paper that examined ethnography for nurse-researchers (Aamodt, 1982). This chapter is a further exploration of the complexities surrounding the use of ethnography for clinical nurse-researchers.

The Essence and Sense of Ethnography

Ethnography is a way of collecting, describing, and analyzing the ways in which human beings categorize the meaning of their world. In other words, ethnography attempts to learn what knowledge people use to interpret experience and mold their behavior within the context of their culturally constituted environment.

In the broadest sense, ethnography is both a craft and an art (Werner & Schoepfle, 1987). Participation in the everyday lives of the people within specific cultural systems, informal conversations, formal interviews, and writing-up the study portray a sense of what novice ethnographers learn about in their early work. Taxonomic structures (Spradley, 1979, 1980) ask for direction from the apprentice. The discipline of cognitive ethnoscience gives reason for naming and linking units of meaning. However, resolving the ambiguities in meanings experienced during long-term field work cannot be accomplished without exploring a world beyond the technology of ethnoscience (Werner & Schoepfle, 1987). Thus the real meaning of what is being portrayed is a lifelong endeavor.

My experiences as an ethnographer began early. Assisting with household tasks often accompanied my mental gymnastics during my teenage years. As I traveled and visited among aunts, grandparents, cousins, and in my own home, I shared in organizing the world we lived in, for example, washing clothes, putting away groceries, and doing other family chores. In retrospect, I am impressed with the diversity in the various categories we used as we washed sheets, pillow cases, black, brown, and yellow socks, diapers, and dishtowels and hung them on the line to dry. Aunt Inga did it one way and, 60 miles away, Aunt Marie did it another. I remember being aware of a skill that belongs to many nurses today, that is, anticipating what the rules are going to be. And I am certain I was not alone—I just do not remember talking to anyone about it. The specialized language and specialized rules in each household and family became a fascination.

Now as I look back as an ethnographer and anthropologist, I know that our ways of categorizing in the midwestern United States were not much different from the ways of human beings in Ali Chuck, on the Tohono O'odham Indian Reservation, in Kristianson, Norway, or in Tucson, Arizona. In a simple way, we can say each cultural system consists of categories of classifying and interpreting experience and generating social behavior. Members of a society learn the rules for appropriate behavior and how to interpret the behavior and events they observe. I still remember that, although anything could go any place in Aunt Marie's refrigerator, the clothes line was another matter, and diapers were not pinned to the same line with towels used for drying dishes.

Today I immerse myself in the texts of my observations and the answers to ethnographic questions of Norwegian-American women and children with cancer. As I struggle to abstract the sense of the linguistic expressions with meaning in a cultural system, I am reminded and impressed by the complexities of the spontaneous thought that led me to my understanding of the similarities and differences of the patterning of those household chores. The scenes were the same, the objects and roles essentially the same, but after a time with Aunt Marie, the categories and the rules made sharing in the chores in Aunt Inga's house a brilliantly different experience. Similarly, today I can view the thought processes and behavior of nurse-researchers, nurse-theorists, practicing nurses, and clients in any and all health care settings and generate a view of the assortment of rules that inform our behavior as we all pursue health, illness, and healing in our personal and professional worlds.

Capturing a sense of the rules for culturally constituted behavior is an adventure that begins with a recognition of settings or social scenes. For example, the settings for caretaking behaviors among children in a day care center take shape with the observation of backrubbing, crackers being offered, or by hearing someone say "I'll help!" From the child's view, the cultural meaning of the motion in rubbing a back, skin contact, doing something for another, or giving food to another all require a system of analysis different from that used by naturalistic observers of behavior, such as ethologists Morris (1967) or Barker and Wright (1955).

Sometimes, such a beginning originates in a chance remark or a passing glance at a social scene in a researcher's personal or professional everyday world. Sometimes a choice is made because of an idea deeply embedded in the mind of the researcher. Of course, the idea will pervade the research whether the researcher wills it or not. Conceptualization of patterning and care are examples of ideas that persist. The work of Leininger (1984), Watson (1987), Newman (1986), Patterson and Zderad (1976/1988), and Rogers (1970) illustrate, for me, the persistence of an idea within one's work.

Another example in nursing is the patterning in human responses. A two-year-old child becomes whiny, flushed in the face, nares flare, retractions or recessions occur at the neck and chest when she breathes, and she refuses to drink fluids. Her parents have watched and worried for several weeks. The nearest nurse or physician is 50 miles away; a medicine lady is next door, and medicine men are available in the village. Nurse-ethnographers may be interested in the subtle details in the social interaction that transpires. Being present as a participant observer introduces a fieldworker to the linguistic expressions that convey the meaning of the objects and events: the three-cornered scarf placed on the child's head, the somber face of the father as he approaches his daughter, the special glass used to tickle the fancy of the sick one. Later the nurse-ethnographer-fieldworker can use formal protocols to elicit information from informants about how care organizes human experience within the culturally constituted environment of the mother, father, and child. Culturally relevant domains of meaning emerge and are written about. Such is the work of an ethnographer.

Then the ethnographer asks, "What don't I have?": patterning of body movement among family members; physiological responses during fear, anger, or passion; metaphors representing the multi-worlds of thinking in human experience, conscious and unconscious; and the multiple cognitive systems operating in the researcher during fieldwork. Thus, with a different set of tools, a different focus of interest (besides care) a different set of scientific assumptions will emerge, and the same scene will construct a different set of principles and meanings for use in understanding the health experience of families.

What Kinds of Ethnographic Data
Can Be Useful in Nursing

Modern nursing learns from the greater world what is useful for the thought-world of nursing scientists. *The Wonder of Being Human* (Eccles & Robinson, 1985), *Women's Ways of Knowing* (Belenky, Clinchy, Goldberger, & Tarule, 1986), and *Perceiving Ordinary Magic* (Hayward, 1984) are book titles reflecting some of the ideas that are helping all of us to "pop a quiff" or skip from one paradigm to another. Humanism, expanding consciousness, subjective involvement, discovery, and patterning are becoming useful conceptualizations as we move along in our present phase of clinical nursing research.

Unlike grounded theory a la Glaser (1978), unlike naturalistic inquiry from the work of Barker and Wright (1955), and unlike phenomenology emerging from the existentialists (Heidegger, 1962), ethnography is grounded in the culture concept and seeks to understand the native's (or human carrier's) view of a cultural system. The language of ethnographers includes, among other terms, cultural scenes, culturally relevant domains of meaning, researcher-informant experiences, and cultural themes. Thus what ethnographers see and seek to know is similar to that of any clinical researcher of the qualitative persuasion, and yet, it is different. The purpose of this chapter is to show how ethnography fits into a social context, generating nursing knowledge. The method is similar to a kind of semantic ethnography, a term I prefer to ethnoscience. Embedded in "semantic ethnography" are meanings associated with language and the philosophical position of knowledge generation when humanism and science meet. Nonetheless, in this chapter the term "ethnography" refers to all forms of anthropological fieldwork grounded in the culture concept.

Two assumptions provide a useful beginning for understanding ethnography: (a) culture is viewed as a system of knowledge used by human beings to interpret experience and generate behavior (Spradley, 1979, 1980), and (b) linguistic expressions used by informants during social interactions are the structural blocks of meaning for constructing systems of cultural knowledge. What people do, say they do, and say they want to do provide beginning ethnographic information to clinical nurse-researchers. Various strategies have been developed for constructing questions, abstracting answers from the informant or the observer of cultural scenes, and transforming data to a different level of abstraction. Abstracting language from its social context requires an understanding of the patterning emerging in the whole of the ethnographic record. Transforming the data requires an understanding of the relational terms that bind together the culturally relevant domains or data.

As illustration, consider the work we are doing at the University of Arizona. My research program is grounded in the question, "What characteristics of care promote human responses for quality human experience?" Other studies using an ethnographic format include: "The child's view of chemically induced alopecia" (Aamodt, Grassl-Herwehe, Farrell, & Hutter, 1984), "The child's view of a pediatric oncology clinic" (Porter, Aamodt, Farrell, & Hutter, 1983), ""The child's view of care during chemo-therapy" (Aamodt, 1984), "Neighboring: Discovering support systems among Norwegian-American women" (Aamodt, 1981), and most recently, "The male view of care during and following an acute illness and/or a major stress experience" (Aamodt, 1987). The focus is always to uncover diversity in conceptualizations of care.

The research question for each study focuses on cultural knowledge, for example, "What cultural knowledge about care informs the behavior of a child during and following chemotherapy?" Thus by "cultural knowledge informs," an empirical world is framed to ensure systematic analysis: Cultural knowledge allows a focus on care conceptualizations of children of a healing scene where children are known to feel fatigued, dizzy, and nauseous (in other words, "lousy").

An ethnographer then proceeds to: (a) observe in the cultural scene identified in the question, (b) develop beginning ethnographic questions, (c) gather linguistic samples from actors in the social scene of study, (d) identify culturally relevant domains of meaning, (e) develop structural questions, and (f) elicit structure for a taxonomy of domains of meaning. These steps represent a beginning protocol for an ethnographer. Spradley (1979, 1980) has written in detail on this format. The reader is advised to study his work as well as the work of others who explicate the many complexities in the goals of ethnographers (Agar, 1982; Basso & Selby, 1976; McCall & Simmons, 1969; Werner & Schoepfle, 1987).

Observing the cultural scene of children experiencing chemotherapy, and what happens to them following chemotherapy, might include thinking about it before coming to clinic, watching the nurse, watching the needle go in, and waiting for the terrible feeling. From these observations, beginning ethnographic questions can be developed. For example, "Tell me about a time when you didn't feel good?" has been extracted from the observational record and, in question form, can decode the child informant, as follows:

1. Tell me about a time when you didn't feel good?
2. Tell me about what you did for yourself?
3. Tell me about what others did?

The next step elicits more specific linguistic expressions from the answers of beginning ethnographic questions. The objective is to help the child informant to talk about "not feeling good," using nonanalytical but complex reports on how they see their experience and how they talk to other children about it. An example of how a seven-year-old boy felt after "chemo" is reflected in the following quotation: "Well, yesterday I had the medicine for my cancer and before I left for home my head started to hurt and I got dizzy and the nurse came and put me on a bed and mother held my head and my hand, that's all . . . ." (Boy 7 Yrs., 2 Mo.)

Developing structural questions is usually accomplished at this time and provides a beginning order for getting to the minute details of the data. The objective is to obtain thick description. Questions that assist in developing lists of "things you like to have," "kinds of feelings," and "what people did for you" are illustrated here:

1. Tell me about the things you like to have when you're dizzy?
2. What other kinds of feelings do you have besides a hurting head and dizziness?
3. What else did people do for you besides putting you to bed and holding your hand?

A single set of terms can be ordered to show a beginning analysis of a domain of meaning. The intent in this discussion is not to explain the complexities of taxonomies and differences among domains of meaning but rather to show some of what might be anticipated as one is listening and observing a child. For example, "things I like when I feel dizzy" are outlined below. This list might come from one child or several children. Given the idea of the culture of childhood, "drinking a little water" or "laying quietly in bed" may be two culturally appropriate ways to behave when one is dizzy:

Things I like when I feel dizzy:
hear a familiar tune
drink some water
have someone near
lay quietly in bed
have complete silence

A second structural feature of ethnographies is cultural themes (Opler, 1945; Spradley, 1980). Cultural themes are patterns of recurring messages that represent the organizing principles in the cultural system under study. Whereas taxonomies are the natives' view of the parts of a cultural system, approximated as closely as the researcher can, the cultural themes are the researcher's view of the whole of the cultural system. According to Opler's view, a cultural system has multiple cultural themes. For example, in the child's cultural system of the cancer clinic experience (Porter et al., 1983), we found "Be good don't mess 'em up," "We wait and wait for docs, needles, feeling bad, and things like that," and "Treat me normal; treat me special."

"Be good don't mess 'em up" tells how children expect to help out the caregivers and exert self-control in the face of pain. "We wait and wait for docs, needles, feeling bad, and things like that" emphasizes waiting. We know only a little about the meaning of "waiting" at this time, but it is a time for focusing on the object of the wait and a time of fantasy, curiosity, and creativity. In "treat me normal; treat me special" (Aamodt et al., 1984) children seem to be saying: "I am the same as I always was, but I am different. Treat me carefully, I am still a real person. It helps when I seem to be normal to you."

A final structural feature of ethnography is an analysis of the researcher-informant experience. Ethnographic research in today's world exploits rather than avoids the contributions of the researcher in the research setting. Reflexivity conceptualizes, in part, who the researchers are, what is going on in themselves, and how a sense of self-consciousness can be put to analytic use in an ethnographic context. In other words, reflexivity focuses on what characterizes the immersion of the ethnographer in the setting, for example, the stress of the observer, fatigue, being "stranger" and "friend" at one and the same time, and ease of adaption to the socialization experience. A researcher-informant experience can be recorded and used in various ways, but assuredly, a log or diary is crucial, pictures are helpful, and comments/letters/reports to family, friends, and colleagues provide an added dimension to the definition of reality in the ethnographic data. An example of a recording is as follows:

> Johnny (age six years) turned away from me as I walked into the house. His mother reported he had been feeling bad and the only one he liked around him was his father, who was now at work. As I left the house after a conversation with Johnny's mother, I reflected on how was I going to get data from this child or anyone. . . . (A.A. 1/4/88)

What Characterizes the Epistemology of Ethnography in Clinical Nursing Research?

When a project has been completed, when we have enough "thick description" (Geertz, 1973), what knowledge is true, or at best useful, for nursing? In other words, what is the correspondence of what we find to reality? Ethnography is one among many of the methods whereby clinical nurse-researchers can generate images of what is "fact," "value," "truth," or "knowledge." In a sense, knowledge is a social achievement. The meanings from ethnography that have "made it" in the written and oral communication systems of nursing are knowledge. Some of the principles guiding ethnography in the generation of knowledge are units of analysis, cultural context, aggregation of data, transformation of data from one level of analyses to another, and applicability of data in the context of research, theory, and practice.

Units of analysis for ethnography are often linguistic expressions or domains of meaning understandable in scholarly communication. Human meaning-making powers expressed in domains of meaning are fundamental to the study of health and healing behavior of individuals and communities. An example is the linguistics expression "working on acceptance" (Berg, 1979), a domain different from the traditional domains of "acceptance" or "nonacceptance." This kind of discovery has allowed nurse-researchers to focus on a process oriented domain constructed from two opposing domains. The label "working on acceptance" changes our language and, in a sense, allows us to think in a different way when trying to understand other human beings.

The cultural context of domains of meaning or cultural themes contributes to the meaning of the domain in the way a genetic system contributes to the meaning of one or more genes within that system. Thus the cultural theme, "the pits of dependency is not being able to scratch yourself when you itch" (Porter, Aamodt, Pergrin, & Prosser, 1981), makes different sense to nurses when placed in the context of their care of the elderly than it does to the elderly who are thinking of care for themselves. For the nurse, the meaning for understanding care for another brings to mind a wide range of interpretations of what may be appropriate, from sympathy to playfulness. For the patient, the message may reflect a context of "take care of me now" to "I want to do it on my own."

The aggregation of data from multiple informants is dependent upon the balance the ethnographer is able to maintain between the assertions they wish to emphasize and how the linkages strike them at the moment. Time in the field and immersion in the data assist in setting the stage for domains and themes to emerge in the mind of the researcher. Understanding the various modes of awareness in human beings assists the researcher in constructing and representing the reality of the people being studied using ethnographic data. In other words, fieldwork is both an art and a craft, and interpretation can take a lifetime (Werner & Schoepfle, 1987, p. 16).

Transformation of data from one level of analysis to another requires a similar sense of awareness and an intuitive sense of the whole of the data as well as the context in which the abstractions will probably be placed. For example, as a category for theory, "working on acceptance" would hardly have been relevant at a time when process was not as popular as it is in today's scientific world.

Thus the epistemology of ethnography is characterized by a different set of assumptions than traditionally oriented clinical nursing research, which is characterized by operational definitions, variables, reductionism, and sampling. Rather, the basic frame for deciding which observations can be judged to be knowledge are formed by the cultural context, the relationship between what people do and say they do, and the influence of the researcher on the knowledge generated. "More or less" and "better or worse," epithets for traditional scientific analysis, have little place in ethnography. Rather, the purpose of ethnography is to understand the relationship between time and space in human experience. In nursing research, the concern is for understanding human experiences associated with human health.

Value of Ethnography
for Practice Theory in Nursing

The usefulness of ethnography for the practice of nursing can be found at several levels. One level is in the real world of nursing practice, and another level is the world of nursing theory. For the ethnographer, the stream of consciousness, as reported by informants about a given social scene, portrays the cultural system of care (if that is the object of study) that is organizing the informants' experience. Such information, translated into a report for the nursing community, provides a map, if not a master plan, for recognizing and evaluating the needs of individuals and groups of individuals and putting into play strategies for quality human experience.

Although cultural knowledge is not a predictor of what will occur or what has occurred, it is an indicator of what can be anticipated to occur. Thus ethnography provides us with an increasingly wide range of possibilities for understanding health behavior and problem-solving among providers and recipients of care. A practicing nurse, using the data associated with the previously mentioned domain, "Things I like when I feel dizzy," will not be surprised by anything a child might ask for or respond to if the member terms are inclusive of everything relevant to a child in such a cultural scene.

However, a different set of principles is necessary for the practicing nurse who chooses ethnographic data rather than cause/effect data. The nurse who uses ethnographic data must place what is viewed as knowledge back into the cultural context of the given social scene, balance the meanings of the objects and events (as well as the physiological and psychosocial responses of the moment) and

the history and potentiality for the future of the meanings. A decision is made with the client (as individual, family, or community)
concerning what assumptions are true. For example, of the alternatives available in "Things I like when I'm dizzy," "complete silence"
and "to be told a funny story" are two possibilities. However, one
precludes or excludes the other. Thus ethnographic data gives the
nurse the structure of a domain, of what is possible, but it in no way
suggests even a probablistic prediction for an absolute outcome. The
humanness of nurses as they apply cultural knowledge in a client-
centered arena is grounded in judgment, insight, and sensitivity.
Thus the researcher-informant experiences in collection and analysis
of data are replicated in part in the application of data (Chenitz &
Swanson, 1986). Culturally constituted human meanings are incorporated into the perceptions of the practicing nurse.

The world of nursing theory is dependent upon the generation of
primitive concepts or constructs from the ideas permeating interaction among human beings. The tools of ethnography provide a
way of capturing these human meanings in a language system useful
for health providers. Theory is composed of substantive terms and
relational terms. The cultural diversity in human health behavior
provides a complex frontier for discovering all kinds of variations,
which can lead to theory generation.

"Working on acceptance," "be good don't mess 'em up," and "the
pits of dependency is not being able to scratch yourself when you
itch" represent domains of meaning suggestive of care, self-care, and
human response. What else might we say of these long phrases? We
need to continue to think about them and others and generate
conceptual structures for what we truly value in nursing practice.

Summary

This chapter has addressed some of the complexities in the use of
ethnography in generating nursing knowledge. A major goal of
ethnography is the translation of the human meaning-making powers of individuals, families, and communities as they confront birth,
health, illness, and death and convert these meanings to make
scholarly sense. Subsequently guidelines can be provided for practicing care providers in intensive care units, rural communities,
emergency rooms on ski slopes, nursing clinics, and for medicine

men and medicine women. The context of a culturally constituted environment provides the meaning and makes ethnographic knowledge different from every other form of knowledge generated in clinical nursing research.

References

Aamodt, A. M. (1981). Neighboring: Discovering support systems among Norwegian-American women. In D. Messerschmidt (Ed.). *Anthropologists at home in North America: Methods and issues in the study of one's own society* (pp. 133-149). New York: Cambridge University Press.

Aamodt, A. M. (1982). Examining ethnography for nurse researchers. *Western Journal of Nursing Research, 4*(2), 209-221.

Aamodt, A. M. (1984). *The child's view of care during chemotherapy.* Unpublished manuscript.

Aamodt, A. M. (1987). *The male view of care during or following an acute illness and/or a major stress experience.* Unpublished manuscript.

Aamodt, A. M., Grassl-Herwehe, S., Farrell, F., & Hutter, J. (1984). The child's view of chemically induced alopecia. In M. Leininger (Ed.). *Care: The essence of nursing and health* (pp. 217-231). Thorofare, NJ: Charles B. Slack.

Agar, M. (1982). Toward an ethnographic language. *American Anthropologist, 84*(4), 779-795.

Barker, R. G., & Wright, H. F. (1955). *Midwest and its children.* Evanston, IL: Row, Peterson.

Basso, K. H., & Selby, H. A. (1976). *Meanings in anthropology.* Albuquerque: University of New Mexico Press.

Belenky, M. F., Clinchy, B. M., Goldberger, N. R., & Tarule, J. M. (1986). *Women's ways of knowing.* New York: Basic Books.

Berg, C. (1979). *Clinical-nurse encounter in ambulatory health care settings.* Unpublished manuscript.

Chenitz, W. C., & Swanson, J. M. (1986a). *From practice to grounded theory: Qualitative research in nursing.* Menlo Park, CA: Addison-Wesley.

Chenitz, W. C., & Swanson, J. M. (1986b). Surfacing nursing process: A method for generating nursing theory from practice. In W. C. Chenitz & J. M. Swanson (Eds.). *From practice to grounded theory* (pp. 24-38). Menlo Park, CA: Addison-Wesley.

D'Andrade, R. G. (1976). A propositional analysis of U.S. American beliefs about illness. In K. H. Basso & H. A. Selby (Eds.). *Meanings in anthropology* (pp. 155-180). Albuquerque: University of New Mexico Press.

Eccles, J., & Robinson, D. N. (1985). *The wonder of being human.* Boston, MA: Shambhala Publications.

Geertz, C. (1973). *The interpretations of cultures: Selected essays.* New York: Basic Books.

Glaser, B. G. (1978). *Theoretical sensitivity.* Mill Valley, CA: The Sociology Press.

Hayward, J. W. (1984). *Perceiving ordinary magic.* Boston, MA: Shambhala Publications.

Heidegger, M. (1962). *Being and time* (7th ed.). New York: Harper and Row.

Leininger, M. M. (1984). *Care: The essence of nursing and health.* Thorofare, NJ: Charles B. Slack.

McCall, G., & Simmons, J. (1969). *Issues in participant observations: A text and reader.* Reading, MA: Addison-Wesley.

Morris, O. (1967). *Primate ethology.* Garden City, NY: Doubleday.

Newman, M. (1986). *Health as expanding consciousness.* St. Louis, MO: Mosby.

Opler, M. E. (1945). Themes as dynamic forces in culture. *The American Journal of Sociology, 51,* 198-206.

Patterson, J. G., & Zderad, L. T. (1976/1988). *Humanistic nursing* (Publication No. 41-2218). New York: National League for Nursing.

Porter, C., Aamodt, A., Farrell, F., & Hutter, J. (1983). *The child's view of a pediatric oncology clinic.* Paper presented at the 11th Annual Research Conference, Tucson, AZ.

Porter, C., Aamodt, A., Pergrin, J., & Prosser, L. (1981). *Client-nurse encounter in ambulatory health care settings for the elderly: Loneliness.* Paper presented at the 9th Annual Nursing Research Conference, University of Arizona, Tucson.

Rogers, M. (1970). *An introduction to the theoretic basis of nursing.* Philadelphia: F. A. Davis.

Spradley, J. P. (1979). *The ethnographic interview.* New York: Holt, Rinehart & Winston.

Spradley, J. P. (1980). *Participant observation.* New York: Holt, Rinehart & Winston.

Watson, J. (1987). Nursing on the caring edge: Metaphorical vignettes. *Advances in Nursing Science, 10*(1), 10-18.

Werner, O., & Schoepfle, G. M. (1987). *Systematic field-work* (Vol. 1 & 2). Newbury Park, CA: Sage.

Dialogue

On Ethics and Validity

BERGUM: When you become involved in your work, the ethical issues become "how are you true to, as in my situation, the women you work with, true to their words and, yet, never hurt them in any way?"

My own experience, in this particular study, was to give the material back to the women that I studied, and this was really difficult. Was I fair? Was I honest? Was I open? So it was an issue of ethics that goes beyond the ethics committee, and is an issue of morality. It is a feeling that has to permeate our research. An ethical commitment that has to permeate our research.

MORSE: Is there a flip-side to that, Vangie—if you give it back to the informants, will they want to delete all the negative and present only their ideal selves? How do you resolve that problem?

BERGUM: The one situation that was really hard for me was the one woman who talked about how hard it was for her to accept the baby, and she, in fact, turned away from the baby at birth, and that was all a part of her story that was recorded. And when I gave it to her, she was very honest and open about what was happening to her, this was the way it was for her. And I tried to say, "This was my understanding about what it was like for you." And she was able to say, "Yes, that's the way it was." And we went on from there. She didn't say I couldn't use it. But I don't know if that situation would always work.

4

Being a Phenomenological Researcher

VANGIE BERGUM

Phenomenological research, a research method that explores the humanness of a being in the world, is a drama, an interactive involvement of both the "researcher" and the "researched." For the researcher, the research drama is experienced as a dialectic between the inner commitment (the interest, the passion) and outer activities (stating the question, establishing the approach, operationalizing the tasks, writing and rewriting). Phenomenological research is an "action-sensitive-understanding" method, which finds its beginning and end in the practical acting of everyday life and leads to a practical knowledge of thoughtful action (van Manen, Bergum, Smith, Ford, & Maeda, 1987). In order to begin to understand how a phenomenological researcher affects and is affected by this research approach, this chapter will explore the lived tension between the inner passion and the outer activities as experienced by a phenomenological researcher. This chapter is based on the recent study of women's transformation to mother (Bergum, 1989), a study that grew out of my personal and professional life and that brought me back to nursing with renewed commitment to women's health care and back to questions of health care ethics.

This chapter will address the importance of the research question, deciding on the research method, and the writing and publishing of the study, while being ever mindful of the ethical commitments to the self, to the women who are the focus of the research, and to the larger scholarly and social community. First, it is appropriate to clarify the phenomenological approach used in the study.

SOURCE: Reprinted from *Woman To Mother: A Transformation,* by Vangie Bergum, 1989, by permission of Bergin & Garvey Publishers, Inc., Massachusetts.

Phenomenological Research

Phenomenological research is a *human* science that strives to "interpret and understand" rather than to "observe and explain," which is an approach normally found in a *natural* science. Phenomenology, which searches for meaning, "was from the very beginning a hermeneutics both of expression and of life-world experience" (Edie, 1984, p. 239). Stated in a simple way, phenomenology has to do with description of experience, and hermeneutics with interpretation of experience. Such simplicity, however, contradicts the depth and complexity of the historical roots from which these philosophical approaches arise. Phenomenology is associated especially with the foundational writings of philosophers such as Edmund Husserl (1970), Martin Heidegger (1962), and Maurice Merleau-Ponty (1962). Others have infused the phenomenological project with a concern for hermeneutics (Gadamer, 1975; Ricoeur, 1973), a concern for a hermeneutical epistemology (Rorty, 1979), power (Foucault, 1975), critical theory (Habermas, 1968), textuality, (Derrida, 1973), and so forth. Most, if not all, of these approaches are fundamentally concerned with understanding the meaning of our life through interpretation of human experience.

Van Manen (1984), an internationally known educator and scholar, says that phenomenological research, "edifies the depthful, the personal insight contributing to one's thoughtfulness and one's ability to act toward others, child or adults, with a tack or tactfulness. . . . [It] is a philosophy of the unique, the personal, the individual which we pursue, against the background of an understanding of the logos of Other, the Whole, or the Communal" (p. ii). The hermeneutic phenomenological approach, used in the present example, is concerned with the description of the experience of transformation of women as they become mothers through childbirth and with the act of interpretation as a way to recover or point to the nature, or essence, of this transformation for women.

Ermarth (1978) says, "Lived experience is the 'originary' way in which we perceive reality. As living persons we have an awareness of things and ourselves which is immediate, direct, and nonabstractive. We 'live through' (*erleben*) life with an intimate sense of its concrete, qualitative features and myriad patterns, meanings, values, and relations" (p. 97). To understand lived through experience is to go beyond the taken-for-granted aspects of life. It is to "uncover meanings in everyday practice in such a way that they are not destroyed, distorted, decontextualized, trivialized or sentimental- ized" (Benner, 1985, p. 6). My study of the transformation of women was aimed at clarifying women's knowledge and realities, and in an effort to more deeply understand who women are as mothers, this study explored the ways in which pregnancy, child-bearing, and mothering change women.

The Research Question

Gadamer (1975, see p. 326ff) reminds us how important the ques- tion is in our search for knowledge. The word "question" comes from the Latin root word *quaerere,* meaning "to seek, to ask, to inquire, to be in the quest of something." Questioning indicates the existence of an unsettled issue, a difficult matter, an uncertainty, a matter for discussion. It also invites a reply, a dialogue, a searching out of opposites and similarities. It opens possibilities and leads, in some sense, to uncertainty, for it throws what may have been thought secure into disequilibrium or imbalance. The nature of the question is important in the phenomenological quest for knowledge.

With questions that search for understanding, there can be no separation of the knowledge of the experience from the meaning of the experience. That is, understanding the meaning of the experi- ence can be understood only by reflecting on the context of the situation, for the "individual both constitutes and is constituted by the situation" (Benner, 1985, p. 7). Marcel says (cited in Zaner, 1971, p. 7) this kind of involvement in research allows no detachment. That is, I, as researcher, cannot place myself outside the problem I formulate. For me, the posing of the question was not something I had to search out. It came from my life. Therefore, a question like "Who are women as they become mothers?" or "How do women come to live as 'mother'?" may not be so far from "Who am I as mother?" or "How do I live as mother?"

Nevertheless, questions in phenomenology do not ask for an inward glance, that is, "precise introspection"; rather, they focus on "seeing ourselves when we observe the world" (van den Berg, 1974, p. 130). There is no gap between a woman, as a pregnant woman, bearer of the child, and living as mother, and her environment with the question of "what is the transformative experience of women who become mothers through childbirth?" It is not a subjective perception that opposes the objective or a question for the re-searched but not the researcher, but rather, it is a search for both knowledge of women as mothers and of oneself as mother.

Questions about being a mother, that is, living as a mother in our present society, have surfaced again and again in my life. Though not easily articulated, the importance of my own mother in my life as a woman appears to be a primary consideration. Interest in mothering persisted for me as a hospital nurse working with women in labor and postpartum. As a student nurse, I recall finding a terrified woman alone on the delivery table in active labor. I wondered, "Do women really forget the pain and the loneliness of that experience?" Then as a career woman, I wondered about the possibility of chil-dren in my own life: "Who is a woman without children?" As I waited for the birth of my first child, I thought of the responsibility: "Could I handle the birth, and could I love enough to give my life for a child?" As an educator preparing other woman for childbirth, I was shocked when a woman asked me, "Why did you not tell me about the pain?"—I thought I had. The question about mothering affected me as a feminist thinking about the place in the world for women as mothers, as a friend attending other birthing women both at home and in the hospital, as a researcher seeking a way to ask useful questions, and as a mother at my desk in the dining room, that is, living with children.

Who are women who become mothers? In the coffee room where I work, a note is placed above the sink. It reads:

Your mother is not here!
Please clean up after yourself!

At first I was angry. My anger stemmed from the mistaken idea that it is mothers who "should" do the dishes, do the cleaning up, do the jobs many people find disagreeable. But then I wondered, "What more was being revealed in these words?" What is it about women who become mothers who would, in fact, clean up after children? Adult children at that! Could it be that becoming a mother changes not *what you do* (changed roles) but *who you are* (changed nature).

Although childbirth may be only one experience that transforms a woman to mother, it appears to be a significant one. As a young girl of perhaps 12 or 13, I recall reading Pearl Buck's *The Good Earth*

(1931). When O-lan, the wife of Wang Lung, said to her husband, "I am with child," I was fascinated. Further on I read:

> She would have no one with her when her hour came. . . . She said no word. . . . The panting of the woman became quick and loud, like whispered screams, but she made no sound aloud . . . [then] a thin, fierce cry came . . . She called him in. The red candle was lit and she was lying neatly covered upon the bed. Beside her, wrapped in a pair of his old trousers, as the custom was in this part, lay his son. (pp.37-39)

However mythical Buck's description of nonwestern, traditional birth may be, birth was different for O-lan than for me and my women friends. O-lan gave birth in the tradition of her time. She gave birth as she understood herself and her life. As women in our society, how do we come to know ourselves as mothers through childbirth? How was O-lan's experience different from those of Gail and Christine (women in my study)? And how do these experiences affect each woman's understanding of herself as mother? Reflecting on the last moments of labor, Gail said:

> Then the team gathered around . . . all women, three midwives, two nurses and they were incredible! There were no stirrups, right! It was all hands-on! Everyone had some part of me . . . . One was holding one leg, one was holding the other leg. I was held by all these women, and I remember only minutes before the last, all of us just laughing; them joking about something. Just before the last contraction grabbed me, I had to stop myself from this big laugh that I was in. It just seemed that there was just so much gaiety . . . that only a whole collection of women together like that could really see the humor of that moment.

Referring to her last moments of labor, Christine said:

> Then things got really busy, seems to me there were three nurses, and there was another doctor assisting with the birth, and Dr. Henry gave me a pudendal block . . . and that was alright. I was in stirrups and they had put the green things on, and were very busy, and everyone was draping me with stuff . . . I know I had my eyes open but I don't remember seeing anyone, and he said, "With the next contraction, I want you to push, I have the forceps on, and I want you to push." I didn't feel him put them on, didn't feel a thing when they were applied . . . and I started to push and that was the worst thing I have

ever felt in my entire life [laughs]. I just felt that everything was being pulled and yanked. The pain was so excruciating, I stopped pushing, and I think everybody . . . Dr. Henry said, "Christine, push," and I can remember him being louder than I had ever heard him. And Nathan said, "Push now," and then what happened was that everything stopped because I stopped pushing. My legs went straight out of my hip (I think I bonked the resident with my foot), my feet went out, and I yelled and yelled and said, "I can't push, it hurts," but I was yelling and then I must have pushed a little bit more and then Dr. Henry told me I was to "push the baby out on my own." He had taken the forceps off and the baby was born . . . . They finished with a zillion stitches, I'm sure. And then he [the doctor] came to my side and said, "Boy, I don't ever want you to do that to me again,"—that is what he said to me.

Of course there are a number of aspects that impact the childbirth experience, such as the position of the baby, the energy of the mother, the length of the labor, the differing cultures, and the general practice, but in each situation, these experiences reflect different forms of knowledge, which affect women's understanding of themselves as mothers. What impact do these experiences have on women as they move to motherhood?

The Method

The subject of birth has, inevitably, its own compelling attraction. No one who has given birth or witnessed it ever quite forgets. Mothers relive it secretly, or reflect on their own experience among each other for many years afterwards. For a story that is, essentially, always the same . . . the essence is always new, always dramatic . . . . It was the same for Cleopatra, for Marie de Medici, for Anna Magdelena Bach and Sophia Tolstoy and Sophia Loren and—Eve. I was in good company. (Sorel, 1984, p. xvi)

To explore the transformation that occurs in women's lives as they become mothers, I asked women to talk about their own lives. The study centered primarily around conversations with six women during their experiences of pregnancy, childbirth, and early mothering. The study attempts to describe "real" life experiences of women, to capture an exact and exhaustive description of the depth of a layer of life as experienced (van den Berg, 1974, p. 123), and to identify themes in which to pursue a hermeneutic analysis that points back to *that* life in a deeper way. The phenomenological method attempts to push off method for method sake, to push off sureness and become unsure, to resist conceptual analysis with the view to explain. As a result, this method becomes an attitude, a way of looking—an attempt "to return to the things themselves" (Merleau-Ponty, 1962, p. ix).

Conversation

The term "conversation" rather than "interview" is chosen to more fully describe the actual process that was used. As opposed to the word "interview," which implies that "one person (an interviewer) asks questions of another person" (Polit & Hungler, 1983, p. 531), the word "conversation" implies a discussion and best captures the attitude of this interaction. Like an interview, the conversation has a central focus, but it is not one-sided. The manner of the conversations not only involved descriptions of experience, but, eventually, they involved reflection by the women on their own descriptions. The conversations began with a discussion about the nature of my interest in the transformation of women. The following questions are given as examples of the ways the conversations were initiated or prompted (if needed):

- If it did, when did the possibility of children first come up?
- What kinds of feelings did you have when you found out for sure that you were pregnant?
- How did others in your life respond?
- What was your experience of body, space, time?
- Did you find yourself seeing or hearing things, or attending to things you did not before?

The atmosphere of the conversations was open and the aim was to have the women speak with as much specificity as possible about their own experience in order to clarify what they meant. In actual fact, the women needed little encouragement to talk; therefore, in order to strive for concreteness of experience, the question "Can you give me an example?" was often my only interjection.

In these conversations (five to eight with each woman), there was a consciousness of the interaction between each woman and myself.

I was not merely a privileged observer, I was involved. All the women were experiencing the birth of a first child; I have two children, 13 and 15 years old. The women were in their late 20s or early 30s; I am over 40. Their everyday lives were filled with work and home; mine with study of their experience, along with a penetrating investigation of the literature about women, childbirth, and phenomenology. I was very interested in their experience, but they were not exploring mine. So, although the mutuality was inevitably skewed by the research intentions, there was a sharing of a common concern and experience.

In conversations of this nature, all participants are immersed in the tradition of their own life history, and it is from a position of shared history that understanding comes into being. Of course, there needs to be full consciousness of the presuppositions and interests that are carried by participants, and there needs to be recognition that these "common-sense preunderstandings, suppositions, assumptions, and the existing bodies of scientific knowledge predispose us to interpret the nature of the phenomenon before we have even come to grips with the significance of the phenomenological questions" (van Manen, 1984, p. 9). Setting aside certain questions and assumptions, I attempted to question the "taken for grantedness" of what I thought I knew about this experience and to discover what was truly being said in the conversation. This type of questioning demands that the researcher acknowledge and attend to one's own presuppositions so as to arrive at the depth of the phenomenon (Kvale, 1984). Such attentiveness to self-questioning of commonplace knowledge or assumptions allows for new understandings and possibilities that may go beyond the reality of the presuppositions.

Stories

Knowledge that holds the breadth and depth of wisdom tends to get lost in the surge toward obtaining "research data" and "information," which to be considered valid must be objective, factual, and replicable. In contrast, knowledge revealed through stories is contextualized, personal, never replicable, and full of life experience that is not explained. As it is with interpretation or analysis, knowledge revealed in stories is not forced on the reader. The reader can enter the story in such a manner that ties the reader to the story in a personal way. Benjamin (1969) says that the loss of storytelling as a valued enterprise is related to the changed "face of death" in present society. He says that people are "dry dwellers in eternity" who are stowed away in sanatoriums or hospitals at the end of their life (p. 94). While once the death of a person could release the story of personal knowledge and wisdom—"the stuff of real life"—the hygienic approach to death has led to a loss of the authority of storytelling. Sometimes I wonder if the hygienic approach to birth also contributes to this loss.

In this study, the woman's story was written in a way to approach the knowledge of this human experience. Each woman's story is unique, with its own tempo, style, individuality, and wisdom. The story's authority is perceived by the readers as they interpret it in relation to their own experience. The stories introduce each woman and tell her story in a way that reveals the landscape of her life, that is, her situation and the context from which her words come. With understanding and respectfulness of the complexity of these women's lives, and all human life, the story that characterizes a particular woman's life is, naturally, recognized as a simplification of that life.

While the writing of the stories comes out of my reflection on our conversations (that is, there is choice in the telling), the words belong to each woman. Nothing was fictionalized. The women were invited to read and comment on their story as it was presented. Each agreed that she was able to see aspects of her experience in the story. As a story captures only a few aspects of a particular woman's life, it is less than a personal story, yet the retelling, the focusing, and the shaping of the story may lead to a different and, in some sense, a better understanding of a particular woman's life. However, I found that as I gave each woman an anonymous name, the story also became distanced from her unique self and became "any" woman's story.

Thematic Moments

Thematic moments arose out of these women's stories, not as a collection of elements but as a way to further explore an aspect of their life as mother. As I read the stories, I began to notice that each story somehow characterized a particular theme. In reflecting on each woman's uniqueness and what stood out of her individual story, I realized that these moments were found in other women's stories as well. The following themes, or thematic moments were identified from each woman's story:

Brenda: What is meant by transformation? Do all women who become mothers experience it?

Christine: What is the nature of the making a decision to have a child?

Jane: How is the presence of the child experienced?

Susan: What is the nature of the pain of separation that leads to integration?

Anna: What is the nature of taking responsibility?

Katherine: What is the experience of mindfulness to a child?

"Thematic moment,"as opposed to "theme," arises from the notion that the word "moment" captures more completely the nature of the experience for women, suggesting a cross between momentous and momentary (O'Brien, 1981, p. 47). Although they occur over time, moments are not chronological periods of time. They are identifiable aspects of becoming that together show the nature of the transformative experience. Yet, each moment invariably results in a description of the whole: "everything is connected to everything else" (van den Berg, 1974, p. 110).

It is important not to make too much of moments or themes. Although the theme of an experience is the principle, or essence, that makes the experience what it is (for example, it is true that coming to a decision about having a child is part of all women's move to motherhood), for each woman, the decision may be experienced differently or may not be thoughtfully dealt with at all. Consider the theme of responsibility. Although responsibility is an important aspect of the move to motherhood, it may be realized in different ways and at different times by individual women. It is also true that there may be other thematic moments that could be identified, such as the woman's relationship with her own mother or the importance of grandparents. Thus themes are not magically appearing essences but are useful focal points or commonalities of experience around which phenomenological interpretation occurs (van Manen, 1984, pp. 20-21).

The Writing

There is a great contrast between the story and the interpretation. The interpretation of thematic moments represents further involvement with the texts of the transscripts and entails tracing etymological sources, searching idiomatic phrases, studying other childbirth literature and artistic sources, and attending to personal experience (van Manen, 1984, pp. 12-19). Through thematic analysis, I searched to discover the forgotten, hidden, mysterious, or ambiguous nature of women's experiences. This hermeneutic project, accomplished through an interaction with the various materials (texts) in a effort to disclose meanings, is one a person cannot easily discover by oneself.

According to Silverman (1984), "phenomenological description is an account of the meaning of something, phenomenological interpretation is the act of producing or establishing a meaning" (p.22). By reading and going back and forth among the various levels of questioning, there is a striving for a thoughtfulness, "a deeply reflective activity that involves the totality of our physical and mental being" (van Manen, 1984, p. 28). In one sense, then, phenomenological research can be said to be an exploration of self, forcing a self-reflective attitude. However, van Manen puts it this way: "To write means to write myself, not in a narcissistic but in a deep, collective sense. To write phenomenologically is the untiring effort to author a sensitive grasp of being itself" (p. 28).

One of the difficulties of writing phenomenologically, then, is that it constantly puts self into question: "How can I write in a way that captures the essence of women's expereince? How can I understand? Am I being 'true' to their and my expcrience?"

The existential themes of temporality (lived time), spatiality (lived space), corporeality (lived body), and communality (lived relationship to others) have been woven into the various thematic moments that were identified. Along with this visual structuring of the writing, the effort was made to search for deeper levels of analysis, to vary examples, and to explore and engage in a dialogical fashion with other phenomenological authors. Immersion in language makes the hermeneutic process possible. Language both reveals and conceals, providing for a unity between what is said and what is left unsaid

(Gadamer, 1975; Ihde, 1983). This means an attentiveness to the silence as well as the talk. It is a project that moves from life toward thoughts, not backwards to the author but forward toward understanding the sort of world it discovers and opens up (Marcel, 1978; Ricoeur, 1973).

The writing and rewriting, the constant search for deeper meaning, changed not only the understanding of the particular part of the study but also the totality of the study, which again required a rewriting. This constant search for new understanding has been called the hermeneutic circle, which contains the possibility of deeper understanding. The recognition that it is not yet finished is very real.

Publishing

> If I can see something, I can be deceived. Only if another sees it too and confirms it for me, do I know that it was no deception. . . . The community and universality of truth means that we engage with others, in full reciprocal openness, and that in such a testing and clarifying dialogue we stand on the common ground of rational discussion. (Bollnow, 1974, pp. 12-13)

The soundness of ideas put forward in phenomenological research is realized through discussion with others. I gave the study to Susan, Anna, Christine, and Katherine for their comments. I felt vulnerable to their critique and was reluctant to present an analysis of their conversations, yet it was an essential activity. Each woman read the study and commented through writing and discussion, in which we explored, clarified, and expanded the various ideas. Although it was not possible, it would have been interesting and productive to have had all the women discuss the work together. Some of the written comments were:

> What I found most interesting was discovering that the other women in the study had many similar feelings and experiences as I did feeling— the vulnerability, a change in treatment by others, and even something as trivial as lack of choice of clothing. . . . All of us had made the decision to have children and then having conceived were struck by the overwhelming feelings of uncertainty. It was reassuring to know other women felt the same. (Susan)

It was indeed a transformation for me. . . . I was interested in those things that seemed common [the inwardness one feels during labor], and how we differed [how we felt about our changing bodies]. There is great strength derived from birthing and mothering, and I think it is an untapped resource. (Christine)

The limitations of a study such as this will only be fully comprehended through continued conversation, in which the data is explored with courage to rethink, discard, clarify, expand, and deepen the ideas researched. These conversations must include partners, friends, practitioners, researchers, and scholars who strive to understand this important experience in women's lives. So the conversations are not finished: publishing the work opens the conversations to a wider group.

Ethical Commitments

As demonstrated by these women's stories, no woman's life is exactly like any other woman's life. Each woman is an individual, and her transformation to mother is unique to her. As I entered into a relationship with these individual women, the search for understanding of women's experience was broader than this unique experience of individual lives. Yet, the appreciation for the individual made it possible to see the importance of the broader issues.

The women signed a consent form to be a part of the research endeavor, and none of the women dropped out after her initial involvement. The ethical commitments to these women permeated my mind and actions throughout the study and still continue. These women could be called informants, but the word "informant" does not capture the depth of sharing of thoughts and personal experiences that these women gave to the study. Using their stories for my research purposes binds me to them in a way that goes beyond the technical comsiderations of how to handle the raw data of research, such as whether the data are stored under lock and key, when the transcripts should be erased, and so forth. The very fact that these women talked about their own experience made a difference in their lives. It raised their own awareness of what they were going through and resulted in reflection that may not have occurred outside the research environment. When they read the transcripts of the conversations, the stories written about them, and the interpretative aspect of the study, these women also focused on their own experiences by comparing their comments and experiences with those of the other women and by reflection on my interpretations. Now, as I publish this study (with their knowledge), I am sensitive to the fact that each woman's words, however anonymous and distinct from the unique women who talked with me, are available to her for her continued reflection. She is not anonymous to herself; she knows herself in the text. While the completed study and the transcripts (which were given to each women) may gather dust on the shelf, it is also possible that they may reread them at some later time, causing renewed reflection. Such possibilities point to ethical commitments that have lifelong obligations, which do not end with the signing of the voluntary consent form and clearance from a university research ethics review committee.

The orientation in the approach to the texts has been to search for an understanding of women in a way that acknowledges the public reality of women's private lives. This public/cultural reality is realized in the care that pregnant women receive. The hermeneutic thrust has aimed at producing a text that reveals a strong version of women's lives, one that shows the possibilities as well as the difficulties that childbearing brings with it. In the attempt to understand (by writing, reflection, and rewriting), there is an underlying recognition that the depth of human life may become flattened, simplified, and even polarized. The goal of this study has been the opposite: It is an attempt to write in a way that reveals the depth of the complexity in a woman's life as she becomes a mother.

Enabled action

Reflecting on those aspects of my life that brought me to pose the question, it seems that I, too, have experienced transformation. As a daughter, I have chosen to carry my mother's name. As a mother, I continually make decisions about my commitment to my daughter and son (e.g., balancing work and home life). As a nurse, I have returned to the profession with enabled courage to question current obstetrical practices: How do health care workers assist women through their pain of birthing? How do we acknowledge the value of labor to women and to society? How do we acknowledge the presence of the child in women's lives both before and after birth?

How are we responsible for our actions without usurping the responsibility and its empowerment that women require to be a mother in today's society? How do we live and work in a way that we remain mindful of the child? As a teacher/professor, I need to explore ways to bring this study of the experience of women into my teaching, perhaps using the story to build curriculum. As a feminist, I am interested in exploring more fully the value of women's knowledge of the world as important to the betterment of society, and as a researcher, I plan to continue doing research that lives the tension between the inner as well as the outer, both of the researcher and the researched.

I have learned that being a mother is a matter not only of the mother role (Barber & Skaggs, 1975; Wolkind & Zajicek, 1981), not only of caring for the child, and not only of caring for a home. It is a matter of a changed understanding of who women are as mothers. Becoming a mother is a matter not only of maternal tasks (Rubin, 1984), not only of developmental tasks (Valentine, 1982), and not only of stressors and satisfactions ((Wilson, 1982), it is a realization and acceptance that "I am a mother."

I have learned that to continue to "live" the questions raised in this study means keeping up the search for understanding, constantly questioning what is taken as secure, accepting the fact that there is still more to learn, and searching for another view of the complex reality of living, which may open further depths of questioning and understanding. It also means continuing the conversations among women and between groups of women who tend to polarize women's issues, such as particular feminist and pro-family groups. It means continuing conversations among women and men about unique and shared ways in which they come to their experience of parenting. It means keeping conversations going among nurses, midwives, and doctors in order to explore forms of knowledge appropriate for each situation, while trying to avoid attachments to knowledge for technical, marketplace, sexist, or economic reasons. It means continuing dialogue between the differing activist and professional groups, such as Safe Alternatives for Childbirth, the Task Force on Midwifery, and the College of Physicians and Surgeons. It means comparing questions of how women live as mothers with questions about the place of children in society. In no way do I expect that this analysis is a conclusive or final commentary on women's transformative experiences of childbirth and becoming mothers. It is offered as one possible interpretation of women's lives, recognizing that there is no conclusion for questions of this nature. Striving for deeper understanding is an ongoing project.

References

Barber, V., & Skaggs, M. (1975). *The mother person.* Indianapolis, IN: Bobbs-Merrill.

Benjamin, W. (1969). The storyteller. In W. Benjamin (Ed.). *Illuminations* (pp. 83-109). New York: Schocken Books.

Benner, P. (1985). Quality of life: A phenomenological perspective on explanation, prediction, and understanding in nursing science. *Advances in Nursing Science,* 8(1), 1-14.

Bergum, V. (1989). *Woman to mother. A transformation.* South Hadley, MA: Bergin & Garvey.

Bollnow, O. (1974). The objectivity of the humanities and the essence of truth. *Philosophy Today, 18,* 3-18.

Buck, P. (1931). *The good earth.* New York: Pocket Books.

Derrida, J. (1973). *Speech and phenomena, and other essays of Husserl's theory of signs.* Evanston, IL: Northwestern University Press.

Edie, J. (1984). Phenomenology in America, 1984. *Research in Phenomenology, XIV,* 233-246.

Ermarth, M. (1978). *Wilhelm Dilthey: The critique of historical reason.* Chicago: The University of Chicago Press.

Foucault, M. (1975). *The birth of a clinic: An archeology of medical perception.* New York: Vintage Books.

Gadamer. H.G. (1975). *Truth and method.* New York: Seabury Press.

Habermas, J. (1968). *Knowledge and human interests.* Boston: Beacon Press.

Heidegger, M. (1962). *Being and time.* New York: Harper & Row.

Husserl, E. (1970). *The crisis of the European sciences and transcendental phenomenology.* Evanston, IL: Northwestern University Press.

Ihde, D. (1983). *Existential technics.* Albany: State University of New York Press.

Kvale, S., (1984). The qualitative research interview: A phenomenological and hermeneutical mode of understanding. *Journal of Phenomenological Psychology, 14*(2), 171-96.

Marcel, G. (1978). *Homo viator: Introduction to a metaphysic of hope.* MA: Peter Smith.

Merleau-Ponty, M. (1962). *Phenomenology of perception.* London: Routledge & Kegan Paul.

O'Brien, M. (1981). *The politics of reproduction.* Boston: Routledge & Kegan Paul.

Polit, D. F., & Hungler, B. P. (1983). *Nursing research: Principles and methods* (3rd ed.). Philadelphia: J. B. Lippincott.

Ricoeur, P. (1973). The task of hermeneutics. *Philosophy Today, 17,* 112-128.

Rorty, R. (1979. *Philosophy and the mirror of nature.* Princeton, NJ: Princeton.

Rubin, R. (1984). *Maternal identity and the maternal experience.* New York: Springer.

Silverman, H. (1984). Phenomenology: From hermeneutics to deconstruction. *Research in Phenomenology, XIV,* 19-34.

Sorel, N. (1984). *Ever since Eve: Personal reflections on childbirth.* New York: Oxford Unversity Press.

Valentine, D. (1982). The experience of pregnancy: A developmental process. *Family Relations, 31,* 243-248.

van den Berg, J. (1974). *A different existence: Principles of phenomenological psychopathology.* Pittsburgh, PA: Duquesne University Press.

van Manen, M. (1984). *"Doing" phenomenological research and writing: An introduction* (Monograph No. 7). Edmonton, Canada: University of Alberta.

van Manen, M., Bergum, V., Smith, S., Ford, J., & Maeda, C. (1987, May). *Research for action-sensitive-understanding.* Symposium presented at 6th Annual Human Science Research Conference, University of Ottawa, Canada.

Wilson, J. (1982). *Perspectives on motherhood: A phenomenological study of women's transitions to motherhood.* Unpublished master's thesis, University of Alberta, Edmonton, Canada.

Wolkind, S., & Zajicek, E. (Eds.). (1981). *Pregnancy: A psychological and social study.* London: Academic Press.

Zaner, R. (1971). *The problem of embodiment: Some contributions to a phenomenology of the body.* The Hague: Matinus Nijhoff.

Dialogue

On Fieldwork in Your Own Setting

MORSE: I think this is an important topic on four levels: The first is doing fieldwork in a setting where you already have a role, and you are working. The second is to go to the hospital down the street and work in the equivalent area there. And that is slightly better but still very problematic. One of the issues is, what do you do with the information that is not very flattering? And the third example is doing research in your own community, and Juliene has done a lot of that work. And the last is doing research in your own culture, and Agnes has done much of that work. I find that nurses are the worst people to send in to do participant observation because they cannot sit in the corner and "do nothing." They have to go and tuck in the bed, take the bedpan, get the water, and before you can turn around, they are working!

LIPSON: I think one of the things that is really important to do, before anyone tries to do research in their own culture, is to go outside it first. I tried to do my very first fieldwork in the psych unit where I was working—it was lousy! I had to go and study the Jesus movement first, before I could figure out what was going on at home. It takes a real effort to figure out what is you and what is not you. I think it can be done successfully, but I think it takes a lot of experience and a lot of hard work to get there. And a lot of exposure outside and a lot of self-exploration to find out where your own values are coming from, what your own behavior is, what you're not seeing, and I think it's a very sticky proposition.

It can be done, and it can be done well, but it should not be done by a novice. It should be done by someone who is very, very well prepared, who has had experiences in various settings, who knows herself very, very well inside, and has a good mentor to bounce things off at all times.

5

The Use of Self in Ethnographic Research

JULIENE G. LIPSON

Reinharz (1981) describes "new paradigm" research as research that encompasses a set of assumptions that contrast with those assumptions of the dominant (positivist) paradigm and use a " . . . variety of methods that fall in the general rubric of qualitative research methodology . . . " (p. 416). Qualitative methods include open interviews, case study, participation observation, life history, oral history, ethnography, phenomenology, and experiential analysis. Researchers using these methods "minimize manipulation of research subjects, limit a priori analysis or definitions of variables, and attempt to develop genuine relationships with the nominal subjects, leaving open the possibility that both will change in the process" (Reinharz, 1981, p. 416).

In the new paradigm research, the researcher's self is acknowledged to be the primary tool for collecting data, and reports often contain methodological remarks about the impact on the researcher of conducting research. In nursing research, however, the dominance of empiricist models has resulted in relative neglect of the impact of the person of the researcher on data gathering and analysis. In written reports of qualitative research, methodological details on the researcher's influence are curtailed or phrased in "objective" terms because authors realize that their papers are usually evaluated according to the presuppositions and values of empiricism.

This conflict in paradigms is obvious; however, the current issue in nursing research goes beyond a common supposition that empirical methods are "objective," therefore "unbiased," and qualitative methods are "subjective." Nurse-researchers have become aware that even the most "rigorous" experimental study is subjective in light of the researcher's theoretical stance, questions asked, and interpretation of findings. The problem is to describe how the biases differ in each style of research and how to account for the effects of such bias.

Among qualitative researchers there are positions ranging from the most "objective" to the most "subjective." Some urge qualitative researchers to increase "objectivity" by taking into account personal biases and feelings: to understand their influence on the research (Field & Morse, 1985; Spradley, 1979). In contrast are researchers who argue that attempting to achieve "objectivity" is based on a false premise; they suggest that subjectivity should not be considered a limitation, and personal responses to the social setting can be capitalized on as a rich source of data and an avenue of learning about the setting (Cassell, 1977; Lipson, 1984; Reinharz, 1979; Reynolds & Farberow, 1976).

The three most common qualitative designs used in nursing research—ethnography, phenomenology, and grounded theory— share the goals of describing the complexity of human experience in its context, with emphasis on describing daily events of peoples' lives using their own words. Each design emphasizes learning from "informants" rather than approaching "subjects" with preset hypotheses. Each design depends heavily on the researcher's use of self, but there are differences in what is described and how the self is used.

Phenomenologists use themselves to obtain an essential description of a lived human experience, developing relationships in which they intensively interview relatively few people. They deal with their own biases by "bracketing out" the self, examining their prejudgments and commitments so as to be a clear receptor of the phenomena (Cohen, 1987). Bergum (this volume), however, whose position resembles Reinharz's (1979) experiential analysis, suggests that the researcher's own experience is an important source of phenomenological data and a guide to analysis.

Grounded theorists describe complex social processes and phenomena using theoretical sampling, participant observation, and interviewing. Researchers use themselves as both data elicitors and processors who do ongoing analysis for the purpose of generating categories of data for theory construction. Interviewers must be flexible and constantly alert to elicit data that are needed for the growing picture.

Ethnographers focus on cultural description: " . . . what the world is like to people who have learned to see, hear, speak, think, and act in ways that are different" (Spradley, 1979, p. 3). The most typical use of self is as a participant observer who gathers data through both informal interviewing and on-site participation.

While the ethnographic literature states that the researcher is the major instrument in data collection, until recently, there has been little guidance for learning to use self as an instrument. In the past, fieldwork was considered a "rite of passage" akin to an initiation ceremony; anthropology students were expected to learn to do fieldwork only through doing it. In the past 15 years, however, anthropologists have attempted to address this problem by focusing on the experiential nature of ethnography (e.g., Freilich, 1970; Golde, 1970; Junker, 1960; Powdermaker, 1966; Spindler, 1970; Wax, 1971). Most of these accounts are the personal experiences of individual field-workers, which highlight the influence of the researcher's own values and personality on the study. These accounts provide insight by example and anticipatory guidance to other field-workers. Fewer writers provide guidance on use of self on a more abstract level (e.g., Agar, 1980; Freilich, 1970). The term "reflexivity" (referring to observers/interviewers being part of, rather than separate from, the data and exploiting self-awareness as a source of insight) suggests that researchers need to be conscious of their role as actors and their own internal state (Aamodt, 1983; Reinharz, 1979).

Why is a discussion of the use of self important? The literature assumes that because the self is the major instrument for data collection one must "tune" this instrument so that it is able to collect "valid" data. Freilich (1970) suggests that:

> The internal mental state of the anthropologist is a prime determinant of his presentation of self in the research community. His presentation of self leads to a public image that attracts or repels valid data. Indirectly, therefore, the anthropologist's internal mental state greatly affects the nature of the messages that are "sent to him." Further, his internal mental state is an important determinant of what happens to the data that are sent: how much of it he "receives," what meanings he gives to it, and the closeness of fit between the "meanings" informants intend and the "meanings" the anthropologist decodes. (p. 35)

While most writers recognize the influence of personality and values on qualitative research (Ablon, 1977), few describe exactly how one goes about dealing with personal style, issues, values, biases, and the other "cultural baggage" that we all carry around. Ethnographic researchers observe the interaction between themselves and the observed so all observations include some of the researcher. This chapter addresses the following questions: If the self is the major research instrument in ethnographic research, what are the influences on that self that make it more or less accurate or sensitive? What are some of the more difficult issues in the use of self? What kinds of strategies can be used to improve this instrument?

Background and Assumptions

Three assumptions, apparent in this discussion, are related to the broad use of the term ethnography, the importance of the researcher's background, and similarities in use of self in ethnography and nursing. First, ethnographic research includes more than traditional ethnography, in which the field researcher is immersed in a "foreign" culture for an extended period; it may be conducted in urban subcultures, organizations, small communities, or clinical settings. Such research can be conducted full- or part-time, and the researcher can be similar or different in background to the group studied. However, even when the focus is on individuals, there is a strong emphasis on cultural themes within the sociocultural and environmental context.

The second assumption is that readers should know something about a writer's background or, as a chapter of Agar's (1980) book is entitled, "Who are you to do this?" With regard to this chapter, my background is in psychiatric nursing and medical anthropology. My research has been ethnographic in style, if not classically ethnographic in scope. In the Northern California urban groups I have studied, my focus has been on mental health aspects of developmental and situational transitions. With the exception of the Middle Eastern immigrant study, which uses both structured instruments and qualitative interviewing techniques, I have always used participant observation and informal and semistructured interviews to elicit informants' views of their lives and situations. Participant observation and life history interviews were used in my first study, which concerned Jews for Jesus (1972-1974). Next, I participated in two caesarean support groups and the La Leche League (1978-1981) and used qualitative techniques to interview their members; I participated in another breastfeeding support group until 1986. And in 1982, Afaf Meleis encouraged me to begin a study of Iranian immigrants. Following this study, we collaborated on a study of five groups of Middle Eastern immigrants, and in 1987, I began a study of Afghan refugees.

The third assumption is that there are many similarities between use of self in ethnography and in clinical nursing. Aamodt (1982) points out that the assumption that "everyone can do ethnography" is a myth. While simply being a good clinician does not a good ethnographer make, there are skills common to both endeavors: good interviewing and careful listening; astute observation and interpretation on several levels simultaneously (e.g., verbal and nonverbal behavior, meaning, and context); and intentional use of self. Although the goals of ethnographic research are different from clinical nursing goals, the skills and qualities that enhance rapport and trust are similar and will yield better data, whether for research or clinical assessment.

Psychiatric nursing skills can be excellent training for ethnography. The most useful perspective is the "therapeutic use of self" that views a trusting relationship between nurse and client as a form of therapy that allows the client to grow. The relationship is ideally based on nurses' genuine use of their own personalities, blended with a disciplined use of techniques for helping clients change. Improving therapeutic use of self requires both observing how one's own behavior and feelings affect clients and being aware of one's own style of interaction, values, and attitudes. Similarly, in ethnographic research, the best data grows out of relationships in which informants trust the researcher and in which the researcher has a grasp of his or her own influence on the interaction. Researchers need to know how they themselves behave, verbally and nonverbally, and the impact of their own feelings and reactions on data-gathering and analysis.

Influences on the Use of Self

Among factors that influence the use of self are the characteristics of the fieldwork setting (e.g., urban or rural), the characteristics of the population (e.g., sophistication of informants), and the structure of social relationships. The data elicited through ethnographic methods are influenced by the informants' evaluation of the researcher. Informants make judgments on many levels about what is safe or acceptable to tell researchers. At first, they may judge the researcher in terms of such external characteristics as cultural background, age, gender and social status, obvious personality features, and, perhaps, professional background. As relationships deepen, the personality and culture of the researcher have more impact than "externally obvious" characteristics.

Informants' Perceptions of the Researcher

Ethnographers often have little control over informants' perceptions of them, particularly in the first phases of a study. Because there is much literature on the topics of entry and establishing a role, I will limit my points to the informant's perception of the ethnographer as a person. Because an interview is an interpersonal encounter, it is vastly improved by mutual understanding, rapport, and trust. With Middle Eastern immigrants, for example, the more the informant trusts the interviewer, the better the data will be. If trust is minimal, some of the data may be a fabrication tailored to what the informant thinks the interviewer expects. This is not to say that informants are making a conscious attempt to deceive; instead, they are showing courtesy by giving "answers" that please the interviewer (Lipson and Meleis, 1989). With increased trust comes more candid conversation.

In addition, Middle Easterners respond more strongly to the whole context of the interviewing situation than to the researcher's stated role. If the interviewer is to be trusted with personal information, the informant first wants to know who this person is. I have spent up to an hour chatting before an interview in order to establish rapport. Earning the trust of Middle Eastern and Afghan immigrants depends partly on my comfort in answering their questions about my spouse, children, job, and sometimes income.

What informants think the interviewer will understand relates to their perception of his or her cultural background and personal attributes. Similarity of background can be beneficial or detrimental, depending on the group, the situation, and the individuals involved. The long-standing debate about "insider ethnography" (Aguilar,

1981) addresses such issues as ease of entry, common understanding and language, subjectivity, and "political problems." Even if there is no language barrier, there are things an informant can express only to an interviewer of similar background. In my caesarean study, for example, the women being interviewed were very open, and these data were incredibly rich because they perceived me as someone who had "been there" and could understand what they were unwilling to share with anyone else (Lipson, 1984). When interviewing Iranians about why they came to the United States, my Iranian research assistant was often given the "real reason" (i.e., the politics in Iran); whereas, I was often told they had come for their children's education.

Dissimilarity between ethnographer and informant has advantages in other situations. Some informants will be more open if they perceive the interviewer as a "foreigner," particularly in groups in which gossip is common and feared. A few Iranian informants shared with me some sensitive information that might reflect on the family (e.g., having sought counseling) that they would not admit to my Iranian research assistant. I had little access to the informant's network of family and neighbors, with whom I might gossip, and also, I was seen to be able to "keep a secret."

In addition to ethnic and/or experiential background, other "given" characteristics influence entry, role, and availability of data. Golde's (1970) collection of personal essays by women ethnographers was the first to focus on the importance of gender and the impact of subjectivity in fieldwork in an unfamiliar culture. Age and perceived status are also important, as is education in some groups, for example, Middle Easterners. In our study of immigrants, Afaf Meleis was presented with enormous amounts of information in both English and Arabic because of her reputation in the Arab-American community and status as a respected professor. Although I was accorded less trust, because I am a middle-aged married mother of sons, which is the ideal of a mature woman in the Middle East, and because of my academic status, I still obtained fairly good data. The younger single women interviewers had difficulty getting more traditional older informants to be open with them. They also encountered other problems, such as attempts to marry them off to male relatives (Lipson & Meleis, 1989).

Researcher Characteristics

Agar (1980) says that:

It is clear that the ethnographer's culture-personality background, though increasingly acknowledged as critical, is the greatest unknown in ethnographic research. To make things worse, it's not clear how to integrate it into discussions of ethnographic methodology. . . . Conflicts in cultural rules can make the ethnographer uncomfortable, or blind you to what is really going on. (p. 44)

A good example of this occurred while I helped to plan a refugee health project with a group of highly educated Afghan men. Following a meeting, I reacted with anger to what I perceived as a sexist lack of regard for my expertise and intellect. Later, I realized that "this is reality" in working with Afghans; I needed to forget about taking an instrumental role in this group and, instead, note the circumstances in which lack of respect for women's intelligence occurred and use it as ethnographic data.

It is particularly difficult to handle one's emotional responses when faced with behavior contrary to one's own values (Ablon, 1977; Keiser, 1970). In describing his experiences studying a ghetto gang, Keiser says:

Although intellectually, I felt my values were not demonstrably superior, I still could not stop my emotional reactions. These reactions often made it difficult for me to retain objectivity. More important, I was never completely sure if Vice Lords sensed my reactions and in turn, reacted to them. Thus, I was not always certain if my feelings affected the events I was trying to observe. Although I tried to control my responses as much as possible, I'm still not sure how successful I was. Undoubtedly, some bias crept into my observations, and probably certain events I was trying to observe were changed in subtle ways in response to my emotional reactions. (p. 235)

Keiser's point about control is important. "Controlling" emotional responses is not only difficult but exhausting, especially over a period of time. I doubt that ethnographic researchers are ever able to totally hide their responses from their informants. Who knows how attempts to control feelings are perceived and what effects they have on informants? Is it better to try to control strong feelings or to more openly acknowledge them and try to explain one's reactions? Either way affects both the relationship and the data gathered. For example, when I arrived for my first lunch with an Afghan refugee family in San Francisco, I was greeted at the door with my hosts' shocked exclamation, "Where is your family?" I suddenly realized that their invitation meant that they did not consider me to be an individual but part of a family. My embarrassment at this social gaffe and my attempt to cover my feelings of guilt at having put this financially struggling family to great trouble and expense preparing an elaborate and very large meal, as well as their obvious disappointment, made for an awkward and difficult meal and a spoiled research opportunity.

In addition to emotional responses, data-gathering is influenced by the researcher's personality. Agar's (1980) description of what makes a good ethnographer is apt. Good ethnographers often have a high tolerance for ambiguity and uncertainty, are able to maintain a kind of detached involvement, and are able to cope with culture shock. He thinks that more stress is involved in domestic research: "When you work in your own society, you cross the line between the field and home . . . rapidly . . . [experiencing] . . . frequent mini-doses of culture shock in the place of the one huge jolt that you usually get in more traditional forms of fieldwork" (pp. 52-53). What is critical is the ability to tolerate uncertainty because uncertainty creates anxiety, and a willingness to make mistakes, which is " . . . really a tolerance for uncertainty with a personal cost attached" (p. 53). I think people who do not take themselves too seriously and are able to laugh at themselves are better field-workers, as are those whose self-esteem is relatively less dependent on others' opinions or reactions to them.

Another major influence on the ethnographer's use of self is professional training. Schein (1987) notes that "in practice, clinical and ethnographic roles can become highly intertwined, but this in no way implies that the roles are conceptually similar" (pp. 28-29). In an effort to separate these roles, nurse-researchers probably have more difficulty with the issue of intervention than field-workers trained purely in the social sciences (Byerly, 1969). Although this might be the case, most ethnographers experience "occasional moral dilemmas when needing to decide whether to continue acting in the role of 'marginal native' or whether to temporarily assume the role of 'real native' who can behave in ways he thinks are 'right,' 'just,' and 'human' " (Freilich, 1970, p. 22). For one thing, informants often pressure a nurse into a helping role, unless the nurse conceals this background; but concealment raises ethical questions if not personal conflict. Making the choice to intervene in a health situation is particularly difficult for novice researchers, but for everyone, this issue necessitates examining one's own values. My position is that I will not forsake necessary intervention or an advocacy role for the sake of "research purity"; I handle non-emergencies by separating intervention from data-gathering by time or by referral, depending on the situation (Lipson, 1984).

However, the influence of clinical experience is more subtle than simply deciding whether or not to intervene. Less obvious are "therapeutic responses" that come so easily to nurses, particularly when interviewing people who are in some kind of distress. Such responses can discourage further divulging or change the direction of an interview. For example, when I acknowledged the unexpressed feelings behind an Afghan refugee's description of his life in Kabul with high social status and a university professorship as compared to his life in the United States (his inability to speak English and get any kind of a job), he became wary and changed the subject with "It's OK here. I am safe."

Socialization into a helping profession before becoming an ethnographer cannot be erased. The choice of research and perspective shows through in the writings of ethnographers with backgrounds in nursing. For example, when hearing a presentation or reading a paper by a medical anthropologist, I am sometimes struck with the thought that "this writer is a nurse," even if the author has not acknowledged this background. In such a case, I want to know more about "Who are you to do this."

With these issues in mind, how can ethnographers improve the way we account for the impact and use of ourselves? This chapter concludes with two areas: increasing self-knowledge and improving interactional skills.

Improving Use of Self

What does the person of the ethnographer bring to the research? How does personality affect what data are elicited and how the data are interpreted? How can ethnographers be aware of what they look like when angry or anxious? How do these feelings affect their perception and communication? Self-knowledge, particularly with regard to the field-worker's cultural background and personality, is basic to good fieldwork. Lack of self-awareness is probably to blame for some of the more glaring inaccuracies in ethnographic data and analysis. Agar (1980) complains that, while psychoanalysts must first go through analysis before they are considered competent to analyze others, "ethnographers are allowed to go into a situation with no awareness of the biases they bring to it from their own cultures and personalities" (p. 42). He wonders if ethnographers should go through therapy first. Reinharz (1979, pp. 240-263) urges social researchers to undergo some form of systematic self-analysis as part of their training.

Self awareness and fieldwork are reciprocal. Self-awareness is not only necessary for good fieldwork, but fieldwork itself is a potent source of self-awareness. Gulick (1970) points out that:

> life in the field involves the same emotions as life at home; elation, boredom, embarrassment . . . . To these are added, however, the necessity of being continually on the alert (of not taking one's surroundings and relationships for granted), and the necessity of learning new routines and cues. These necessities are likely to force a heightened awareness of facets of one's personality of which one had not been aware before. This can be an emotionally devastating experience, but it is by no means inevitably so. (p. 124)

Fieldwork brings one face-to-face with one's own values and how they change. For example, I was puzzled about the ease with which I learned to use the Iranian custom of *taro'of,* an exaggerated stance of politeness and hospitality, illustrated by a common expression, "I sacrifice my life for you," even in situations of obvious dislike. While I recognize that my fieldwork is more proficient because I can behave properly (which Evelyn Barbee, personal communication, 1987, jokingly calls being a "cultural swinger"), my 1960s values nag at me anyway: "Why am I behaving dishonestly and not sharing my real feelings? Have I simply become an actress without personal integrity for the sake of my fieldwork?"

In addition to day-to-day awareness, fieldwork has the potential to significantly change people both in their own eyes and in the eyes of others. Evelyn Barbee (personal communication, 1987) shared the following example of an experience she has not written about because "one cannot talk about initiation ceremonies to those who have not been initiated." Pointing out that race and ethnicity are often ignored in ethnography, she said that as an African-American she was afforded an opportunity that would not have been available to a white researcher in Southern Africa. A month after beginning fieldwork she was initiated into the Masikoma Women's regiment of the *baTswana* in the town of Mochudi in Botswana. The experience changed her social status from that of "professional stranger" to a member of the society; she was viewed as an adult, the "daughter" of the chief's wife, and a permanent part of the group. But the experience also changed her as a person. She says:

> I felt very much part of the group, I was no longer a stranger. I even felt different physically, but I can't explain why. It gave me an experiential comprehension of the whole notion of reciprocal obligations; I don't know how long it would have taken me to discover this by asking questions. (Barbee, personal communication, 1987)

Grappling with personal changes can be disturbing. Freilich (1970) notes that many social scientists believe that some kind of psychotherapy is a valuable adjunct to other forms of fieldwork training and that anything that increases a field-worker's reality orientation makes him or her a better field-worker. I do not disagree, but I think that one's self-awareness can be increased by other means, such as a journal, field notes, experiential training, or disciplined introspection.

In addition to regular observational field notes, many ethnographers suggest using a journal to record personal experiences to recognize the influence of personal biases and feelings on the research (e.g., Agar, 1980; Field & Morse, 1985). Included in such a journal are "ideas, fears, mistakes, confusions, breakthroughs and problems that arise during fieldwork. A journal represents the personal side of fieldwork; it includes reactions to informants and the feelings you sense from others" (Spradley, 1979, p. 76). Werner & Schoepfle (1987, p. 273) suggest keeping not two but three kinds of records: (a) transcriptions of interviews, including conversations; (b) external observations; and (c) internal observations or a record of the state of the ethnographer as an instrument of observation.

A journal also allows one to grapple with the deep and lasting effect that fieldwork produces in the ethnographer, which is often more evident when analyzing the data than when collecting it. During the months I spent transcribing 27 lengthy taped life-history interviews of members of Jews for Jesus, I was forced to continually examine my own relationship to Judaism and religion in general. While I could put off my informants' questions about my "position with God" by saying "I'm not ready to consider this commitment," alone with my typewriter and those convincing tapes I asked this kind of question many times: "Why not me? Sarah is so like me in background and abilities. She has found such peace, purpose, growth, and understanding in life because of her commitment. What am I afraid of?"

In addition to introspective journal writing, experiential training, such as training in cross-cultural communication, is another way to recognize what one brings to an ethnographic study. Through structured exercises one has a chance to examine one's values and behavior in a relatively safe situation. Experiential training can be surprisingly difficult and enlightening despite its cloak of simplicity.

Finally, the most important kind of self-awareness training is the ongoing effort, by various means, to note both content and process of interactions, including one's reactions to various incidents and observing their effect on others. This cannot be constant because too much introspection interferes with life. However, a useful practice is frequently checking in and noting what is occurring inside, what one is responding to, and seeing if the reactions are interfering with what is being observed. I learned to do regular checks on myself when learning to function in psychiatric practice; at first, such checks required disciplined attention (e.g., like process recordings), but with practice, they could be made quickly and unobtrusively and did not interfere with the interaction process. Katharyn May (personal communication, 1987) calls this "processing at two levels in real time." Reinharz (1979) says that "one person both participates and observes by being simultaneously on two levels" (p. 153). Ideally, the researcher should master this skill in other than the primary research setting so that it becomes a natural activity during fieldwork. Clinical practice provides excellent opportunities to use this skill. But by whatever means, some effort should be made on a regular basis to increase one's understanding of one's self as a research tool. If nothing else, it might decrease "countertransference," or writing down the researcher's own problems and preconceptions as data.

However, increased self-awareness by itself is not enough. Consider how this knowledge is used to improve the ethnographer's use of self in fieldwork. Inherent in this suggestion is the need to relinquish the "lone field-worker" stance and use the help of others in preparing for and conducting the study. For example, in our Middle Eastern immigrant research, we began by interviewing each other and the bicultural interviewers, which served both to refine the interview guide and to sensitize us to potentially difficult areas. After we had each done a few interviews, we met to discuss our experiences, which helped each of us to fine tune our interviewing styles (Lipson & Meleis, 1989).

Modeling helps in preparing a new interviewer. For example, I helped to train an Iranian doctoral student by using her own interview schedule with her acting as the subject. During the interview, I focused on content and process. Encouraging her to talk about the feelings that were elicited by some of the questions allowed her to gain insight about her own relationship to the interview content in this study of psychological adjustment of Iranian immigrants. I also focused on the process of the interview by stopping to explain how I was reading the ongoing interaction and how I adjusted questioning as we went along.

It is helpful to involve more than one ethnographer in a study so they can complement each other's observations and analysis, observe each other in the context of the social setting, and bring each other's biases to light. In situations in which interviewing an individual is impossible (e.g., Afghan refugees often insist on having the whole family present), one researcher can be the primary interviewer, and the other can observe and engage other family members.

Videotaping is another good way of improving use of self. Ideally, a colleague would include the researcher in a videotape of a social setting, which offers another window on the use of self, particularly nonverbal communication. And if teamwork is not possible in data collection, using the help of another ethnographer for ongoing data analysis can alert the researcher to potential biases and overlooked themes.

It would also be helpful to arrange peer supervision on a regular basis. Two ethnographers could work together in a process that resembles supervision for therapists in training. One field-worker selects a portion of the field research, often a complex or puzzling segment, and presents it to the other field-worker; the second asks questions that help to uncover the researcher's difficulties and suggests ways of improving use of self for data gathering. Tape-recorded segments are even better because tone of voice and process are available for analysis.

Related to peer supervision is the time-honored practice of having a chief informant teach the ethnographer how to act in various settings (impression management). Awareness of one's behavior and the ability to continually adjust it in the field situation are important skills; for example, drama training could be helpful in improving the field-worker's performance, particularly in settings in which strong feelings are stimulated by others' behavior or values, or in which nonverbal communication or interactional style is very different from the researcher's own. Disciplined training in knowing what one's face and body are doing in which situations and the skill of manipulating nonverbal communication could prevent some difficulties.

Finally, I concur with those who strongly encourage ethnographers to publish what they experience in fieldwork. This not only allows the data to be understood in a broader context but would be helpful for other researchers. In addition, Freilich (1979) suggests that writing about the field experience

> demands introspective thought that will help the anthropologist develop a deeper and more objective self-awareness. As he relives fearful, stressful and tension-producing experiences, he will get deeper insight into his fears and experiences, allowing him to handle similar field situations in the future . . . a kind of self-analysis; an analysis of internal mental states focused around experiences in the field leading to superior field adaption. (p. 34)

In summary, there are numerous factors that influence data collection and analysis in ethnographic research. Some of these factors are out of the control of the researcher, such as a group's political or social interaction patterns. Other factors relate to who the researcher is as a person; some of these factors are out of the researcher's control, such as age and gender, but others may just be "out of consciousness." It is these kinds of influences, such as the researcher's personality, cultural background, and use of self, to which this chapter speaks. This is not to suggest that ethnographic researchers should attempt to change their values or personality style, but rather, they should become progressively more aware of how these affect the field setting. Ongoing efforts to bring the person of the researcher into consciousness, noting both inner and outer data, is like developing musical expertise. Assuming that the field-worker is basically a sound instrument, picture the difference between a novice musician, who can play the right notes and rhythms and get the job done, and a master musician, who makes the instrument express a broad complexity of colors, feelings, and tone that really speaks to a broad audience. The ethnographer as a research instrument is capable of progressively finer tuning with effort and time.

References

Aamodt, A. (1982). Examining ethnography for nurse researchers. *Western Journal of Nursing Research, 4*(2), 209-221.

Aamodt, A. (1983). Problems in doing nursing research: Developing a criteria for evaluating qualitative research. *Western Journal of Nursing Research. 5*(4), 398-402.

Ablon, J. (1977). Field method in working with middle class Americans: New issues of values, personality and reciprocity. *Human Organization, 36*(1), 69-72.

Agar, M. (1980). *The professional stranger: An informal introduction to ethnography.* New York: Academic Press.

Aguilar, J. L. (1981). Insider researcher: An ethnography of a debate. In D. A. Messerschmidt (Ed.). *Anthropologists in North America* (pp. 15-28). Cambridge: Cambridge University Press.

Byerly, E. (1969). The nurse researcher as participant observer in a nursing setting. *Nursing Research, 18*(3), 229-236.

Cassell, J. (1977). The relation of observer to observed in peer group research. *Human Organization, 36*(4), 412-416.

Cohen, M. S. (1987). An historical overview of the phenomenological movement. *Image, 19*(1), 31-34.

Field, P. A., & Morse, J. (1985). *Nursing research: The application of qualitative approaches.* London: Croom Helm.

Freilich, M. (1970). Fieldwork: An introduction. In M. Freilich (Ed.). *Marginal natives: Anthropologists at work* (pp. 1-37). New York: Harper & Row.

Golde, P. (Ed.). (1970). *Women in the field.* Berkeley: University of California Press.

8

The Use of Self in Ethnographic Research

89

Gulick, J. (1970). Village and city fieldwork in Lebanon. In M. Freilich (Ed.). *Marginal natives: Anthropologists at work* (pp. 123-152). New York: Harper & Row.

Junker, B. (1960). *Field work: An introduction to the social sciences.* Chicago: University of Chicago Press.

Keiser, R. L. (1970). Fieldwork among the Vice Lords of Chicago. In G. Spindler (Ed.). *Being an anthropologist: Fieldwork in eleven cultures* (pp. 220-237). New York: Holt, Rinehart & Winston.

Lipson, J. G. (1984). Combining researcher, clinical and personal roles: Enrichment or confusion? *Human Organization, 43*(4), 348-352.

Lipson, J., & Meleis, A. (1989). Methodological issues in research with immigrants. *Medical Anthropology, 12,* 103-115.

Powdermaker, H. (1966). *Stranger and friend: The way of an anthropologist.* New York: W. W. Norton.

Reinharz, S. (1979). *On becoming a social scientist.* San Francisco, CA: Jossey Bass.

Reinharz, S. (1981). Implementing new paradigm research: A model for training and practice. In P. Reason & J. Rowan (Eds.). *Human inquiry* (pp. 415-433). New York: John Wiley.

Reynolds, D., & Farberow, N. (1976). *Suicide: Inside and out.* Berkeley: University of California Press.

Schein, E. H. (1987). *The clinical perspective in fieldwork.* Newbury Park, CA: Sage.

Spindler, G. (Ed.). (1970). *Being an anthropologist: Fieldwork in eleven cultures.* New York: Holt, Rinehart & Winston.

Spradley, J. P. (1979). *The ethnographic interview.* New York: Holt, Rinehart & Winston.

Wax, R. H. (1971). *Doing fieldwork: Warnings and advice.* Chicago: University of Chicago Press.

Werner, O., & Schoepfle, M. (1987). *Systematic fieldwork.* Newbury Park, CA: Sage.

Dialogue

On Nursing Phenomena

BRINK: When people get sick, they respond to their illness. They go through a life-style change. At what point do we look at that transition and do research on it and give it a name that explicates the process? I'm thinking of culture shock, dying, widowing, grieving—any kind of response to loss—any kind of response to change, compulsivity, recovery from alcoholism, the addictions, overeating, and so forth, are all *process* phenomena. The only way to get at process is to do longitudinal research, the nurse who goes in week after week, after week, after week—the Hospice concept—sitting with the people and talking, collecting information over time. Asking "What's going on with you today?" in order to track what's happening. And you can't say this convalescent period is a single phenomenon, except as a global term.

AAMODT: Is it the question or the kind of data that comes out [that is the problem]? And is it the matter of getting the kind of data that describes these kinds of human responses that you are really talking about?

MAY: It might be a "both" problem, because in my experience, working with "baby" phenomenologists (students) is that they are unwilling to take their analysis—a grounded theorists would call it "taking it up a level"—so that then you begin to see the skeleton of an overriding process. They don't want to make that jump, and as a grounded theorist I want to, and so it gets lost in the middle. It turns out to be *wonderful* description, but not much else!

ANDERSON: Well, it depends—there is "good"phenomenology and "bad" phenomenology.

BRINK: Are you telling me that there is a process phenomenology and a content phenomenology? And is the process of data collection different?

BERGUM: Well, let me use an example of "mediocre" phenomenology. In my own study I looked at a concept of transformation—which is a process—and what I found was not a process in a linear way, but a process in a holistic way. It's not any way linear. Is that a concept or a process?

6

Doing Fieldwork in Your Own Culture

PEGGY ANNE FIELD

Over time, several researchers have presented some key issues relating to the process of doing fieldwork (Dobbert, 1982; Wax, 1978; Whyte, 1955, 1984). With the increasing number of nurses using qualitative methods that involve fieldwork techniques to address nursing research questions, the unique problems associated with studying one's own culture need to be explored. Field research strategies needed by the ethnographic researcher include making the initial contact, establishing community and client expectation and attitudes related to the researcher's role, collecting and analyzing data, identifying respondents, and developing trust (Evaneshko, 1985).

In a series of ethnographies, James Spradley studied distinct and different subgroups in contemporary North American society, such as skid row bums and cocktail waitresses (Spradley, 1970, 1975, 1980). With David McCurdy, he encouraged students to learn ethnographic techniques through the study of unique groups within their own society, such as jewelers and grade nine teachers (Spradley & McCurdy, 1972/1988). This type of study has encouraged nurses to examine nursing as a subculture of society, and selected areas of nursing as subcultures of nursing. The methods of ethnographers are also being used with increasing frequency to examine selected concepts critical to the provision of nursing care.

One of the major purposes of field research is to sensitize the researcher to the parameters and nature of the community, including the language. This means the researcher can observe nursing as it occurs in its naturalistic settings.

Aamodt (1981) points out that, while one cannot claim the role of privileged stranger in one's own community, it is an ethnographic mistake to assume that in doing research in one's own society, one may be considered a native. She further notes that even when doing research in one's own society, the linguistic variables that carry social information are network specific. For example, Soares (1978) has demonstrated that the shorthand language used by nurses in intensive care keeps nurses from other areas functioning as outsiders when they are sent to the unit on a casual relief basis. Thus it is evident that one may need to learn the subcultural language of an institution, nursing unit, or specialized area in order to conduct one's study. Problems will arise if the researcher enters the study believing that the culture is already familiar as important pieces of data will be overlooked. It is also important to determine the nature of research that is being conducted. For example, instructors who interview patients in order to evaluate care cannot be considered to be undertaking ethnographic fieldwork. In this chapter the issues of bias, advantages, and disadvantages of studying a peer group; difficulty in role separation; levels of involvement of the researcher; and effects of a third party on transactions will be considered.

Bias in Insider Research

Arguments are presented against insider research for several reasons; the most important one being that such research is inherently biased (Aguilar, 1981). While there is some evidence in a few studies of bias in relation to selection of data and formulation of conclusions, Aguilar claims the examples are few and that there seems to be no evidence of deliberate dishonesty; further, he points out that the risk of such bias occurs in all research. Aguilar and Aamodt (1981) agree that ethnic insiders are generally not as much inside the cultural settings they study, as outsiders have implied, and that because society is formed of many subgroups, with each geographically isolated group differing culturally from its neighbor, no researcher is likely to be a complete native of the group under study. It is probably preferable that, if a problem is identified in one's own work setting, the research should be conducted in a similar setting but in a different institution; this decreases the risk of thinking that the researcher already knows the setting. In a new setting, one must enter as a stranger, thus one has already acknowledged that one does not totally know or is not completely comfortable with the group to be studied.

Study of a Peer Group

In ethnography and most areas of nursing, results of interviews and sensitivity to the behavior of the informant or client are critical sources of data. At the same time, self-consciousness and the personal approach in ethnography are being increasingly emphasized (Lipson, 1984). To explore the issues of role conflict and subjectivity in studying a peer group, Lipson examined the social organization, functions, and membership of two caesarcan support groups. From her perspective, advantages of being in a peer group included: "ease of entry, avoidance of disruption of normal group processes, prior knowledge of some relevant research questions, and an enhanced capacity to elicit in-depth data" (p. 349). Her personal experience of having a caesarean section, when elicited by informants, resulted in a free flow of return information. It must be noted that Lipson was already an experienced researcher when she conducted this study.

In the situation where the researcher has personal experience, it is possible to become, on occasion, one's own expert informant, being able to focus on both what is happening in the group and on one's own response. There were times when emotions influenced Lipson's ability to take field notes in the group setting, but this led to an understanding of the effect of a first meeting of a peer self-help group on other women. A colleague was used to monitor the tape recordings made at the sessions to determine if the personal involvement of the researcher in the topic had influenced the discussion. However, Lipson did experience some difficulty recognizing the significance of some group phenomena. When behavior is familiar, there is a risk that it will be taken for granted (Stephenson & Greer, 1981). Thus Lipson found both advantages and disadvantages in studying a peer group. Her sensitivity to the effects of being a peer led to her using a colleague to increase objectivity in relation to interpretation and analysis of the data. In an earlier work, Wax (1978) cautions against the danger of becoming totally immersed in the culture being studied. Lipson points out that a delicate balance is required when researching a familiar area, a balance between subjective judgment due to over-involvement in the group being studied and the need to use resources to maintain one's objectivity.

Being an Observer in Your Own Setting

Four levels of observation have been described, ranging from total participation of the researcher in the informants' activities to one of complete nonparticipation (Pearsall, 1965). Unlike the social scientist who strives "to maintain a consciousness and respect for *what he is* and for what it is his hosts are" (Wax, 1978, p. 259), the nurse is not a total stranger within the culture. As a result, nurse-researcher conflicts arise when one is in the participant-observer role. Several authors (Aamodt, 1981; Lipson, 1984; Schein, 1987) have spoken of both the advantages and the difficulties of separating the researcher and clinical roles. The difficulty of separating practice from research, in clinical situations where one thinks one should intervene, has been noted by Crowley (1986). She identifies the problems of role confusion between the nurse as a scientist and the nurse as a practitioner.

When a nurse is a researcher and is observing in the clinical setting, it may be difficult for nurses or patients serving as informants to differentiate the two roles, particularly if the researcher is already known in the setting where the observation is taking place. It is also hard for the researcher to step back and look at the setting from a research perspective. Nurses do not find it easy to sit in a corner and do nothing, particularly in an area that is busy and one they know well. This problem is of particular significance when the researcher is an inexperienced student learning to use ethnographic skills because it is likely that she will not yet have developed the adequate skill to recognize subjective bias.

A second difficulty is seeing a setting objectively when one is already familiar with that setting. Someone once said, "If you want to study water, don't ask a goldfish." Nurses already know how nurses are expected to speak and behave; unless the observed nurses do not conform to the expected norms, it may be difficult for the nurse as observer to examine the situation scientifically rather than clinically. On the other hand, the researchers' expectations of the behavior of colleagues as professionals may create difficulties in relation to objective detachment from the situations at hand.

Recently, a graduate student (Estabrooks, 1987), who had been a head nurse in an intensive care unit for five years, investigated the touching behavior of intensive care nurses. She used participant observation for a three-week period (in addition to interviews) as the fieldwork phase of her study. The observation period planned for this study had to be reduced because the investigator found herself unable to function effectively as a detached observer in the intensive care setting. In her study, she describes three processes that interfered with her ability to successfully assume the observer role.

First, it was difficult to achieve the balance between the role of participant and the role of observer, reducing the effectiveness of the observations. Also, familiarity with nursing made it difficult to separate nurses' actions into discrete activities and to recognize touch, the focus of the study, when it occurred—the "goldfish phenomenon" mentioned earlier.

Second, familiarity with the setting as a head nurse did influence the role change to observer. Events were perceived from the perspective of the head nurse rather than the perspective of the researcher, and Estabrooks suffered feelings of "frustration and impotence" when she was unable to respond or intervene.

The final problem encountered by Estabrooks was the inability to achieve adequate distance from the emotional aspects of the conditions of patients in the intensive care unit. The complex defenses constructed when working in the unit were not sustained in the observer role; old experiences and feelings were triggered, which made data collection difficult; and from the investigator's perspective, objectivity was impossible to achieve (Estabrooks, 1987, p. 146). When you are observing and not doing a task, you cannot release pent-up energy through action.

While the researcher is already, to a large extent, a native within the culture, it is still possible to suffer culture shock when one steps out of the practitioner role into the role of observer. Mechanisms that one has developed as a protection for one's psychological self are stripped away when one is observing in the setting. Moral dilemmas arise if the observer sees clients receiving care that is either less than optimal or potentially harmful. If the client knows the researcher is a nurse, there may also be the expectation that the researcher will not allow any preventable untoward events to occur.

Another graduate student (Toohey, 1984), who was observing in an emergency setting, was shocked by the negative behavior that the nurses she was observing exhibited toward accident victims who were responsible for their own injuries. This was particularly evident if alcohol or drugs were thought to be involved. The behaviors she observed were a contradiction of her own professional beliefs and values. While this study focused on preschool children and their parents, she needed the time and opportunity to talk about her reaction to the social (backstage) conversations she encountered as a participant observer in order to reduce her own frustrations.

The Effect of a Third Party on the Interaction

One of the purported difficulties in using the participant-observer role has been assessing the effect of a third party on the observed interaction. When observing nurse-client interactions in my own study (Field, 1980), it was evident that the clients generally ignored the observer once the interaction with the nurse commenced. This concurs with Luker's (1978) findings from her study on health visitor-client interactions. It seemed that once the researcher was introduced as a nurse-researcher the client merged the researcher role with the nurse role, so the transaction became a dyadic rather than a triadic relationship for the client. This merging of roles has implications for informed consent; if clients see the researcher primarily as a *nurse,* they may divulge information that they might have withheld if the researcher role had remained dominant. This process suggests that the fact that the researcher is a nurse should be mentioned with caution in this type of research. The fact that the researcher is a nurse may also have a greater affect on some cultural groups in which people may feel obligated to tell professionals personal data that they would not normally share with other people.

The nurses seemed more aware of the observer than the clients. Being observed often carries with it the threat of evaluation or judgment of their nursing care. This may be a reflection of the student-instructor experience during the nurses' education. My study (Field, 1980) continued over several months so that acclimatization of nurses to the observer's presence seemed to occur. The fact of being observed indicates a potential area for distortion of data if observations are only to be conducted over a relatively short period of time. A period of time for the informants to become accustomed to the researcher's presence may be critical before data gathering is started. This is a problem of concern to all field-workers, but it may be compounded when nurses are studying nursing as the researcher may be seen as evaluating care rather than studying a particular phenomenon.

Involvement as an Insider

In doing studies within one's own setting, difficulties arise when one is seen as a nurse by one's informants. In the previously mentioned study (Field, 1980), it was also difficult keeping the role of observer and nurse separated. The researcher needed to demonstrate credibility as a nurse in order to gain acceptance in the setting; but once that credibility was established, the nurses expected the investigator to act as a consultant if they encountered a client who had an unfamiliar problem. As the study focused on the nurses' beliefs about nursing and the influence of those beliefs on the provision of care, intervention by the investigator was not desirable and was considered a serious threat to validity, yet refusal to provide information had the potential for destroying relationships with the nurses.

Informants may also expect the researcher to act as go-between on their behalf. In one situation, there was conflict between the nurses and the nursing supervisor (Field, 1980). The nurses wanted the researcher to intervene on their behalf to improve the situation. At the same time, the supervisor wanted the researcher to gather information that she could use. Both groups viewed the researcher as a colleague and wanted the researcher to become an insider acting as mediator in the group dispute. This situation was resolved by persuading the nurses and the supervisor to use the services of a mental health consultant skilled in group work. This incident presented a dilemma for the researcher, and it was the greatest threat to remaining detached from the group that occurred over the seven months of observation in the setting. Although the study was not focused on the organization, the functioning of the group undoubtedly influenced the nurse-client situations, which were the subject of study. The insiders perceived the researcher as a source of help, which conflicted with the researcher's need to remain detached from the group. At the same time, refusal to help could have alienated the major informants and destroyed the process of inquiry.

Termination of a Relationship

In a situation where the nurse as researcher has clients as primary informants, confusion between the clinician and researcher role may also exist. In a recent study (Brady-Fryer, 1988), mothers with newborns were interviewed in the neonatal nursery. One baby died following discharge, and the mother called the researcher, asking for a further interview. The researcher reacted as a nurse, feeling she had a responsibility for talking with the mother. As Schein (1987, pp. 35-36) points out, when ethnographers try to help clients with problems they have uncovered, they may make themselves liable for malpractice. Schein goes on to say that both roles can be played if the individual has competence in both areas, that is, in this case, as nurse and as ethnographer. It would seem, however, that while the nurse is in the ethnographer role, referral to an appropriate colleague is probably the safest approach. The way in which counseling problems will be handled should be stated, in the consent to participate in research, when this is likely to be a problem associated with the research. The consent then acts as a contract to guide both informant and researcher.

When nurses are studying parents, the issue of suspected child-battering or elderly abuse may also need to be considered. Usually child-battering must be reported by law. This creates conflict between agreements relating to confidentiality of data and the legal requirements. Legal requirements can be a problem for all researchers, but further dilemmas can be created for the nurse who may debate whether "suspicions" should be discussed with the community health nurse. This is a further point that may need consideration when developing the consent for participation: When can data no longer be considered confidential?

Advocacy Roles

When the nurse is studying nursing, decisions will also have to be made in relation to whether the researcher can take the advocacy role. Again, this is a moral dilemma. If there is, in the researcher's opinion, evidence that elderly patients are being maltreated (for example, the inappropriate use of restraints), what course of action does the researcher take? Does the researcher report the findings to administration prior to completion of the study, jeopardizing the study's outcome? Should the researcher approach the nurses? This could also jeopardize further cooperation. Is the researcher, as a nurse, basing her judgments on her own standards of practice? Is the situation one in which the patients have no other advocates? The non-nurse observing the situation may not have the knowledge to identify the concerns; the nurse, having identified them, is placed in a moral dilemma by virtue of her two conflicting roles.

Interviewing and Analysis: Nursing and Research Approaches

Clinical and ethnographic perspectives require a different focus for the interview and, therefore, a different approach to the way in which data are collected. In the hospital setting, the intake interview performed by the nurse is highly structured, and the purpose is to obtain facts. The clinical perspective is geared toward the perspectives of the client's health, illness, and the related factors that may influence them. The focus is frequently the identification of problems for which nursing intervention is required. The interview, by its nature, is frequently highly directive. As Schein (1987, pp. 54-55) has suggested, the clinical interview is theory-linked and provides the filter through which data are interpreted.

When clients become informants and are interviewed for ethnographic purposes, the nature of the interview changes dramatically. The questions are broad rather than specific, and the interpretation is rooted in the meaning the informant gives to events, rather than being rooted in nursing or related clinical theory. The nurse who chooses to study nursing must change from a clinical to a research approach, perhaps within the same setting and often with the same type of clients with whom she has previously used a nursing focus when utilizing the interview process.

In mental health areas, the nurse as researcher must stop using therapeutic techniques in interviews. The researcher must be totally open and neutral with respect to the kind of data that will be listened for and observed. In analyzing the data, the nurse as researcher must move away from using data for nursing diagnoses or formulating the client's problems in terms of a medically oriented theoretical model. At the same time, the nurse may have to break herself from the habit of using the interviews to teach or counsel the informant as she would do if the informant were primarily in the role of a patient or client.

The nurse, as ethnographer, must be open to what is to be found in the setting to be investigated. The investigator will have research goals, but the concepts and categories must arise from the data. Yet, the researcher will have expectations, based on experience, which may create selective listening and influence what will be seen and understood. The ethnographer must consider the total context of the situation, and the interpretation is more likely to be linked to an anthropological or social theory than to a medical theory.

This whole change in emphasis in both interviewing and data analysis requires a major mind shift for the nurse who enters her own setting as a researcher. It is more difficult to be objective, but once it is achieved, the richness of data can be enhanced because of the nurse's knowledge based on her previous insider's perspective. It is probable that learning to do interviews in one's own culture is more difficult, and this difficulty is compounded for nurses having to unlearn behaviors required from them as nurses. It is often easier for the nurse-researcher to study a very different culture as a first fieldwork experience so as to learn the skills of observing more broadly and objectively. Preparation of the nurse to enable her to be a successful researcher in the field is critical. Using role play, preparation should include practice in explaining the study and obtaining consent, undertaking research interviews, and participating in data analysis (using other data sets) prior to undertaking the first study.

Work with case studies, which focus on moral and ethical dilemmas that researchers may encounter in the field, also prepare the neophyte for the reality of field work. Examination of the dilemma of being a researcher and being a nurse may also be undertaken, using a case study approach.

Taking Field Notes

There appear to be several areas of difficulty related to taking field notes in one's own culture. Both Lipson (1984), an experienced researcher, and Estabrooks (1987), a graduate student, noted that on occasion they were unable to take field notes because of emotions aroused in the study setting. Maintaining objectivity under these conditions may be difficult, and measures need to be built into one's research protocol that allow for verification of interpretations by a second noninvolved researcher. This emotional reaction may be a form of cultural shock to a world not normally observed when the nurse is absorbed in the work situation.

If the researcher is inexperienced and has previously worked in the study area as a clinician, there is a tendency to record field notes as a clinician rather than as a researcher. The notes may be recorded in a shorthand form, with the focus on clinical observations, which do not capture the interactions that are critical to the study and are occurring in the setting. It may be that more attention needs to be paid to the differences between clinical and research observations in the educational preparation of the researcher.

The beginner researcher is frequently afraid that taking field notes or making a recording may influence the subject's behavior. Practice observing in a setting and then withdrawing and dictating one's observations may be needed as preparation for fieldwork so that the researcher does not try to record during an actual observation.

Graduate Students' Involvement in Their Own Culture

When graduate students wish to do studies in their own culture, the problems become intensified, particularly at the first level of research preparation. Some experienced researchers suggest that it may be preferable to encourage a student to look at a different research area first. As noted earlier, it may be extremely difficult for a first-time researcher to translate the role of clinical observer into that of research observer. Observation in the actual setting where the student has worked (or is working) is not recommended. However, if a student identifies a clinical problem that is of critical interest, it may be inappropriate to discourage the student from undertaking the study, but the student must be encouraged to conduct the research in another institution. In this case the research supervisor needs to be sure that the student does not have unresolved feelings related to the topic she selects for study; otherwise, the supervisor will have to invest a great deal of time and effort separating the student's objective and subjective interpretations of the data.

Students need to be encouraged to use their committee members frequently to help resolve feelings of culture shock and to identify biases. Field notes should be checked with the study supervisor for completeness and to ensure that they contain adequate detail for research purposes. Formulating a retrievable record is a learned skill, and it is possible that it may be more difficult when one is learning in one's own culture. But these difficulties should not be used to discourage graduate nursing students from undertaking this type of research if it is the most appropriate method to answer the research question.

It is important that the research question be sufficiently delineated so that the student has a clear focus. A general ethnography of an intensive care unit or emergency ward does not provide adequate focus for a beginner. The previously mentioned studies of the use of touch by intensive care nurses (Estabrooks, 1987) or the interaction of nurses with parents of preverbal children in emergency (Toohey, 1985) provided a focus for these students. A focused topic will not eliminate the problems of being an observer in your own setting, but it will simplify the process of fieldwork because it will provide a focal point for observation.

Student research within an area with which they have great familiarity needs careful planning. Questions arising from clinical experience need to be researched, but the thesis supervisor will need to maintain a close involvement with the student in the data collection and analysis phases. The difficulty in making the change from clinical observation to research observation must not be underestimated. Care must be taken to see that the student is not studying a previously unresolved problem (such as their own feeling of anger related to an unexpected event, like a miscarriage). Despite the problems, ethnographic research can have long-term, beneficial results for nursing in that it enables the researcher to integrate research into the clinical role.

Conclusions

Doing fieldwork in one's own culture has several advantages, and one of the most obvious advantages is that being perceived as a nurse by one's informants may enhance one's ability to gain entry. However, it is essential to make one's role clear, that is, one is acting as a researcher and not as a nurse. When the patient is to be the informant, it is particularly critical that the limitations of the professional role be spelled out. The previous experience of the researcher is likely to have a critical effect on the outcome, and there are some experienced researchers who firmly believe students should not be allowed to do ethnographic research in their own subculture, group, or setting. Other experienced researchers believe it is valuable to allow students to study problems that arise from practice. The critical factors would appear to be that the problem is clearly defined and that the parameters are identified prior to the commencement of the study, and that the student is aware of potential problems. It is also critical that the student receives close supervision and support as data collection proceeds.

In some types of research, there is a risk that the researcher may be viewed as a potential threat, acting in the role of evaluator of the care provided. This would be particularly evident where the research was related to organizational structure or policy. It would probably be inadvisable for nurses to do fieldwork related to policy decisions within their own clinical agency. If the findings were seen by the agency as unacceptable, the researchers, as employees, could be left in a difficult situation or find themselves without a job.

Interviewing skills and methods of analyzing data will need to be changed from the predominant problem identification mode used by the nurse to the open-ended model used by the ethnographer. If researchers are aware of the effect of their experience and their own socialization on the research process, if the researcher remembers that one is not a native, although familiar with the situation, new insights will be developed into aspects of nursing that are as yet poorly understood. Insider research is valuable, but it is not easy. As with all research, being aware of bias is critical. The success or failure of the project will depend to a large extend on the experience, skill, and maturity of the researcher.

References

Aamodt, A. (1981). Neighbouring: Discovering support systems among Norwegian-American women. In D. A. Messerschmidt (Ed.). *Anthropologists at home in North America: Methods and issues in the study of one's own society* (pp. 133-152). Cambridge: Cambridge University Press.

Aguilar, J. L. (1981). Insider research: An ethnography of debate. In D. A. Messer-schmidt (Ed.). *Anthropologists at home in North America: Methods and issues in the study of one's own society* (pp. 15-28). Cambridge: Cambridge University Press.

Brady-Fryer, B. (1988). *An exploration of maternal attachments to the newborn premature infant.* Unpublished master's thesis, University of Alberta, Edmonton, Canada.

Crowley, D. (1986). Perspectives of pure science. In L. H. Nicholl (Ed.). *Perspectives on nursing theory* (pp. 169-172). Boston: Little, Brown.

Dobbert, M. C. (1982). *Ethnographic Research.* New York: Praeger.

Estabrooks, C. A. (1987). *Touching behaviors of intensive care nurses.* Unpublished master's thesis, University of Alberta, Edmonton, Canada.

Evaneshko, E. (1985). Entree strategies for nursing field research studies. In M. Leininger (Ed.). *Qualitative methods in nursing research* (pp. 133-148). London: Grune & Stratton.

Field, P. A. (1980). *An ethnography: Four nurses' perspectives of nursing in a community health setting.* Unpublished doctoral dissertation, University of Alberta, Edmonton, Canada.

Lipson, J. G. (1984). Combining researcher, clinical and personal roles: Enrichment or confusion? *Human Organization, 43*(4), 348-352.

Luker, K. A. (1978). Goal attainment: A possible model for assessing the role of the health visitor. *Nursing Times Occasional Papers, 74,* 1257-1259.

Pearsall, M. (1965). Participant observation as role and method in behavioural research. *Nursing Research, 14*(1), 37-42.

Schein, E. H. (1987). *The clinical perspective in fieldwork.* Newbury Park, CA: Sage.

Soares, C. (1978). Low verbal usage and status maintenance among intensive care nurses. In N. L. Chaska (Ed.). *The nursing profession: Views through the mist* (pp. 198-204). New York: McGraw Hill.

Spradley, J. (1970). *You owe yourself a drunk.* Boston: Little, Brown.

Spradley, J. (1975). *The cocktail waitress: Woman's work in a man's land.* New York: John Wiley.

Spradley, J. (1980). *Participant observation.* New York: Holt, Rinehart & Winston.

Spradley, J. P., & McCurdy, D. W. (1972/1988). *The cultural experience: Ethnography in a complex society.* Chicago: Science Research Association.

Stephenson, J., & Greer, L. (1981). Ethnographers in their own cultures: Two Appalachian cases. *Human Organization, 40*(2), 123-130.

Toohey, S. (1984). *Parent-nurse interaction in the emergency department.* Unpublished master's thesis, University of Alberta, Edmonton, Canada.

Wax, R. (1978). The ambiguities of fieldwork. In N. K. Denzin (Ed.). *Sociological methods: A sourcebook* (pp. 258-268). New York: McGraw-Hill.

Whyte, W. F. (1955). *Street corner society* (2nd Ed.). Chicago: University of Chicago Press.

Whyte, W. F. (1984). *Learning from the field.* Beverly Hills, CA: Sage.

Dialogue

On the Evolving Nature of
Qualitative Methods in Nursing

MAY: Nurse-scientists have deviated considerably from the original "analytic drivers" in grounded theory, so that I can talk to Benner and understand what she does with data as a phenomenologist, and she understands what I do with data as a grounded theorist. She tells me that I think more like a phenomenologist than a grounded theorist, and I ask: "Why should that surprise you?" I think one of the problems of grounded theory methods as done by sociologists includes too much macroanalysis, which, frankly, I find *not* very useful in my work. I am more interested in microanalysis, so that my work ends up reading more like phenomenology than a sociologist's grounded theory; and if you can mess with that concept, that's where some of the confusion lies. I'm not interested in Basic Social Processes but more about how the individual constructs reality. And Glaser and Strauss didn't give me the language that I need to do this.

BRINK: I think we should develop a standardized system of labels for the phenomena that we study that is uniquely nursing. We could then train the rest of the nursing world about what qualitative methods are. I think we do a different kind of qualitative method than what other people do. For example, most qualitative studies [in other disciplines] are studies of content that look at a single phenomena, at a single moment in time. In nursing we look at process variables. We look at how people respond to illness, and that's a process!

It's not static, and you can't get at it as a cross-sectional piece of research, because you *have* to look at it over time. Now, we don't have a good handle on estimating reliability and validity on a variable that changes by, virtue of development, by generation. I think we could develop terminology for these kinds of studies that have never been dealt with before.

7

Qualitative Clinical Nursing Research When a Community is the Client

JUDITH A. STRASSER

Community health nursing is a holistic approach to communities and aggregates, as well as to individuals and families, which emphasizes health promotion through the synthesis of public health and nursing sciences (Archer & Fleshman, 1985, p. xvi). Such a diverse clinical practice arena, which includes both geopolitically and ideologically defined communities, requires multiple theoretical and methodological approaches to research. Epidemiologic as well as other quantitative and qualitative studies are all needed to answer a myriad of researchable questions. Evaluation research using multiple methods is also needed to determine the efficiency, effectiveness, adequacy, and appropriateness of community health nursing programs. Studies of nurses and nursing, information management, population risk factors, disease and its determinants, marketing forces, and select groups are all possible research foci in community health nursing. Nurses in community health collaborate with other health professionals in many kinds of research studies, and increasing efforts are being made to involve both nursing faculty and clinical practitioners in the conduct of community studies (Cross, Northrop, & Strasser, 1983).

AUTHOR'S NOTE: The author acknowledges the award of a Nursing Research Grant #1 P21 NU-00829 from the Division of Nursing for the study used as illustration. This study is titled *Growing Up in a Rural Black-American Community: Implications for the Developing Family*. Dr. Mary Virginia Ruth is codirector of this study. Both researchers acknowledge the consultative help of their Black American colleagues Dr. Marcus Walker, Dr. Hazel Blakeney, and Ms. Johnny Hicks, and the kind support of Dr. Patricia Maloof, consultant and medical anthropologist.

While qualitative community studies should be an integral part of any community agency's research program, they seldom are. There are many reasons for this, including: a dearth of people prepared to conduct qualitative studies, insufficient funds, lack of time, and pressure on nurses and agencies to do other things. Despite such barriers to conducting qualitative studies, there is strong justification for addressing basic research questions, such as: "What is this?","What is happening here?", and "What is the meaning of this?" (Diers, 1979, p. 52).

This chapter will discuss justification for doing qualitative community studies, the costs/benefits of qualitative community studies, and examples from one qualitative community study illustrating the implementation of a community study and the challenges of fieldwork.

Justification for Qualitative Studies of Community

If Archer and Fleshman (1985, p. 2) are on target with their notion of community health nursing being *of* and not merely *in* the community, then a thorough assessment of the unit of care is a prerequisite to good nursing service that is grounded in theory and based on the knowledge derived from research.

Diers (1979, p. 54) describes four levels of inquiry. These levels of research arc analogous to Dickoff and James's (1968a, 1968b) levels of theory development, and they encompass a qualitative-through-quantitative continuum. The levels are not meant to imply values of high or low, good or bad; instead, they are meant to clearly differentiate the required research approach based on the kinds of questions asked.

Kinds of questions asked in qualitative studies involve the discovery of meaning and understanding through the revelations of informants and a thorough analysis of emergent themes. When disseminated, such understanding helps nurses to approach groups in the community with greater knowledge about systems of meaning through which culturally appropriate care and services can be provided.

Qualitative studies of communities are helpful in locating at-risk groups, in describing health beliefs, life-styles and practices, in

exploring the meanings of health, disease, and illness for the community, and in discovering what and who the community is. Such
knowledge can be invaluable in delivering nursing care and in
program planning with community members as partners.

The Cost and the Rewards of
Community Study

Justification for qualitative community studies in nursing can be
found in the benefits of this type of research for the community and
nursing caregivers. Unfortunately, clinical agencies are not usually
in a position to support large research ventures. As a result, researchers must look for public and/or private funds.

Funding a study is a value-laden issue related to whether a given
kind of study is worth the investment. This investment is high
because most community studies in nursing are complex and benefit
most from a team approach, which is costly. Moreover, community
studies often require a longitudinal approach rather than a one-shot
view. This type of approach is labor intensive. In short, community
studies are expensive and time-consuming ventures. Also, many
community studies have been criticized as not being relevant to the
real world of community health nursing. While Archer and Fleshman
(1985) advocate nursing of communities rather than merely nursing
in communities, Fleshman (Archer & Fleshman, 1985, chap. 7) describes the problems and situations encountered in qualitative research that examines the context of community rather than the
community itself. Community health nurse clinical practitioners
often focus on the problems of individuals or select groups while
viewing the bigger picture from an epidemiologic perspective. With
this in mind, it is understandable that Fleshman emphasizes research
concerning contextual themes and problems rather than holistic
community studies.

This emphasis on themes, problems, and epidemiology provides
valuable information that can benefit nurse caregivers, but it yields
insufficient information for understanding the meaning of health,
illness and health care, life ways, and care practices. Often, community health nursing practice, like the rest of health care, follows the
funds. Despite the fact that holistic studies might help identify and

limit the duplication and cost of health services, few community health nurses actually focus on the needs of whole communities or neighborhoods. Community studies in nursing, conducted by nurses with preparation in qualitative field methods, seem worth the investment. This view is supported by the literature that espouses care *of* the community and the experiences of community health nurses who work in neighborhoods where "at-risk," unidentified, underserved, and little understood people live.

Time

Qualitative community studies, whether they are holistic or concerned with selected themes, take time, and time is expensive. Faculty who are in need of documentation for promotion, and practitioners who are pressured by paper trails and the need for clinical solutions, are both under great time pressures. Time, however, can be negotiated, if the funding is available, with a plan for conducting multiple mini-studies, and time can be used to the researcher's advantage in developing a long-term research interest in a community. Such mini-studies are immediately publishable and can yield an abundance of helpful facts as well as aid in the discovery of health-related belief systems. Existing tools, with supported validity and reliability, can form a logical adjunct to the central qualitative study.

Rewards

Many potential rewards exist for both researchers and informants. For researchers, a long-term study can function as the research thrust for an entire career. For informants, there is the opportunity of working with nurse-researchers who may be able to provide some ideas for strengthening the community or helping families in need. For example, in a study of a rural Black-American community by Ruth and Strasser (in progress), several women thanked one researcher for bringing together four generations of women to discuss maternal orientation to menarche. The women and one young girl said that they had never talked like that before and were grateful for the opportunity.

Both professional and personal rewards are readily available during the course of qualitative community studies. Learning from and with informants provides a unique experience of stimulation and growth. Using oneself as a research instrument provides satisfaction when hurdles are overcome and skills are refined.

Implementing a Qualitative
Community Study

There are a wide variety of considerations when conducting a qualitative community study. First, of course, is formulating the research question(s). Once that is accomplished, funding is a consideration. A two-year field study of a small, rural Black-American community on the Eastern shore of Maryland, which was conducted by Ruth and Strasser (in progress), will be used to illustrate how to implement a community study and the challenges of doing fieldwork in this setting. The researchers, who are both White-Americans, were interested in families and kinship, health beliefs and practices, child rearing, social supports, work, religion, education, male/female roles, and the growth and development of both families and the community itself. In preparing to undertake this qualitative study, the researchers planned to use the community as the unit of study, with some specific research questions directed toward selected themes concerning the health practices related to family and community development.

Three approaches to community study are evidenced in the literature. The first is a holistic approach to the community, as seen in West's *Plainville, U.S.A.* (1945) and Warner's *Yankee City Series* (1959). Other more recent works (Aschenbrenner, 1975; Dougherty, 1978) explore themes in the context of community or are comparative studies (Ellis, 1986). All approaches are of value for community health nursing since an understanding of the whole, the parts of the whole in context, and the community compared to other communities are relevant for nursing practice whether of or in the community.

After determining the research questions and approach to the study, considerations of funding, ethics, and sensitivity to the culture were addressed by the research team.

Funding

Funding for the study was obtained from the Division of Nursing. This particular study was part of a larger project consisting of several studies supported by the Nursing Research Emphasis Grant, all of which were concerned with developing families. Incorporating a qualitative study into a larger umbrella project consisting primarily of quantitative research is one way to obtain funding. Other ways include seeking support from private foundations, benefactors, or other public sources. Five thousand dollars was received from the Division of Nursing, $3,000 was obtained from other sources, and additional costs involving transportation were covered by the researchers themselves.

Ethics

With regard to community studies, ethical questions concern the protection of the community as informant as well as protection of individuals within the community. Cassell (1980) states that in fieldwork "power is shared between investigators and subjects, with subjects having somewhat more power to frustrate research than researchers have to compel them to participate. Subjects control the setting of research and influence the context, with interaction flowing comparatively freely in both directions" (p. 31). While this statement is generally true, when the researcher is also a nurse and when nurses are perceived as authority and/or caring maternal figures, the perceived power can shift somewhat in favor of the nurse-researcher. As the researcher's participation in the life of the community increases, informants may forget that research is the investigator's main purpose and may share personal experiences and pain with the investigator as with a friend. This can present an ethical dilemma for the researcher: to report or not to report. If the decision is to report, the question becomes how to report so that the truth is revealed and the informant is protected. Such an ethical dilemma is time- and energy-consuming and not always amenable to anticipatory planning.

In terms of the whole community, it is important to protect the identity of the community itself. Even though presented data may appear innocuous to the researcher, it may not prove to be so for some or all informants. Once the community is identified, individuals within it can be spotted in the data.

Punch (1986) points to the fact that science is not necessarily neutral or beneficial, as evidenced at the Nuremberg trials. Issues of consent, deception, privacy, and confidentiality must be considered before, during, and after fieldwork. Harm to informants can result from ignoring the implications of study goals or procedures.

Another dilemma encountered in community studies involves participation in community ritual when values and beliefs contrary to those of the researcher are publicly celebrated. For example, at a church service, sexual abstinence for teens is advocated as the only "right" way of preventing teenage pregnancy. Does the researcher, if not in agreement, say "Amen" with everyone else, nod but say nothing, look pleasant, disagree in public or in private, or make some other choice?

Cassell advocates the categorical imperative as a test for ethical adequacy in studies involving qualitative fieldwork. That fellow human beings should be approached as ends in themselves rather than the means to the end is the ideal. However, in the field setting, this ideal requires frequent introspective moments on the part of the researcher. Informants are people and are to be respected rather than used. But researchers do use people. The critical difference may be that informants freely agree to be used once they know the general goals of the researcher in their midst and if they perceive some benefit in participating in the study.

Cultural Sensitivity

The term "cultural sensitivity" implies an awareness of one's own culture of orientation as well as an astute alertness to the variations of perception, values, and beliefs of others. In certain situations, cultural sensitivity imparts to the researcher the responsibility of orienting himself or herself to past work by researchers from one's own ethnic or cultural group concerning the people studied, as well as to critiques of the work by study group members. For example, Billingsley (1968) describes the negativistic and distorted fashion in which white researchers have described back North American families. Billingsley attributes this flawed research to political, religious, and philosophical ideologies and to Euro-American ethnocentrism.

When there is a history of the biased use of statistical data, with economic and political ramifications for the people in question, the researcher must be particularly careful to prevent recurrence of bias. Besides developing insights into one's own ethno-, socio-, and individual "centrisms," the use of coinvestigators from the group in question, use of consultants from the group in question, a broad brush use of triangulation to validate findings, and personal insight and sensitivity might reduce the chance of researcher bias.

General Challenges in the Field

In conducting this community study, the researchers encountered many challenges. Some were anticipated, and some were clearly unexpected. The challenges to be discussed here are: (a) finding and defining the community; (b) seeking an acceptable role; (c) balancing participation and observation; (d) sticking to the plan; (e) serendipity as a gift or an annoyance; (f) sequencing ethnologic field techniques; (g) ordering and recording field notes; (h) stressors, anxiety, and blunders; (i) working with a team; (j) passing the test; and (k) owning the community.

Finding and Defining the Community

Finding the community to study presented the first challenge. The researchers had determined that the community should be stable and small (about 50-100 families), represent a variety of age groups, be contrastive in terms of the researchers' background, ethnicity, and culture, and be open to the researchers.

Using maps and available census data, the researchers selected several small communities for review. Following an interview with an informant from the local health department who referred us to an indigenous health worker, we were on our way. The local community health worker, who later became one of our central informants, helped us narrow the field to three communities. One of these communities was rejected because almost all of its residents were elderly, and a second was eliminated because it had the reputation of being closed to outsiders.

Defining the community was not easy. It took the researchers several weeks to learn that geography was not the primary determinant for defining the community. Being from Farmville (fictitious town name) meant that one was from any of six proximate regions, interspersed with people who were not viewed as belonging to the community.

Seeking an Acceptable Role

Another task of the researchers was to arrive at a role that could be understood and accepted by the people. This was accomplished through a formal introduction in the local church. An informant made the initial introduction to the minister, who gave each researcher time during the service to state her name, purpose for being there, and a brief description of how she would go about her task. The researchers introduced themselves as nurses and researchers who were interested in the town and the health of its families. The researchers mentioned that they would be exploring families' health practices, the peoples' knowledge of the history of the town, and that they would be attending church services. The minister then welcomed the researchers to their church and town, and after the service, they were greeted by the people.

Balancing Participation and Observation

McCall and Simmons (1969) state that it is probably misleading to regard participant observation as a single method. These authors refer to participant observation as:

a characteristic blend or combination of methods and techniques involving some amount of genuinely social interaction in the field with the subjects of the study, some direct observation of relevant events, some formal and a great deal of informal interviewing, some systematic counting, some collection of documents and artifacts, and open-endedness in the direction the study takes. (p. 1)

Achieving the most effective blend of methods and techniques is the goal of the researcher when conducting a community study. It stands to reason that observation most often comes before participation. Even during the initial periods of observation, informants need to have some sympathetic identification with the researcher. (Kenny, 1978)

With this beginning, researchers may be invited to more and more participation. Participation itself can be either active or passive-benevolent. Full, active participation is hard to pull off when the community studied contrasts greatly and visibly with the researcher's own cultural experience.

Participant observation is like a dance. Knowing when and how to move, when to be still, and how to gracefully recover when somebody's toes get stepped on are central to a smooth operation.

Sticking to the Plan

Table 7.1 presents the data collection timetable used in the study. The Table summarizes the two years of the study and identifies researcher or consultant, time and sequencing of activities, researcher activity and technique, informant, and central theme or focus. It is a good illustration of a "best laid plan." While report deadlines were generally met, there were several factors that called for increasing flexibility when following the plan. These factors included the consultant's relocation from the East to the West coast, a crisis in the community, the need for reciprocity in the form of transportation, difficulties obtaining interviews with males (for the female researchers), and responding to requests for help.

Each of these factors affected the smooth progression of the plan. Moreover, because of some tension in the area, the researchers did not access public documents until most of the community data were collected. This was done to diminish the researchers' public visibility. Each hurdle was dealt with as it occurred, and although some barriers were never completely overcome, data collection and reports required by the funding agency were completed.

Serendipity

Serendipity was another factor that interfered with the smooth running of the plan. When the researchers encountered an individual who had undergone a sex-change operation, they needed to explore the notion of deviance in the community. However, the researchers had no previous knowledge of gender-crossing and were obliged to review the literature on the topic. In the long run, this unanticipated investigation provided both fruitful insights into the functioning of the community and new knowledge for the researchers concerning the phenomenon of gender-crossing.

While serendipity provided some worthwhile information concerning the study community, it did require some unplanned sidetracking into areas that were new to the researchers. The following question remains for investigators to answer. When is the thread of serendipity worth the price of unraveling, and when is it best left tangled?

Sequencing Field Techniques

The data collecting procedures timetable (Table 7.1) describes a general initial approach to demographic community data, followed by oral histories, observation, participation, and use of selected measures. Efforts were made to achieve a sense of balance among the type and number of informants, the degree of researcher involvement, skills of the researcher, and the specific type of technique employed. These four factors aided the researchers in modifying the timetable in terms of appropriate field techniques. Table 7.2 presents a cursory view of the methods used to plan and review accomplishments.

Ordering and Recording Field Notes

Field notes, a personal diary, and a log of contacts, dates, phone numbers, and pertinent information such as informant work schedules, were kept by each researcher. Field notes were recorded as soon as possible following each field experience, and whenever possible, notes were written in the field. Field notes were quickly transcribed by hand in a rough fashion on contact cards or note pads. Next, information was filled in and remembered details added. Both researchers reviewed the field notes for accuracy if both participated in the same field observation. Descriptive data based on the research questions were recorded on blue cards, and analytical reporting, including related literature, was placed on yellow cards, which were cross-indexed with related descriptive data. This method worked well for the researchers since living quarters were not suitable for housing a computer, and funding did not provide for one.

TABLE 7.1 Data Collection Procedures Timetable

Time	Researcher/ Consultant	Research Function/ Techniques	Informant/ Samples	Central Theme
Week 1 day 1	1, 2, 3, 4	Team will meet to refine plan, evaluate level of study, and clarify reporting procedure	n/a	n/a
Week 1 day 2 until month 4	. 2, 3	Focus is on community. Demographic information will be obtained from primary and secondary sources. Observation and reporting with gradually increasing participation will be conducted. Frequent monitoring will occur.	Researcher 2- pregnant females, female community members, town leaders, and secondary sources, such as, newspapers, community library, courthouse, church records.	1, 4
	3		Male community members, expectant fathers	
Months 2-4	1	Life histories will be elicited which focus on the 4 themes.	2 elderly females 2 elderly males	1, 2, 3, 4 3, 4
	1, 2, 3	Observation and participation will continue. Team will meet frequently to review progress and refine plan.	Community informants	
End of 8th month (one day)	4	Progress evaluated with team. Additional suggestions and plans for progress will be made.	n/a	n/a
		Field notes will be reviewed and possible new emergent themes evaluated.	n/a	n/a

(Continued)

TABLE 7.1 (Continued)

Time	Researcher/ Consultant	Research Function/ Techniques	Informant/ Samples	Central Theme
Months 8-12	1, 2, 3	Participation in and observation of rites of passage. Particular emphasis will be placed on courtship, pregnancy, marriage.	Pregnant female expectant fathers, parents, and/or grandparents	3, 4
		Incorporation of female into health care system will be observed.		
		Ethnographic interviews of males and females concerning health, child-bearing, and child rearing practices will be conducted.		
End of month 12 (one day)	1, 2, 3, 4	Team will evaluate progress to date and prepare plan for final report.		
Months 12-24	1, 2, 3	Data will be analyzed and put into final form.	Selected informants	
		Occasional field visits will be made to clarify data and to aid in termination		
End of month 24 (one day)	1, 2, 3, 4	Final product will be reviewed by team and informants.		
		Effects of fieldwork on researchers and informants will be reviewed		
		Particular attention will be paid to ethical considerations.		
		Implications for nurses and nursing interventions will be reviewed.		
		Changes in manuscript will be made where necessary.		
		Team will arrive at closure.		

*Researchers #1 and #2 were the study investigators. Researcher #3 was a male doctoral student research assistant, and #4 was the consultant, a medical anthropologist with expertise in the study of mothers and infants. Central themes are: #1 community, #2 kinship, #3 rites of passage, and #4 folk beliefs and practices.

Stressors, Anxiety, and Blunders

Stressors encountered when conducting a community study may vary depending on whether the study is conducted in a contrastive culture or in a culture similar to the researcher's own. In each case researchers have to deal with questions of role. For instance, in a non-contrastive culture, researchers expend energy in reframing observations and in analyzing data in as unbiased or bias-aware way as possible. In a contrastive culture the researcher has to cope with being a marginal person, being viewed by informants in terms of some specific image or stereotype, and with constantly monitoring one's behavior in order to achieve an acceptable fit with the cultural group in question.

In McCall and Simmons's (1969) book on participant observation, Schwartz and Schwartz (p. 93) address the notion of anxiety and distractions as contributing to a sense of distortion. This function was clearly at work when the researchers compared notes after attending their first church service in a contrastive culture. Both researchers came from religious experiences where minimal participation in church was required, and both were somewhat apprehensive about being asked to testify at the service attended. While this participation was not requested, the anxiety surrounding the possibility of such a request, and what to say if asked, served to create a situation of tunnel vision, where only selected events were observed while obtaining a general impression. Each researcher focused on very different parts of the ceremony. Moreover, weeks later when an informant spoke with one of the researchers and mentioned that she was sitting beside her at the service, the researcher had no recollection of ever having seen the particular informant before.

In addition to perceptual distortion, anxiety can also cause social blunders. For example, when attending a church service, both researchers left their purses in the trunk of the car. This was a common practice for the researchers in their native inner-city habitat, but it was probably interpreted by community members as a lack of trust. It was a definite faux pas that required making amends. Another blunder occurred when one researcher brought her six-year-old nephew to the site and he spotted a dog with a dead rat in its mouth. Although he had been prepared for the visit, he commented (and continued to comment as only a child can) on something that the researcher would have soft-pedaled.

TABLE 7.2 Data Collection and Procedures Accomplishment Table

Time	Research Function/Techniques	Planning and Accomplishments
Week 1 day 1	Team will meet to refine plan, evaluate level of study, and clarify procedure.	Completed according to schedule.
Week 1 day 2 until month 4	Focus is on community. Demographic information will be obtained from primary and secondary sources. Observation and reporting with gradually increasing participation will be conducted. Frequent monitoring of progress will occur.	Demographic (including health) information obtained in nearby metropolitan area. No demographic data was obtained from county seat because of local tensions. This was accomplished in the second year of the study. Tour and mapping of the area, with one or two central informants initiated.
Months 2-4	Life histories will be elicited which focus on the 4 themes.	Four life histories were begun. These were not completed until the first half of year two.
	Observation and participation will continue. Team will met frequently to review progress and refine plan.	Observation and participation continued with assessment of cemeteries, completed mapping and weekly participation at church services.
End of 4th Month (one day)	Progress to date will be evaluated with team and possible use of additional measures will be assessed.	Team met to evaluate progress. Problems with finding a suitable shelter for storing data were discussed. People in the rooming house had access to our field notes. New housing was obtained by the end of the 4th month. Consultant moved to west coast. Genealogies, ethnographic interviews, ritual reports, and cultural inventories begun.
	Some suggested measures are: genealogy, ethnographic interviews, ritual reporting, event analysis, rites of intensification and incorporation, cultural inventory, photographic techniques.	
	Plans will be refined for the next data collection period.	Accomplished.
	Field notes will be reviewed, evaluated, and suggestions for future will be presented and discussed.	More work still to be done on oral histories. More emphasis needed on the town's history.

(Continued)

TABLE 7.2 (Continued)

Time	Research Function/Techniques	Planning and Accomplishments
Months 4-8	Increasing participation emphasized. Researchers will attend church services, recreational activities, gossip centers. Selected research measures will be applied.	Participation in church services has been almost twice weekly since the third month. Several interviews were held, which included neighbors and friends who dropped in. Oral histories are continuing. Questions about nutrition, meals need to be developed. Premastication of meat for infants is practiced. Exchange, with regard to sharing water and transportation, needs to be explored. One town recreational event was attended. Further data on clubs needed.
End of 8th Month (one day)	Progress evaluated with team. Additional suggestions and plans for progress will be made.	Research consultant is on the west coast so this meeting was postponed until the end of the 12th month.
	Field notes will be reviewed and possible new emergent themes evaluated.	Field notes were reviewed with two informants and with faculty consultants. Aspects of deviance and social control need to be explored.
Months 8-12	Participation in and observation of rites of passage. Particular emphasis will be placed on courtship, pregnancy, marriage.	Reincorporation of a former church member was observed. No expectant mothers were living in the community at this time. Mothers of newborns were interviewed several times.
	Incorporation of female into health care system will be observed.	Ethnographic interviews were conducted with female informants concerning incorporation into health care system. Observation could not be scheduled. Four males were interviewed.
	Ethnographic interviews of males and females concerning health, child-bearing, and child rearing practices will be conducted.	

(Continued)

TABLE 7.2 (Continued)

Time	Research Function/Techniques	Planning and Accomplishments
End of month 12 (one day)	Team will evaluate progress to date and prepare plan for final report.	Fieldwork continued and plans for final report were discussed.
Months 12-24	Data will be analyzed and put into final form. Occasional field visits will be made to clarify data and to aid in termination.	Data were being reviewed and analyzed as the study progressed.
End of Month 24 (one day)	Final product will be reviewed by team. Effects of fieldwork on researchers and informants will be reviewed. Particular attention will be paid to ethical considerations. Implications for nurses and nursing interventions will be reviewed.	Data are still being collected. Final report for the funding agency is completed. Implications of field experience were discussed and ethical considerations were addressed. Implications for nursing practice were discussed. Plans were made to complete the written history of the town for town residents. Genealogies were reviewed and revised by informants.
	Changes in manuscript will be made where necessary.	The preparation of the manuscript is in progress. The expected date of completion is now the summer of 1988
	Team will arrive at closure.	The team has not arrived at closure. Researchers have set their sights on study completion in 1989. Clinical intervention projects based on study findings will be explored.

These were not the only errors to occur; however, a completely blunderless and anxiety-free community study may not be a realistic expectation. Informants knew that the researchers were not perfect and continued to relate to us despite our occasional failings. Moreover, informants were more understanding when they saw that the researchers were open to learning and, when appropriate, changing.

Working with a Team

One advantage of working with a team is that such an approach is an aid to getting closer to holism. Hammering out things together and following up when perceptions differ are clearly beneficial activities for improving study outcomes.

Reconciling apparent conflicts between the two team members was at times a trying process. The task was made more difficult because limited time was available to discuss the study. Since both researchers worked together, it was very easy to get sidetracked to other work-related topics. Conscious efforts in setting aside time exclusively for the study were mandatory. One thing that the researchers did not anticipate was the personal time required to record field notes and to analyze one's own feelings about the process after an interview or period of participation. Both researchers worked at a university full-time, and although sufficient time was allocated for the study, there seemed to be difficulty in acquiring breathing space before and after plummeting from the field back to the office and classroom.

Freilich (1977) states, "It is important that one have a planned strategy for data collecting and recording and the storing of field notes" (p. 311). Planning is certainly necessary, but it is not sufficient. Perseverance is the added ingredient without which the daily, or twice or more daily, recording of field notes would not happen. Without persistence in overcoming distractions, obligations, fatigue, and the vagaries associated with being in a strange place, good field notes will not materialize.

Besides planning and perseverance, the location of field notes in the context of the entire study, the writing, reading, and refining of notes, linking the field notes with analysis, and the continuing review of method and techniques are relevant for the study's meaningful evolution.

In the reported study of the rural community, field notes concerning the observations and participation were central to the study. Moreover, when reviewed by the team, the field notes acted as the guide for determining the use of additional techniques. Writing field notes in a car, when one is fighting to stay awake, or frantically fast, when one realizes the tape did not work after all, is not easy. Days later, it may not even be possible to read one's own writing. Notes written hurriedly require rapid review, clarification, and refinement in order to conduct responsible analysis. Holding back the tendency to analyze, synthesize, and publish data before categories are saturated is difficult when one experiences the first thrill of an "Aha!"

When new discoveries emerge from the data, one additional difficult decision arises: to read or not to read? Exploring the literature in an emergent area can violate the *tabula rasa,* and yet, it may stimulate the asking of highly relevant questions. A team approach to the community study will presumably arrive at the best solution.

In the course of conducting fieldwork, some mark of acceptance of the researcher should occur. At times, this happens in a structured way, such as, a rite of incorporation or passage. In the rural community study, the researchers were formally accepted as members of the local church after attending a specified (but unknown to the researchers) number of services. After six weeks of conducting interviews in a study of "new age nurses" who practice witchcraft (Strasser, in progress), the researcher was permitted entry to a "craft room" where the informant's cat (a familiar) walked counterclockwise around the researcher. This circumambulation was observed by another member of the witchcraft group, and it served as a formal rite of incorporation, which allowed the researcher to continue the interviews over time.

Passing the test is important, and if some indication of acceptance is not received, the researcher and the study are in trouble.

Owning the Community

Once the researcher is accepted by the community, a kind of reciprocal relationship develops, with the potential for jealousy on both sides. Researchers and informants can begin to feel some mutual possessiveness, accompanied by the fear of rejection "now that we have gotten this far." One indication of this is a reference to "my community" and "our researchers, friends, and nurses."

Owning is a part of the research process that can serve to protect both the researcher and the informants, but it is not the end of the process. As in any relationship, work is required to free all to change, to grow, and to open boundaries to new influences. As in any relationship, there is a time to let go.

This chapter has identified selected issues and challenges in the field when conducting qualitative community studies. None of the issues were examined fully; however, a general overview of selected areas was presented, the need for more funded qualitative community studies in nursing was addressed, and problems and solutions in the field were described.

References

Archer, S., & Fleshman, R. (1985). *Community health nursing* (3rd ed.). Monterey, CA: Wadsworth Health Sciences.

Aschenbrenner, J. (1975). *Lifelines: Black families in Chicago.* New York: Holt, Rinehart & Winston.

Billingsley, A. (1968). *Black families in white America.* Englewood Cliffs, NJ: Prentice-Hall.

Cassell, J. (1980). Ethical principles for conducting fieldwork. *American Anthropologist, 82,* 28-41.

Cross, J., Northrop, C., & Strasser, J. (1983). How community health nurses spend their time. *Nursing and Health Care, 4,* 314-317.

Dickoff, J., & James, P. (1968a). A theory of theories. *Nursing Research, 17,* 197-203.

Dickoff, J., & James, P. (1968b). Researching research's role in theory development. *Nursing Research, 17,* 204-206.

Diers, D. (1979). *Research in nursing practice.* Philadelphia: J. B. Lippincott.

Dougherty, M. (1978). *Becoming a woman in rural black culture.* New York: Holt, Rinehart & Winston.

Ellis, C. (1986). *Fisher folk—two communities on Chesapeake Bay.* Lexington: The University Press of Kentucky.

Freilich, M. (Ed.). (1977). *Marginal natives at work: Anthropologists in the field.* New York: Halsted Press.

Kenny, M. (1978). *Guideline for reporting on a ritual in USA Culture: Lectures and discussion.* Washington, DC: The Catholic University of America.

McCall, G., & Simmons, J. (Eds.). (1969). *Issues in participant observation: A text and reader.* Reading, MA: Addison-Wesley.

Punch, M. (1986). *The politics and ethics of fieldwork.* Beverly Hills, CA: Sage.

Ruth, M. V., & Strasser, J. (in progress). *Growing up in a rural black community: Implications for the developing family.* Nursing Research Emphasis Grant.

Schwartz, M., & Schwartz, C. (1969). Problems in participant observation. In G. McCall & J. Simmons (Eds.). *Issues in participant observation: A text and reader* (pp. 89-105). Reading, MA: Addison-Wesley.

Strasser, J. (in progress). *New age nurses.*

Warner, L. (1959). *Yankee city series* (Vols. 1-4). New Haven, CT: Yale University Press.

West, J. (1945). *Plainsville, U.S.A.* New York: Columbia University Press.

Dialogue

On Terminology

BRINK: And measurement—I looked it up and found that it meant "judgment," so that if we take that meaning of the word, then qualitative researchers do measure!

AAMODT: It would be helpful if we could have words that we could all use—

BERGUM: Yes, but I think that's really the problem. I appreciate what you are saying about measurement, and the definition being something broader than "judging numbers." But the common terminology of measurement is one that I think is a difficult one, and to slide into "Well, we don't really understand it that way, we understand it differently" is to almost change the term. I would think it might be more valuable to do that! I wish we could all talk the same language, but maybe there's strength in not doing that!

MORSE: I agree, Vangie. Especially in phenomenology, where everyone uses the right words and then thinking, because they are using those words, that they are doing phenomenology.

126

8

Strategies for Sampling

JANICE M. MORSE

The selection of a sample has a profound effect on the ultimate quality of the research. This relationship has been most clearly described in quantitative studies, where the sampling method has a direct bearing on the reliability, validity, replicability, and generalizability of the study. Thus, in quantitative research, prescriptive rules for selecting samples and models for calculating adequate sample size have been developed. In qualitative research, the selection of an adequate and appropriate sample is also critical, and again, the quality of the research is contingent upon the appropriateness and adequacy of the sample, that is, from whom, how much, and what is the quality of the data obtained. However, in qualitative research, the rules for selecting samples have not been discussed in depth; in fact, this topic is not addressed in many qualitative texts.

The lack of clear guidelines on principles for selection of a sample has resulted in much confusion. Some qualitative researchers have used quantitative methods to select a sample, for example, some form of randomization (e.g., see Leininger, 1985, p. 202). However, if such techniques are rigidly adhered to, the research may be placed in "double jeopardy." A small randomly selected sample violates both the quantitative principle that requires an *adequate* sample size in order to ensure representativeness and the qualitative principle of *appropriateness* that requires purposeful sampling (i.e., selecting the informants best able to meet the informational needs of the study) and a "good" informant (i.e., one who is articulate, reflective, and willing to share with the interviewer).

A second approach that has been used is quota sampling (Brink & Wood, 1988, pp. 128-129) or statistically nonrepresentational sampling (Trost, 1986). When using this technique, the researcher a priori prepares a sampling frame constructed with "independent" variables designed to ensure heterogeneity of the sample. Unfortunately, variation is usually selected from demographic and other sociological characteristics, such as age and sex. Consequently, rather than taking cues from the study as it progresses, the researcher makes deductive assumptions about the characteristics that contribute to theoretical variation and enters these characteristics, which are frequently inappropriate and insignificant demographic variables, into the sampling frame. The system of selecting "negative cases" (Glaser & Strauss, 1967, p. 138) in order to elicit variation is a much more rational and valid method for identifying variation in qualitative research because it is not dependent on the chance selection of an uncommon event, which, considering the small sample size, may be exceptionally remote.

Quota sampling also poses another real threat to validity. The researcher may become so preoccupied with finding informants that meet the criteria of the sampling frame in order to fill the cells that the criteria for completion of the study becomes one of *sample size* rather than the *development of a theory* (Agar, 1980, p. 121). Furthermore, excellent and knowledgeable informants may be ignored because the researcher has already interviewed the required number of those "types" of informants. As it is assumed in quota sampling that informants can only speak from their own experience and cannot compare personal experience with the experience of others, a technique such as quota sampling ignores an informant's interaction with others and does not use the informant's observational and analytical skills. For example, if, in a study of the adjustment phases of becoming divorced, the interviews are restricted to just a man's or woman's *own* experiences and adjustments, there will be a loss of important information. In order to avoid losing any valuable information, the participant should be given the opportunity to reflect on and provide information about his or her experiences in comparison with other divorcees. It is these insider comparisons (i.e., self-reflections about the similarities and differences in his or her situation that have eased adjustment or made the adjustment more difficult) that add important richness and theoretical variation to the research.

Thus sampling techniques that ensure the quality of a quantitative study should not be used for qualitative research; in fact, using quantitative sampling techniques may invalidate a qualitative study. Therefore, the purpose of this chapter is to examine the principles of sampling in qualitative research and to consider threats to validity and special problems that occur when making sampling decisions.

Types of Samples

In qualitative research, four types of samples are commonly used: the purposeful sample, the nominated sample, the volunteer sample, and the sample that consists of the total population.

Purposeful Samples

When obtaining a purposeful (or theoretical) sample, the researcher selects a participant according to the needs of the study (Bogdan & Biklen, 1982, p. 67; Diers, 1979, p. 87; Glaser, 1978, p. 36; Glaser & Strauss, 1967, p. 48). Initially, the researcher may choose to interview informants with a broad, general knowledge of the topic or those who have undergone the experience and whose experience is considered typical. Then, as the study progresses, the description is expanded with more specific information, and participants with that particular knowledge are deliberately sought. Finally, informants with atypical experiences are sought so that the entire range of experiences and the breadth of the concept or phenomena may be understood. Thus, rather than selecting a sample using criteria based on typical or representative population characteristics such as age, economic status, or level of education, the sample is selected according to the informants' knowledge of the research topic. Therefore it is essential for the researcher to discover who will be the most appropriate informant before beginning interviews.

Nominated Samples

Nominated, network, or snowball sampling (Bogdan & Biklen, 1982, p. 66; Brink & Wood, 1988, p. 128; Taylor & Bogdan, 1984,

p. 83) is a common method of obtaining a qualitative sample. Nominated samples are obtained by eliciting the support and assistance of a single informant already in the study to assist with the selection of another participant. The first informant who is interviewed is invited to suggest another participant, and the researcher uses this referral to solicit the second person to be a part of the study. The new participant is approached in one of two ways: Either the researcher approaches the next informant, using the first informant as a reference, or the first informant approaches the new informant on the researcher's behalf. Thus the selection of participants is partly controlled by the participants enrolled in the study. In a nominated sample, the underlying assumptions are that those within the group can distinguish the "insiders" from the "outsiders," know who is most knowledgeable about certain topics, and therefore are most qualified to recommend the person who can provide the most information and the best interview.

When using nominated samples, the researcher does not have to spend time with groups of potential informants (getting to know about their background and so forth) in order to identify the best informants. In addition this technique has the advantage of easing the introductory phase of the interview and helping with the development of researcher-informant trust. If trust can be established with the first informant and that informant introduces the researcher as a "good guy" to the next informant, then the new informant is more likely to agree to be interviewed. Thus nominated sampling is an especially appropriate technique to use when the informants are difficult to identify or when informants may not wish to be identified, such as in studies involving homosexuals, witches, drug dealers, and so forth.

The strength (as well as the weakness) of this method of sampling is that the identification and selection of participants is controlled by the population of potential informants. The strength of the method is that researchers who want to contact a group, which may otherwise be difficult to contact, can gain access to the entire group by initially gaining the trust of one member of the group. On the other hand, if the first participant does not trust the researcher, then that person may protect the group by deliberately making an inappropriate referral and sending the researcher off on a false lead.

Volunteer Samples

Volunteer or solicited samples (Agar, 1980, pp. 156-157; Diers, 1979, p. 86) are frequently used in nursing research when the potential informants may not be known to the researcher or to each other. The researcher must rely on the potential participants (that is, those who might be presently going through or have had the particular experience of interest) identifying themselves. For example, a researcher might wish to study incontinence, managing breastfeeding while working, or the experience of dieting. While it may be possible to obtain the sample through a physician's caseload or through support groups, such as La Leche League or Weight Watchers, it is possible that those informants may have a different experience from those who do not use such services. Placing notices in newspapers, on television, and in supermarkets, requesting that people with the desired experiences contact the researcher, increases the types of participants and therefore broadens the potential range of experiences available to the researcher.

Total Population

A sample consisting of the total population is used when all the informants live or work within a confined area. For example, all the members of a nuclear family may be interviewed, regardless of family size, or all the staff members and patients on a single unit might be interviewed (e.g., the study of the cancer unit [Germain, 1979], or a neonatal intensive care unit [Hutchinson, 1984]).

In qualitative research, it is only possible to use the total population as the sample if the number of potential informants is not large. Although it is recognized that some of those interviewed may not have the information needed by the researcher, it is also recognized that *not* interviewing some of those present may be rude or offensive, making some of the participants feel left out, or it may make those who did participate more easily identifiable and thus reduce anonymity. After the interview has been conducted, the researcher should review the tape and decide whether the information obtained is worth including in the study. If the information is worth including in the study, then the tape should be transcribed; if it is not worth including in the study, the tape should be stored. This process is known as the "secondary selection" of the sample.

Qualities of a Good Informant

Regardless of the type of sample employed, informants must be selected or carefully chosen according to specific qualities (Agar, 1980, pp. 84-87; Hammersley & Atkinson, 1983, p. 46). Informants must be *knowledgeable about the topic* and experts by virtue of their involvement in specific life events and/or associations. The informants may have experienced the event that is being studied (for example, have experienced a heart attack or breastfed successfully for a long period of time) or been closely associated with someone who has undergone the experiences (for example, a relative of the patient or a nurse working on a coronary care unit).

A "good" informant is not necessarily an expert in the usual sense, that is, possessing in-depth theoretical knowledge or a particular sociological characteristic. Rather, as well as being someone who has undergone or is undergoing the experience, a good informant is one who is able to reflect and provide detailed experiential information about the phenomenon. Thus merely experiencing the condition is not sufficient enough criteria to make one a good informant. For example, a patient who has cardiac problems and is denying the experience would not make a good informant because the denial process itself would interfere with the self-examination and diminish or inhibit the descriptions of the experience in the interview situation. Good informants must be willing and able to critically examine the experience and their response to the situation, and this process may be painful or stressful, or it may be therapeutic. The second quality of a good informant is that he or she must be willing to share the experience with the interviewer.

Third, the willingness to talk is also related to the interviewee having enough uninterrupted time for the interview and sufficient patience and tolerance to explain and answer the researcher's questions. Repeated unstructured interviews require great blocks of time, and interruptions from the telephone, from children, or from other commitments distract the interviewee and severely reduce the quality of the data. In participant observation, having the researcher "hang around" is an imposition and possibly an intrusion. Although the researchers may not feel that their presence is an imposition, it does take some of the participant's time to introduce a researcher to others, provide orientation to the setting, and explain the norms and informal rules that are necessary for functioning in the setting.

Unfortunately, people agree to participate in a research project for many reasons other than to "contribute to science." For example, they may be curious about the purpose of the research and may suspect that the researcher has a hidden agenda. These people may volunteer to be in the project so they can discover the *real* reason for the research or so they can be in a position to monitor the activities of the researcher first-hand. They may also volunteer to add a little prestige or variety to their otherwise uneventful lives. It is flattering to be invited to express an opinion (even though revealing one's true feelings may be painful), and it is a pleasant boost to one's self-esteem to have an attentive interviewer listening to and recording one's every word. Informants may also agree to participate out of curiosity, just to see what is going to happen during the data collection phase. A poor informant would be one who speaks superficially or exaggerates the real experience for the sake of holding the researcher's attention while at the same time being unwilling to trust the interviewer and reveal his or her true feelings.

If the informant agrees to participate in the study, yet proves to be a poor informant, and the researcher is not getting the information needed, then the researcher uses *secondary selection* (see this chapter). The interview is terminated, or the researcher does not make arrangements for follow-up interviews, and the participant is dropped from the study. The researcher then decides whether to have the interview transcribed or to exclude it from the analysis. As a precaution, however, it is recommended that the tape of the interview be kept until the analysis is completed. As insights are gained, a poor interview may become an excellent example of a patient in a particular stage of denial, or whatever, and may eventually be useful. However, it is nonproductive to continue interviewing a participant who is not giving new information: It wastes the researcher's time and transcribing funds.

Group Interviews

The appropriateness or inappropriateness of conducting group interviews depends on the *type of knowledge or information sought*. If the researcher is seeking factual information, such as information on how something is done or what happened, it may be advantageous because informants can correct one another, and this process may help to jog memories. For instance, group interviews may also be helpful when examining intergenerational changes in infant feeding practices as discussions contrasting practices between the elderly women and new mothers may be enlightening (see Raphael & Davis, 1985). However, even with such nonthreatening topics, such factors as cultural rules for polite behavior may prohibit the younger informants from expressing contrary opinions and may interfere with data collection.

Group interviews, however, may cause problems when the information sought is intimate or highly emotional. Husbands and wives have different views on many topics, and these perspectives may not necessarily be shared with each other. (An excellent example of such perspectives is presented by Stinson and Stinson [1979/83] in their diaries written during the months that their premature infant received care in the neonatal ICU.) In such cases, the information presented to the researcher in joint interviews may be the dominant partner's perspective, or a view that both consider to be acceptable to others, but not their innermost thoughts. As such, a joint interview is an untenable threat to validity. Finally, interviewing each partner separately and then later interviewing the participants together as a couple creates many ethical dilemmas for both the interviewer and the participants. Awkward situations are created when the individuals have first confided possibly discrepant views to the researcher and then find themselves in a position of having to conceal the earlier position.

The last danger of joint interviews involving families or married couples is that the researcher may fall into the trap of providing counseling to reconcile differences or to get at the "real truth." Counseling changes the relationship of the researcher and the informants and is not the purpose of the research interview. The best way to avoid this type of situation is to avoid joint interviews.

Methods for Evaluating Samples

The method of sampling in qualitative research must be both *appropriate* and *adequate* (Morse, 1986). *Appropriateness* refers to the *degree to which the choice of informants and method of selection "fits" the purpose of the study as determined by the research question and the stage of the research. Adequacy,* on the other hand, refers to the *sufficiency and quality of the data.*

Tests for Appropriateness

As the study progresses, the criteria for the selection of informants changes. As stated at the beginning of the study, the researcher may elect to interview an informant with a broad knowledge of the situation or concept. Later, as the analysis develops and the research is approaching completion, the researcher may deliberately select informants with particular knowledge of some aspect of the topic in order to fill a gap in the developing theory or to confirm the researcher's hunches; therefore, an appropriate sample is guided by *informant characteristics* and by the *type of information needed by the researchers*. A test for appropriateness is, *do the methods used to select a sample facilitate understanding?* The appropriateness of a sample is evaluated by examining the methods of sampling and determining if the methods used and the sample obtained facilitate understanding of the research problem.

Test for Adequacy

In a qualitative project, adequacy refers to *informational adequacy,* that is, the *sufficiency and quality of the data obtained.* To ensure adequacy, one assesses the *relevance, completeness, and amount of information obtained.* If the data are adequate, then there are no "thin" areas, and the resulting theory is complete. Most researchers refer to this stage as *saturation* and use indicators, such as the researcher's "not hearing anything new" or becoming bored during interviews, to recognize saturation. Thus in qualitative research *informational adequacy* is ensured by the completeness and the amount of information rather than, as in quantitative research, by the number of cases. The test for adequacy is, *was saturation achieved and does the theory make sense?*

Researcher Control Over Sampling

In qualitative research, in order to ensure that the sample meets the criteria for appropriateness and adequacy, the *researcher must have control over the composition of the sample.* This is ensured by primary selection, that is, controlling who is selected to be interviewed. Alternatively, if the researcher does not have the opportunity to assess the informant's suitability before the interview has commenced, he/she uses *secondary selection,* that is, deciding whether to continue with subsequent interviews, or even whether to include the information obtained during the first interview, during or at the end of the first interview. If the decision is made not to include the interview, then it is not transcribed. But even if it is not used, the taped interview should not be erased because the information might be significant at a later stage in the research.

Primary Selection

With primary selection, researcher control is maintained because the researcher has a relationship with prospective informants, is aware of which members of the group have the knowledge required, knows who would be "good to talk to," and knows who would probably be willing to participate before inviting them to participate in the study. For these reasons, the "response rate" is high, usually 100% (Morse, 1986), and primary selection is the ideal method of sampling for purposeful or theoretical sampling in ethnography, participant observation, grounded theory, and phenomenology. Primary selection is clearly efficient, and because of this efficiency, the sample size is as small as possible.

Secondary Selection

This sampling strategy is used when the researcher does not have control over who will be interviewed at the commencement of the interview, for example, volunteer, nominated, and quota samples, and samples that include the total population. In these cases, the selection of informants is done *after* the interview has commenced. With these sampling strategies, some poor informants will be interviewed because the researcher does not know if the participant has the required knowledge or the qualities of a good informant. Thus in order to maintain the quality of data, the researcher must decide whether to include data obtained from a poor informant during the interview or at the completion of the interview. As stated, transcribing poor data is a waste of grant funds. In addition, collecting too much information quickly makes the data unmanageable; and poor data "buries" the significant data, making the process of analysis difficult.

In special circumstances if too many people volunteer, or if the list presented is too long to make it feasible to interview everyone, those participants first interviewed may be randomly chosen; however, this process alone does not ensure adequacy or appropriateness. After commencing the interview the researcher must still maintain control over the selection of informants, continuing interviews with those who provide the "best" information.

A problem that may arise with advertising in a newspaper or on the radio for participants is that the researcher may be overwhelmed with callers. For example, Williams and Morse (1989) conducted interactive interviews with mothers who had made the decision to wean their infants, and a newspaper article about the study resulted in more than 400 responses. In addition to those who were undergoing the experience of weaning, other "experts" called. For example, although the advertisement specifically requested that mothers who had made the decision to wean should call, one grandmother, who had weaned nine children, and many mothers who had completed the weaning process responded to the call for study participants. The investigator should make decisions about including these people in the study before the advertisement is placed. It may be advantageous to keep a list of their names should, for example, a sample be required later in the study to validate the emerging theory.

With nominated samples, because the newly invited participant has the privilege of choosing whether to enter the study, neither the first participant nor the researcher has initial control over the sample. However, if the second participant does not suit the research needs, then the researcher uses secondary control and drops the participant from the sample.

As stated, the ideal method of sampling for qualitative research is primary selection; however, this is frequently not possible for focused ethnography, grounded theory, or interactive interviews. In these research methods the sample size must be increased using secondary selection in order to compensate for the participants from whom little or no information is obtained. However, for phenomenology, because the sample size is very small and because of the time involved with repeated interviews, the researcher should be reasonably confident of the quality of the sample before beginning the first interview. Therefore phenomenology usually uses only primary selection.

TABLE 8.1 Comparison of Types of Samples Used in Qualitative Research

Type of Sample	Method	Selection	Researcher Control
Purposeful, Theoretical	Ethnography	Researcher	Primary
	Participant observation	Researcher	Primary
	Grounded theory	Researcher	Primary
	Phenomenology	Researcher	Primary
		Researcher	Primary
Total Population	Ethnography	Participant	Secondary
	Grounded theory	Participant	Secondary
Nominated, Snowball	Ethnography	Participant	Secondary
	Interactive interviews	Participant	Secondary
Volunteer, Solicited	Interactive interviews	Participant	Secondary

The types of samples used for different situations in which qualitative research is conducted and the amount of control the researcher has over the initial selection of the participant are listed in Table 8.1. This process of primary or secondary control of informant selection is essential to ensure that the interviews do not contain a lot of irrelevant information and that the data collection process is relatively efficient.

Special Problems in Sampling

The Control of Bias

The major criticism of volunteer, purposeful, and nominated samples is that the samples are "biased" by virtue of the selection process (either self-selection or researcher-selection). The criticism is valid—these methods facilitate a certain type of informant with a certain knowledge being included in the study, but *that is the purpose and intent of using those methods*. This is ideal; and in qualitative research, bias is *used* positively as a tool to facilitate the research. As mentioned, an unbiased sample, perhaps chosen randomly, violates the qualitative principle of obtaining information from experts *and* of sample size adequacy.

Nevertheless, special sampling strategies are used in qualitative research to ensure that all sides of an issue are represented. This includes either the deliberate seeking out of negative cases or seeking informants who had atypical experiences, bad experiences, or in some way a different experience. To ensure that the analysis is not distorted toward one perspective, several techniques are used to manage variation. It is important to understand that theoretical variation disregards the quantitative regard for proportions or percentages. Theoretical richness has nothing to do with "how much or how many," has nothing to do with the most common or least common experience, has nothing to do with likelihood; rather, the researcher seeks to describe the experiences as richly and accurately as possible. It is a serious error to exclude an experience because it is uncommon or appears to be an exception to the developing theory; rather, to ensure validity, all cases must fit the explanatory model.

Managing Variation Descriptively

Managing variation descriptively may be accomplished by using thick description to explain a concept. In the research report, the researcher carefully and fully describes all possible perspectives or types of experiences revealed. Of course, this description is more than a series of case studies; instead, depending on the level of analysis, it may be a compilation of scenarios or an explication of explanatory concepts presented as a detailed generic description.

Explaining Variation Diagrammatically

The grounded theory technique of constant comparison enhances the identification of indicators within a concept that may or may not be present. Glaser (1978, pp. 65-70) recommends developing 2 × 2 matrices to assist with constructing typologies (see Stern, this volume). Other methods include mapping (Artinian, 1986), the process using a flow chart or developing a model to show the relationship of various types of categories and the relationship between them (Corbin, 1986).

Using Secondary Samples

Another technique is to confirm hunches about the developing theory with a secondary sample. For example, in grounded theory when the researcher finds a negative case or has *a thin part in the data set,* that area is targeted, and further information on that topic alone is deliberately sought from additional informants. For instance, conformation of a hunch would be sought by quickly finding a person who has not previously been interviewed and asking him or her: "Some people tell me that____, is this true for you?"

Confirming

The last method of ensuring that the data are complete and all parameters of the experience are described is to confirm the findings with the participants. This may be done individually; although, if conducted in a group setting, the resulting dialogue between participants comparing their experiences with each other assists in removing interviewer bias and confirms the accuracy of the researcher's interpretation. Because it is often necessary to return to participants for additional or confirmatory information, it is important not to terminate or to lose track of the sample until the study is complete.

The Use of Multiple Sites—One Sample or Two?

Sometimes it is necessary to select two sites so that the sample will be large enough to obtain adequate informants. This introduces the questions of the dependence of qualitative research on the context of a study and of whether these two sites should be compared, or considered a single setting with data from both pooled. Again, it depends on the research question and the similarity of the two settings. For example, if the researcher wishes to compare the response of males and females to major surgery, then a male and female unit should be selected and the obtained data compared; however, if the second site is selected to increase the potential pool of participants and the researcher cannot identify any reason that the sites may be different, then the data could be pooled.

Occasionally it is necessary to select multiple sites so that one part of the data collection will not interfere with another. For example,

English and Morse (1988) and Estabrooks (1989) selected two settings: In one setting, the researchers interviewed and observed the
patients; and in the other setting, they interviewed the nursing staff.
This dual strategy was deliberately used to prevent reactive effects
from the research process changing the practice of the nurses or the
behavior of the patients during data collection phases, and this
strategy strengthened the generalizability of the study.

The Myth of Saturation

Although most researchers stop sampling when saturation is
reached, it is not uncommon at that point to confirm the findings
with another group, only to find that the secondary sample adds a
new perspective on the experience that had not been reported by
the original participants. The researcher is then faced with a dilemma: Has saturation really been attained? Should the new information be treated as a negative case, or should the researcher
conduct further interviews? Only the researcher can make this decision. In reality there are a myriad of experiences that may or may not
be pertinent or significant, and only the researcher is in a position to
decide whether or not the new information is significant.

The Myth of a Random Sampling

The principle underlying random sampling is that everyone will
have an equal chance of being selected, and so, the sample is more
likely to be representative of the population. However, for qualitative purposes, the potential informants within a population do not
have an equal amount of knowledge or equivalent experiences.
Furthermore some members of the group are more willing to be
interviewed and to share their experience. Random sampling, therefore, is a problem because it violates the quantitative principle of
sample size, violates the qualitative principle of selecting the most
experienced and knowledgeable informants, and violates the principle of selecting the best informant with the "qualities of a good
informant." Also, although those in quantitative research are inclined
to retain as many subjects as possible in their study (to improve
the "response rate"), if the participants in a qualitative study were
chosen randomly, the researcher might be reluctant to use secondary
selection and, instead, might cull the sample by removing poor

informants. Thus random sampling may jeopardize the quality of the research.

The Myth of Demographic Variation

Samples are typically described in terms of demographic characteristics, such as sex, age, martial status, and education level, so the reader can identify the type of population from which the sample was drawn and, if desired, replicate the study. These characteristics are used as indicators of the cultural or subcultural groups from which the informants are derived; and in qualitative research, such indicators are insufficient to identify the population from which the sample was drawn. In qualitative research demographics have little significance, and more descriptive methods of describing the participants and the context should be used (see Hutchinson, this volume).

Excluding Participants

Recognizing the significance of cultural beliefs and values in qualitative research, and the dependence of the results on the representativeness of the information obtained, should a culturally distinct participant be included in the sample? For example, when doing a study of the family experience of the incarceration of one parent, does the researcher select families of a single cultural group?

There is no obvious answer to this question. Some of the effective aspects of the research topic will cross cultural boundaries; others will not. It may or may not be important to know this information, and the researcher should carefully consider the research question and the purpose of the research. If the participants are from many cultural groups, and if it was not the intent of the researcher to do a cross-cultural study, then the study may become more difficult to interpret and unnecessarily complex. Therefore, unless the researcher is having difficulty in locating participants, those potential participants who are not a part of the cultural group should be excluded from the study or should be used as a comparative group.

Discussion

Ignoring the principles of qualitative sampling can be costly in terms of the reliability and validity of the study, compromising the quality of the resulting theory, and in terms of expense and researcher time. An example of the consequences of disregarding qualitative principles of sampling was recently noted in a study of clinical decision making (Prescott, Dennis, & Jacox, 1987). In this study, the researchers chose a quota sampling frame: At least two short-term general hospitals were selected from six geographically distinct cities (15 in total), but no rationale was provided for the city selection. Within each hospital, six patient care units (representing low, average, and high nursing vacancy rates at that hospital) were selected by administrators; and within each unit, three staff nurses, two physicians, the head nurse, and the supervisor were selected as participants. Thus the investigators were committed to a quota sampling frame based on demographic and regional factors assumed to contribute to variation. This research design resulted in a total of 560 interviews. The data obtained, however, were so voluminous that the study was unmanageable. Even at the stage of data collection, adequate resources were not available for transcription and analysis. The investigators' solution was to randomly select transcripts to be included in the analysis (Prescott et al., 1987, Footnote 1, p. 57), apparently disregarding the variation in the quality and the contribution of individual interviews to the theoretical development of the study.

The neglect of choosing a sampling method, which would allow theory to determine ongoing selection of participants, resulted in an extraordinary waste of collected interviews in the study, and the sample did not meet the criteria of adequacy or appropriateness required for a qualitative study. Furthermore the one-shot approach to analysis (conducted after the collection of data was complete) denied the principles and purpose of a qualitative study. A better design, one that would have met the researchers' needs for both exploration and generalizability, would have been a two-phase project. The first phase would have consisted of an in-depth qualitative project conducted in one institution using a small, purposeful sample to determine "What is going on?" From these data, a survey could have been developed and administered to a larger, representative sample during a second, quantitative phase.

When conducting qualitative research, it is most important to be vigilant and aware of the state of the project, of what is known and not known, of the thin areas of the data, and of the needs of the developing theory. Sampling is a process that goes on continually throughout the concurrent data collection and analysis phase, and the selection of informants is critical to the ultimate quality of the research. In qualitative research the key to maintaining an appropriate and adequate sample is the researcher's control over the sample. Primary control of the sample is ideal and most efficient, with the researcher controlling who is interviewed, when, and how often. If primary control is not possible, then secondary control should be used, with the selection process actually taking place after the interview has commenced. If the interview is not productive, then the interview should be terminated as soon as possible, and a decision should be made concerning the inclusion of the data in the study. Special techniques are used to manage variation and to prevent bias. These techniques are used to elicit and to describe the dimensions of variation within the phenomena or concept, rather than to convey the weighing, the proportions, or the statistical significance of different responses or experiences within the domain. At the conclusion of the study, the researcher describes the sample in relation to the context and the nature of the participants' experiences, rather than using population demographic indicators.

References

Agar, M. (1980). *The professional stranger: An informal introduction to ethnography.* New York: Academic Press.

Artinian, B. M. (1986). The research process in grounded theory. In W. C. Chenitz & J. M. Swanson (Eds.). *From practice to grounded theory* (pp. 16-23). Reading, MA: Addison-Wesley.

Bogdan, R. C., & Biklen, S. K. (1982). *Qualitative research for education: An Introduction to theory and methods.* Boston: Allyn & Bacon.

Brink, P. J., & Wood, M. J. (1988). *Basic steps in planning nursing research: From question to proposal* (3rd ed.). Boston: Jones and Bartlett.

Corbin, J. (1986). Coding, writing memos, and diagramming. In W. C. Chenitz & J. M. Swanson (Eds.). *From practice to grounded theory* (pp. 102-120). Reading, MA: Addison-Wesley.

Diers, D. (1979). *Research in nursing practice.* Philadelphia: J. B. Lippincott.

English, J., & Morse, J. M. (1988). The "difficult" elderly patient: Adjustment or maladjustment? *International Journal of Nursing Studies, 25*(1), 23-29.

Estabrooks, C. (1989). Touch: A nursing strategy in the intensive care unit. *Heart & Lung, 18*(4), 392-401.

Germain, C. (1979). *The cancer unit: An ethnography.* Wakefield, MA: Nursing Resources.

Glaser, B. G. (1978). *Theoretical sensitivity.* Mill Valley, CA: Sociology Press.

Glaser, B. G., & Strauss, A. L. (1967). *The discovery of grounded theory.* New York: Aldine.

Hammersley, M., & Atkinson, P. (1983). *Ethnography: Principles in practice.* London: Tavistock.

Hutchinson, S. (1984). Creating meaning out of horror. *Nursing Outlook, 32*(2), 86-90.

Leininger, M. (1985). Southern rural Black and White American lifeways with focus on care and health phenomena. In M. Leininger (Ed.). *Qualitative research methods in nursing* (pp. 195-216). Orlando, FL: Grune & Stratton.

Morse, J. M. (1986). Qualitative and quantitative research: Issues in sampling. In P. Chinn (Ed.). *Nursing research methodology: Issues and implementation* (pp. 181-193). Rockville, MD: Aspen.

Prescott, P. A., Dennis, K. E., & Jacox, A. K. (1987). Clinical decision making of staff nurses. *Image: Journal of Nursing Scholarship, 19*(2), 56-62.

Raphael, D., & Davis, F. (1985). *Only mothers know: Patterns of infant feeding in traditional cultures.* Westport, CT: Greenwood Press.

Stinson, R., & Stinson, P. (1979/1983). *The long dying of baby Andrew.* ???: Atlantic-Little, Brown Books.

Taylor, S. J., & Bogdan, R. (1984). *Introduction of qualitative methods: The search for meaning* (2nd ed.). New York: John Wiley.

Trost, J. E. (1986). Statistically nonrepresentative stratified sampling: A Sampling technique for qualitative studies. *Qualitative Sociology, 9*(1), 54-57.

Williams, K. M., & Morse, J. M. (1989). Weaning patterns of first-time mothers. *Maternal-Child Nursing, 14,* 188-192.

Dialogue

On Replicability

MUNHALL: Phyllis, when you did your study on stepfathers—how long ago was that?

STERN: 1976.

MUNHALL: Do you think you generated theory from that?

STERN: Yes.

MUNHALL: Yes, I think you did, too. And if somebody wanted to do that same study 20 years later, would they have different results?

STERN: No—I think the kind of thing you generate in grounded theory will stand in time. The main point about step-families, for instance, is that they're not integrated when they come together, and they have to *get* integrated. It doesn't matter if it's a hundred years from now, they're still going to have to go through that integration process.

MUNHALL: And 20 years later, it may be easier because society accepts step-families more.

STERN: It may be, but we have to go out and look.

MUNHALL: Right, it's something that we have to do. I'm arguing that things do change, and we should study things, periodically, over again.

STERN: Sure. The situation may change, but the process may remain the same. Take suicide: It's still a process. You can follow Durkheim—he wrote about it before the turn of the century—and suicide is still very much the same process. You either end up dead or you don't!

9

Are Counting and Coding A Cappella Appropriate in Qualitative Research?

PHYLLIS NOERAGER STERN

Heady with our newfound freedom to debate publicly the relative merits of this or that style of naturalistic approach, we can now consider two propositions over which qualitative researchers take issue: (a) whether measuring data by counting, with percentages, or with ratios—that is, quantitative tools have any place in qualitative designs; and (b) whether investigators of a given situation can be trusted to code, form categories, and generate theoretical constructs alone, or whether they must pass the scrutiny of a panel of experts.

I am a grounded theorist of strong conviction, and it is against the tenets of that discipline that I gauge every other. Using grounded theory as a guide, my first thoughts about the subjects at hand were that counting the number of things in a population, or the number of times respondents said a certain word, is not only superfluous to theory development, but this kind of measurement might also get in the way of the analyst. As for coding alone, I maintained that there is no reason why any reasonably bright, trained, mature individual cannot code data accurately, meaningfully, coherently, and solo. Following consultations with colleagues, however, I am willing to entertain the idea that there might be other ways of thinking about counting and coding.

Ways of Measuring Qualitative Data

As qualitative researchers, we not only have to decide how to approach a research problem but we also have to explain ourselves

147

to those who have not learned the jargon of our genre. Translation of our language is necessary when we propose a study, during its conduction, and when we report what we have found (see Munhall, Chapter 15). The task may seem laborious, but we must now translate qualitative language into common English for our methodologically different colleagues. If others fail to understand our language, they will also fail to accept our generated theories, fail to publish our work, and fail to fund our proposals.

We have ways of measuring data exclusive of numbers, methods that require lateral rather than linear thinking. But in our need to make ourselves clear to others, do we need to use numbers? It appears that sometimes we do. Can numbers be helpful to the analysis and interpretation of the data? Yes, but only if the numbers do not blur the vision of the researcher.

Numbers and the Proposal

Whether we are submitting a proposal for funding, ethical review, or to an organization wherein likely informants dwell, there is an almost 100% chance that many of the individuals making up the group we approach will know little about qualitative research. We may criticize numbers as being poor representatives of reality and amenable to machination, but in the instance of the proposal, we assume numbers to be the universal language.

An organization that grants permission to do a piece of research by funding, ethical approval, or supplying research participants, wants number answers to certain concrete questions: How long will the research take? How much of the participants' (and perhaps, organization's) time will you occupy? How many individuals will make up the study population? Qualitative researchers do not know the answers to these questions; instead, they make an educated guess as to what figures seem reasonable and submit them.

Some of my colleagues have philosophical problems with this. They argue that a concrete number can never be offered in advance of a study, for one never knows beforehand the size and shape of a theoretical sample, how long an interview might last, or when the analysis will be complete. Also, some data respond to reexamination after years of being left alone. These colleagues think they should not be forced into the quantitative mode. The answer to this philosophical dilemma is really quite simple. In a sense all proposals are made up of a series of educated guesses. Regardless of the style of approach, the investigator never really knows what she or he is getting into. More basic than that, if the members of the organizational board applied, to read a proposal in other than their own language, then permission to do the study is usually denied. Put that way, filling in the numbers seems a small philosophical price to pay for admission.

Measurement and Analysis: Basic Premise

Our measurements in a qualitative study go beyond numbers into the realm of conceptual manipulation. The symbols we work with are words rather than numbers. We use words, clustering them, ordering them, and building them into a picture of reality. We map data and draw pictures about it, and we try to see how it moves and changes. Continuums, cross-tabulation, and phase analysis are but three examples of qualitative analysis.

Continuums

A continuum can be a handy device for picturing some kinds of data since every process has a polar quality. Every time one tunes in, one tunes out to something else. There will be gradations of the process that can be placed along the continuum. If one thinks of markers between antipodal end points of our continuum, order can be generated about a sane-insane concept. Very few individuals can be classified as feeling insane 24 hours a day, seven days a week. Likewise, the most sane of us have moments of doubt about our balance. Where an individual can be placed on a sane-insane continuum, and how that order of placement might change over time, are the types of things that concern the qualitative researcher.

Cross-tabulations

Glaser (1978) offers a number of ways to picture and, therefore, measure data in *Theoretical Sensitivity*. Glaser uses a four-fold table

Certainty of Outcome

	+	−
Time of Outcome +	Certainty of time and outcome: nothing more to do	Certain time when outcome will reach turning point
−	Certainty of outcome but lingering	Wait and see

Figure 9.1 Cross-tabulation of time and certainty dimensions in the formation of an outcome typology.

Source: Adapted with permission of Barney G. Glaser from *Theoretical Sensitivity* by B. G. Glaser. Copyright © 1978 by Barney G. Glaser.

to illustrate the cross-tabulation of typologies. In analyzing the data for the dying study (Glaser & Strauss, 1965), the concept "outcomes" was enriched through the cross-tabulation of the dimensions "certainty of outcome" with "time of outcome." In *Theoretical Sensitivity*, Glaser states, "We have started out 'wholistically' with the concept death expectations, discovered two dimensions of it, then reduced them to a typology" (p. 66). Figure 9.1 depicts this process.

Phases

The analysis of phases in a given process can be a useful way of thinking about data. For example, identifying the benchmarks in a recovery period following a devastating house fire provides helpful information for both victims and their supporters (Stern & Northrup, 1988).

As one attempts to define the limits of a given variable, one must picture its path into infinity and then follow that path back to the heart of the data. What data make up the path? How was the path constructed? What is the meaning of that path to the participants? Where does it take them—can they refuse to go? The use of continuums, cross-tabulations, and phase analysis help us answer these and many other questions.

Appurtenant Counting

Used with discretion, number symbols may be employed in the analysis and report of a qualitative study, particularly when one discovers an all-or-none phenomenon in the data. Certain aspects of the demographic data, for example, may be subjected to arithmetic manipulation just to see if the results enrich the analysis and report. Boyle's (Chapter 16) picture of teenage mothers is a brilliant example of how numbers can enrich a qualitative analysis. Boyle paints a lifelike picture of the teenage mothers who participated in her study when she tells us about their use of the word "stuff":

> For example, the word stuff occurs over 100 times in the 16 transcribed interviews. It seemed to be a common word used by teenage mothers as they struggled to express their views and perceptions of reality . . . in explaining why they became pregnant "We spent a lot of time together and stuff." Or, in describing their daily activities, "I bathe the baby and stuff" . . . . When describing her relationship with her husband, "We do stuff together. . . . "

When Boyle gives us these bits of datum and tells us that she and her colleagues tabulated 100 indices of the word "stuff," the slang of teenagers comes alive for us, as does the plight of these young women as they grapple with the real and grown-up condition of parenthood while possessed of a half-child mode of speech with which to express themselves.

Ellingsen's study (Ellingsen & Stern, 1988) is another example of the way numbers can enhance a qualitative study. Ellingsen reports that Micmac Indian women's narratives are interspersed with long pauses. The pauses do not indicate a completed topic, and to interrupt the silence with further questioning or offered opinion is considered rude. Ellingsen, who has worked on Micmac reserves as a Public Health Nurse, notes that only individuals familiar with Micmac speech patterns would know about the pauses, and even so, it is often difficult to ascertain how long a silence should last. Only the Micmacs understand. Joyce Carver, a member of our grounded theory seminar and a content analyst, suggested that one could measure the length, interval, and frequency of those silences. In this way one might come closer to discovering the meaning of silence for Micmac Indian women.

Carver's suggestion opened up two avenues for exploration: (a) understanding the meaning of silence for Micmac women may help nurses learn more about what these women want their nursing care to be, and (b) the analysis of content through measuring data in the numerical sense can be a valid method for a qualitative researcher.

Dubious Use of Numerical Measurement

The content analysis method for manipulation of qualitative data was an honest effort on the part of its developers to make indicative research more scientific, rigorous, and scholarly—in other words, easier to control. Content analysis offers the interpreter of data a way of curbing the impulse to zoom off on creative flights of fancy and, at the same time, to know the victory of being able to demonstrate to quantitative colleagues where the final conclusions come from. They come from counting, categorizing units of analysis, and attempting to make them statistically coherent. Content analysts believe that they have captured the best elements of qualitative and quantitative research. Their critics believe that they have separated the wheat from the chaff, and that excess rigor has, in the end, given them the chaff to work with. Polit and Hungler (1987) have described these two schools of thought:

> Whether or not qualitative data should be quantified is a different issue. Some investigators argue that everything can be measured (quantified) and that quantitative analysis is the best way to determine objectively whether relationships between variables exist. . . . Other researchers argue against any quantification asserting that qualitative materials are richer than numbers and offer more potential for understanding relationships and meanings. They also argue that because data collection and coding procedures are not immune to subjectivity, the use of numbers merely disguises potential bias and gives the illusion of objectivity. (p. 352)

Polit and Hungler disagree with both extremes. Because of the valuable contributions of my colleagues, particularly Ramona Mercer's numerous publications (recently, Mercer, Nichols & Doyle,

1988) and the program of research by Ritchie, Caty, and Ellerton (1984), I have been pushed to view content analysis with curiosity rather than disdain. I have come to the conclusion that the success of research outcomes depends more on the scientist than the scientific method used. One must proceed with caution, though, for the researcher who analyzes qualitative data by interpreting numerical measurements does so at her or his own risk. What follows is an in-depth critique of a study which strikes me as going awry.

Bliss-Holtz (1988) attempted to determine the learning needs of pregnant women when she conducted her study, "Primiparas' Prenatal Concern for Learning Infant Care." Unfortunately Bliss-Holtz seems to have had problems with her method of data collection, her analysis, and her interpretation of the findings, and consequently, she seems to have failed to learn what pregnant women think about learning infant care prenatally.

Problem One: Data Collection

Polit and Hungler warn that in quantifying qualitative data "the trick is to develop a system that is consistent with the aims of the research and faithful to the message conveyed in the qualitative materials" (p. 352). Bliss-Holtz was so focused on objectivity that when she collected her data she never got the message she was after. She wanted to test three hypotheses:

1. There is a difference in overall desire to learn infant care in the three stages of the antepartal period.
2. There is a difference in the pragmatic component of the desire to learn infant care in the three stages of the antepartal period.
3. There is a difference in the psychological component of the desire to learn infant care in the three stages of the antepartal period. (p. 21)

To find the answers to these questions, Bliss-Holtz interviewed women in early, middle, and late pregnancy. Instead of simply asking the women what they wanted to learn about infant care, she constructed "an open-ended interview schedule . . . to avoid responses based on what the subjects thought the investigator might want to hear" (p. 21). Participants were asked things like, "If your were going to a fortune-teller, what would you ask her?" and the slightly more focused question, "What information would you like to receive about your pregnancy?" (p. 21).

Respondents generally try to tell the interviewer what they think "the investigator might want to hear." That is, respondents try to provide the information needed. These informants were told that "the purpose of the study was to determine items of concern or interest to women during pregnancy" (p. 21). If the investigator chooses to be less than honest about the intent of the study (in this case, failing to inform about child care information needed), she or he runs the risk of gathering data oblique to the study question. If we picture ourselves as a pregnant woman being asked the fortune-teller question, we may guess that the investigator wants us to predict the future of the stock market. Responding to the second question, we would certainly answer something about pregnancy because the question was about pregnancy and not child care. As the pregnant informant, we would know the investigator was interested in our infant care learning needs only when she gave us the "Child Care Experience Scale" to fill out. By then it would be too late to tell the investigator what we wanted to know about taking care of our expected baby, because the interview would be over and there would not be another one. One cannot recover from this kind of off-the-mark data, and Bliss-Holtz never does.

Problem Two: Analysis

To analyze her data, Bliss-Holtz separates it into thematic units. She explains that "a basic assumption underlying this form of data translation is that the amount of interest each subject has in a topic will be represented by the number of phrases the subject uses to express that interest" (p. 21). To assess the "amount of interest" the pregnant women had in infant care, she used transparent overlays to cover her typed data to see how much space in that typed data interest-in-child care occupied. Bliss-Holtz took no inventory of the intensity of the responses. Put another way, she took great pains to measure her data with care, and in so doing, she completely lost the quality of the message. If we now assume the investigator's point of view, we might discover that many of the women said something like, "Wow, do I need to know more about baby care!" In the method we have chosen to analyze the data, the "wow" and the exclamation mark would be quantified out of this quote so that it would receive only a neutral rating. Consequently we would have to ignore the intensity of the women's remark because we are trapped by the rules of our content-analysis game.

Problem Three: Interpretation of Findings

When Bliss-Holtz discusses her findings, she notes that, although women in the later stages of pregnancy were significantly more interested in both child care and the pragmatics of child care, the "expression of desire to learn infant care was relatively small [and] represented only 5% of the total concerns expressed" (p. 24). Considering how she collected her data, this outcome is not surprising. What is startling is Bliss-Holtz's conclusion that "the practice of teaching infant care during the third trimester must be questioned." She may be right. Perhaps mothers have to get through labor before they are ready to tackle caretaking instruction—one assumes her study grew out of her clinical observations. But the tragedy here is that what may have been perfectly good clinical observation has been put through the scientific method hopper until it is of debatable use to practicing nurses.

Making Numerical Measurement Work:
Going Beyond the Method

Given the Bliss-Holtz example, we may ask, how do some content analysts manage to arrive at findings that have meaning for nursing and for further research? The answer may be that the scientists who use content analysis practice the time-honored custom of stepping back from the method to see the whole picture. DeMillo, Lipton, and Perlis (1979) tell us that the acceptance of a theory is a social process wherein colleagues decide if the theory makes sense. They further argue that the proofs are irrelevant as no one reads them because they are so boring. Those scientists who have contributed so much to our knowledge about our clients and our profession dare to go beyond the proofs to a truth that can be accepted by their colleagues. More of this later when we consider the uses of the panel of experts.

Coding, Categorizing, and Conceptualizing Alone

The question of whether one can code, categorize, and conceptualize alone requires a two-part answer. One aspect has to do with the mechanics of the enterprise, the other with the intent of the work. In the first instance, the task is to get from here, the data, to there, what one finds in it. In the second, one must decide whether one aims to describe phenomena or explain to it.

Coding Alone: Mechanics of the Enterprise

There are two parts to the mechanics of coding alone. One has to do with ability, and given that our analyst has prior or concurrent training, we assume that ability. The second part has to do with whether it is a good idea to do this task alone. Well, it depends. . . .

Ability to Code Alone

Regardless of whether the research is set up as a team or as an independent study, a great deal of the coding process takes place in solitude. The nature of the work is such that, for part of it at least, the intense state of concentration that one can only achieve in isolation is needed to make one's way through the labyrinth of possible meanings and conceptual configurations contained within the data. The passion of dissecting and reassembling the data becomes a 24-hour-a-day occupation. If we refer to the example of the sane-insane continuum mentioned earlier in this chapter, and substitute attention-to-the-here-and-now as the variable measured, analysts working with qualitative data go right off the end of the scale past the preoccupation end-point. This state of being is well known to familiars of the analyst as he or she might, during an important dinner discussion, get a blank expression, reach for a pen, and scribble a note on the wine list.

Is Coding Alone a Good Idea?

Although solitude may be a necessary part of coding in the development of a theory, the best analysis, like the acceptance of a theory, is a social process. As I prepared myself for this chapter, I looked over what I had written about qualitative analysis in the past (Stern,

1980, 1985; Stern, Allen, & Moxley, 1982, 1984; Stern & Pyles, 1986). I discovered that more often than not, I suggested working with a team. For one thing, teamwork is more fun. It can get exciting and fast as the group catches fire with the analysis. Strauss (1987) agrees, and he presents several illustrations of team analysis.

A study-in-progress case of the solo-simultaneous pattern of coding might help clear up the seeming dichotomy between coding a cappella and/or under supervision. As an exercise in collecting and treating data, students in a master's course in qualitative research offered by teleconferencing analyzed the special qualities of this medium of course delivery. The course was delivered to 29 master of nursing students in three provinces of Eastern Canada: Nova Scotia, New Brunswick, and Prince Edward Island. Over the phone, we coded and categorized data about the teleconferenced class. Students had been thinking about this and other teleconferenced courses and, therefore, were quick to offer both data and a way of organizing it.

Data involving students traveling to teleconference sites in major blizzards, for example, were categorized as *constancy*. Lacking visual interaction, students compensated by a particular care in reading the assigned and other material. This was categorized as *preparedness*. The necessity of activating their microphone to join the seminar made students feel they had to speak in well-thought-out sentences. When I, as the course professor finally said, "I don't understand some of this junk very well either," students found this *self-disclosure* helped them relax. On-campus, full-time students complained that they had made sacrifices in order to gain the intimacy of a traditional seminar medium of delivery and that they were not getting that closeness. Afraid the on-campus students might indeed be missing something, I began phoning the authors of our readings long-distance during class time and connecting them to our conference call so that these authors could join our seminar for an evening. We labeled this *guest stars*. We named all of these categories as a group exercise.

Next we tried to decide on the core variable. One student suggested that the core variable in our teleconferenced course was networking. But we were not entirely satisfied with that. I thought about our analysis solo over the week, and it hit me that the class was about overcoming impaired communication. Switching to the group mode again, I tried out this core variable on two or three students in the class and on some of my professor colleagues familiar with distance technology. By the next class period, I was ready to spring it on the group. The group of 29 participants and analysts accepted the core variable. A few weeks later, Judith Wuest, a member of the class, and I submitted an abstract of our analysis for consideration by the jury panel of a research conference. We compared our separate readings of the data, and after we talked over what the class had found, I had the nagging fear that we had committed premature closure on the study. I worked alone for a while, going over the data, the categories, and the analysis until the phrase, "Accommodating to a fear of omission" came to mind. I whooped because I knew that phrase was exactly right for describing the process. You see, as a class, we were so afraid we were going to miss something because the work was phoned in that we all tried extra-hard to make it work.

In our class, we analyzed, as individuals and as a research time, the social/psychological processes inherent in broadcasting a seminar over the phone in the cultural climate of Eastern Canada. The process went back and forth. We submitted our preliminary findings for research conference review (Stern & Wuest, 1988). The final step before presentation was to circulate an abstract of our revised theoretical scheme to the 29 members of the team for their ideas about the further expansion of the analysis. We followed Rennie, Phillips, and Quartaro's (1988) advice that "independent categorizing by research collaborators can be useful as a check on the perceptual field of the primary investigator" (p. 148). The research team, then, is our panel of experts.

The Panel of Experts

Pamela Brink makes a convincing case for using a panel of experts or a judge panel elsewhere in this book. As I understand her, I agree with Brink. When a researcher's mission is to *describe* a given unit, consistency within the component parts is important so that the description of the same unit will be equivalent if tackled by another researcher.

A panel of experts enters nicely into a descriptive equation for it represents outsiders who know little of the research. As such, the panel adds a research component as objective as any quantitative design. We must, however, be mindful of Minnis' (1985) caution: "Most research remains overwhelmingly descriptive. The focus is narrow with emphasis on particular institutional problems. . . ." (p. 190).

If we elect to follow Minnis's lead and *generate theory,* a panel of outside experts would be inappropriate because developing a well-integrated theory demands a thorough knowledge of the data, the categories, and the discovered hypotheses. Authors often speak of being immersed in study data. If one accepts this term, then no panel of experts could possibly be immersed with enough data to be able to judge the suitability of categories. Rather, reality testing of the developing theory with "research collaborators" (Rennie et al., 1988, p. 143) provides a good check of how accurately the emerging theory depicts the action in the scene under study. The use of 29 participant-analysts above illustrates this concept. The ultimate experts in judging the validity (are the findings true for the group under study) and reliability (will the findings be valid over time) of a developing theory are the study informants. One must never override their judgment. As Brink points out, this validity check is built into many qualitative designs.

The value of using objective expert panels in theory-generating qualitative designs is less clear to me. I have acted as expert for a study of nurses' use of empathy. McKay, Hughes, and Carver (1990) asked me and another colleague to act as jury for their categories. Unfamiliar with the fine points of the content analyses research design, my judge colleague and I nattered on about how we could give a better opinion of the categories if we saw the data in context rather than in what is called "units of analysis," this case, parts of sentences.

Nevertheless, we did as we were asked and apparently provided good inter-rater reliability. In the report of the study, however, there were elements that caused concern. In conversations between nurses and their patients on a burn ward, there was content that McKay, Hughes, and Carver would categorize as having a "feeling tone" (emotional in nature). These feeling tone data appeared rarely, but when they did, they were supercharged. They usually came up in discussions about significant others. Unfortunately, by the rules of their method, feeling tone rated a low frequency or percentage score in the overall analysis.

"Thank God! A panel of experts!"

Figure 9.2 A panel of experts may prove to be inappropriate for certain research questions

What to do? These researchers had followed the rules. They had sought the advice of a panel of experts, and still, an element in the data (feeling tone) failed to achieve the importance it deserved vis-à-vis its intensity. MacKay et al. did what good researchers everywhere do: They stepped back from the method to take in the whole picture. They were then able to tell their audience that although nurses and their patients on a burn unit rarely discuss feeling tone issues, when they do, the intensity of the patient's emotional involvement is so apparent that it is clear the empathetic nurse would pursue these feeling tone areas. The contribution of the panel of experts in the example above (as those in Figure 9.2) may or may not have added to the validity and reliability of the study findings. It was the investigators themselves, however, who can be credited with moving outside the method to render a real and true final report.

Conclusions

At the beginning of this chapter, we posed two questions: (a) whether measuring data by counting, with percentages, or with ratios—that is, quantitative tools—have any place in qualitative designs; and (b) whether investigators of a given situation can be trusted to code, form categories, and generate theoretical constructs alone, or whether they must pass the scrutiny of a panel of experts. In our attempts to answer these questions, we have woven a tapestry with a predominant pattern reading, "it depends."

As qualitative researchers, we find the imprecise nature of our methods endlessly fascinating. This imprecision matches the very nature of our study informants, for humans can only be correctly coded as individuals. The flexibility of qualitative methods, then, allows us to bend and sway and, in so doing, to follow the leading rhythm of the people we want to find out about—to finally find their truth.

We may see that phrases such as "bend and sway" fit poorly with the lexicon of granting agencies. Clearly, there are portions of a proposal and study findings that can be translated into the universal language of numbers. As for that other part of the proposal, we can assure validity and reliability by first establishing whether our purpose is description or theory generation. Then we must describe, in clear, precise, English terms, how we hope to achieve either of those ends.

We may have unearthed some of the reasons why we as qualitative researchers come to the decisions we do when designing our studies. There may be something here that will help us describe our study designs clearly and winningly, and then help us find our informants' truth by standing back from that design prior to concluding our studies.

References

Bliss-Holtz, V. J. (1988). Primiparas' prenatal concern for learning infant care. *Nursing Research, 37*(1), 20-24.

DeMilo, R. A., Lipton, R. J., & Perlis, A. J. (1979). Social processes and proofs of theorems and programs. *Communications of the Association for Computing Machinery, 22,* 271-280.

Ellingsen, R., & Stern, P. N. (1988, November). *Variables affecting Micmac Indian women's health.* Paper presented at the Third International Congress on Women's Health Issues, Tampa, FL.

Glaser, B. G. (1978). *Theoretical sensitivity.* Mill Valley, CA: Sociology Press.

Glaser, B. G., & Strauss, A. L. (1965). *Awareness of dying.* Chicago: Aldine.

MacKay, R. C., Hughes, J. R., & Carver, E. J. (1990). *Empathy in the helping relationship.* New York: Springer.

Mercer, R. T., Nichols, E. G., & Doyle, G. C. (1988). Transitions over the life cycle: A comparison of mothers and non-mothers. *Nursing Research, 37,* 144-151.

Minnis, J. R. (1985). Ethnography, case study, grounded theory, and distance education research. *Distance Education, 6,* 189-198.

Polit, D. F., & Hungler, B. P. (1987). *Nursing Research: Principles and methods* (3rd ed.). Philadelphia, PA: Lippincott.

Rennie, D. L., Phillips, J. R., & Quartaro, G. K. (1988). Grounded theory: A promising approach to conceptualization in psychology? *Canadian Psychology/Psychology Canadienne, 29*(2), 139-150.

Ritchie, J., Caty, S., & Ellerton, M. L. (1984). Concerns expressed by acutely ill, chronically ill and healthy preschool children. *Research in Nursing and Health, 7,* 265-274.

Stern, P. N. (1980). Grounded theory methodology: Its uses and processes. *Image, 12,* 20-23.

Stern, P. N. (1985). Using grounded theory in nursing research. In M. M. Leininger (Ed.). *Qualitative research methods in nursing* (pp. 149-160). New York: Grune & Stratton.

Stern, P. N., Allen, L. M., & Moxley, P. A. (1982). The nurse as grounded theorist: History, processes and uses. *The Review Journal of Philosophy and Social Science, 7,* 200-215.

Stern, P. N., Allen, L. M., & Moxley, P. A. (1984). Qualitative research. The nurse as grounded theorist. *Health Care for Women International, 5,* 371-385.

Stern, P. N., & Northrup, D. (1989, May). *Burned out: Variables affecting a positive outcome following loss of home by fire.* Paper presented to the International Council of Nursing, Seoul, Korea.

Stern, P. N., & Pyles, S. H. (1986). Using grounded theory methodology to study women's culturally based decisions about health. In P. N. Stern (Ed.). *Women, health and culture* (pp. 1-24). New York: Hemisphere & McGraw-Hill International.

Stern, P. N., & Wuest, J. (1988). *Overcoming impaired communication in a tele-conferenced graduate seminar in qualitative research.* Abstract submitted to a conference.

Strauss, A. L. (1987). *Qualitative analysis for social scientists.* Cambridge: Cambridge University Press.

Dialogue

On Issues About Reliability and Validity

BRINK: The issue that I would like to lay on the table is the issue of
           terminology. In the literature on reliability and validity, I
           found the terminology execrable! We have so many terms to
           cover exactly the same concept. Nobody is talking to any-
           body. Anybody who does anything at all on reliability and
           validity makes up a new term to cover what has previously
           been discussed in another setting and in another field. There-
           fore, in my chapter, I decided to use the reliability and validity
           terminology that was used in the original Selltiz (Selltiz,
           Wrightsman, & Cook, 1976) works that underpin most of
           psychology. And as you know, both Selltiz and Kerlinger
           (1973) were the two major psychologists that nursing has
           used for research texts for years, and so we still have hang-
           overs in many of our quantitative papers from both Kerlinger
           and Selltiz.

           The basic reason for my using Selltiz is that most of us have
           to write for quantitative people. We have to get our articles
           published, and most of the reviewers are quantitative re-
           searchers. We need to get our research funded. Most of the
           reviewers on review boards are quantitative and will under-
           stand terminology if we use quantitative terms. So what I tried
           to do in this chapter was to take quantitative theory of
           reliability and validity and translate it for qualitative methods.

On Hard Data

STERN: I haven't yet sorted this out very well, but there seems to be
           some sort of notion out there that what people say, and what
           they think about what they say, and the symbolic meaning of
           what they say to one another is not as real as the stain on the
           cell or the chemical compound that may, in a few years, turn
           out not to be the basic compound that we thought it was.

10

Issues of Reliability and Validity

PAMELA J. BRINK

I had just left the field and was writing up my doctoral dissertation when I had occasion to compare notes on "fieldwork" experiences with a fellow doctoral student. I was grousing about the fact that I was able to live with the Northern Paiute for only seven months, and he felt sorry for me because he said he had spent three years in the field. He was a descriptive linguist and had worked with a woman informant to transcribe her language, and if he needed verification on any words or meanings, he would ask her children. He was very meticulous about his verification procedures. But then he mentioned that she lisped, and later, he mentioned that he was able to go to the field to collect data only during the summer months when he was not in school.

This incident puzzled me so much that I wrote a paper about it, called "How Many Informants and What for?" What I was grappling with, without knowing it, were issues of reliability and validity. How could one have a valid description of a language if the chief informant lisped! All verification was from the offspring of that same woman. Instead of validating the language of the people she was supposed to represent, were her children just validating her language? Would it not have been more valid to have sought verification from persons other than her own children? And what, by the way, made her a good chief informant? On what basis was she selected? How many people were needed to document a language, or anything else, for that matter? Finally, I was disturbed that his three years

AUTHOR'S NOTE: I am grateful to Gail Ardery for her cheerful persistence in editing all drafts of this manuscript.

of fieldwork actually totalled only nine interrupted months. How could I believe him and his work with this kind of reporting?

Ever since that time, I have been concerned with issues of reliability and validity (Brink, 1987; Brink & Wood, 1978, 1988) and have listened to every "methods" report with my "third" ear. To what degree can I trust the reporter that the research is true? To what degree can I believe that all possible occurrences of error were minimized rather than "built into" the design?

I am certainly not alone in my concern. Oscar Lewis (1951) challenged Robert Redfield (1930), and Derek Freedman (1983) challenged Margaret Mead (1928) on just these issues. The problem was, of course, that neither Lewis nor Freedman found what their predecessors had found and, therefore, challenged the validity of the previous work. Neither, of course, could prove that the previous work was invalid. Both Lewis and Freedman had completely different sampling frames from their predecessors, asked different questions of different informants, and lived in different locations. Regardless of the issues of validity raised, such sampling differences alone would account for the discrepancies. When probability samples are used in highly quantitative correlational studies, different results are obtained, depending upon the sample selection procedures and the size of the sample. When both procedures and size are identical, different people belonging to the same group may respond differently to the same questions, thereby yielding different results. The point that both Lewis and Freedman missed was that they were arguing reliability issues while challenging the validity of their predecessors' reports. Their reports were, in fact, no more valid than their predecessors' and could be challenged by still others with the same results. Because of these two famous cases, however, qualitative methodologists are now documenting methods, rather than simply assuming everyone knows what has been done, and that is not a bad thing.

The first general methods book in anthropology to treat issues of reliability and validity with any consistency was, of course, the work by Pelto(1970) and, later, by Pelto and Pelto (1978). Prior work (McCall & Simmons, 1969), although dealing with these issues, did not discuss them in great detail. Today, there are a number of books, notably published by Sage (Agar, 1980; Borzak, 1981; Brinberg & McGrath, 1985; Fielding & Fielding, 1986; Kirk & Miller, 1986; Lincoln & Guba, 1985; Miles & Huberman, 1984; van Maanen, 1982; van

Maanen, Dabbs, & Faulkner, 1982; Whyte, 1984; Yin, 1984), that go into reliability and validity in qualitative research in detail.

Sources of Error in Research

Initial work on reliability and validity came from concerns of early educators and psychologists that their measuring instruments might not reflect the true differences in their subjects and might instead be some kind of error either in relation to the characteristic being measured or in the measurement process itself (Selltiz, Wrightsman, & Cook, 1976, chap. 6). When educators designed tests to identify students' levels of intelligence, their concern was that the test actually measured IQ (Intelligence Quotient) and not something else. They were also concerned that the same test, given at different times, would yield essentially the same results. When psychologists sought to develop tests for personality types, they found that they had the same concerns. Not only is measurement a matter of discovering the true differences in subjects, but it is also the minimization of error at all phases of the research process. The process of measurement is easily affected by error, particularly when the concepts being measured are abstract and may not be fully understood.

Error affects both reliability and validity and can permanently damage the research project, whether the error is either serious or superficial and easily corrected. The error can be obvious to any external reader or it can be hidden away from everyone. Error can be a major problem or a minor irritant. In any case, every researcher attempts to avoid as much error as possible during all phases of the research in order to increase the credibility of the results. For example, while transcribing field notes, the researcher might type "quantitative" rather than "qualitative" and not notice the error when reading the transcription. Although this is an example of a simple typing error, the impact on the reader could be great and might affect both the reliability and validity of the final report.

The key notion in reliability and validity, therefore, is the idea of "error." Error that occurs anywhere during the research process compromises the outcomes of the study and limits the usability of the data. The greater the degree of error, the less "truthful" the results. Using a table, Bailey (1978, p. 63), demonstrates just where error can, and often does, occur (see Table 10.1).

TABLE 10.1 Sources of Error in the Research Process

Phase of the Research Process	Type of Error
1. The Research Question The Research Problem Operational Definitions	1. Lack of Face Validity
2. Construction of measurement instrument (questionnaire)	2. Faulty or ambiguous wording of questions Categories not mutually exclusive Not representative of content Alternate form questions missing
3. Sampling	3. Lack of external validity a. Sampling error b. Not representative
4. Data collection Failure to control	4. Reliability issues. a. Environment (lighting
5. Coding	5. Coding errors, such as missing data, incorrect recording, illegible coding Failure to establish the rules for coding that represent the universe of content.
6. Data analysis	6. Incorrect statistics Faulty interpretation of data measurement in Qualitative Research

Source: Adapted with permission of The Free Press, a Division of Macmillan, Inc. from *Methods of Social Research* by Kenneth D. Bailey. Copyright © 1978 by The Free Press.

Measurement in Qualitative Research

A second notion in reliability and validity is the notion of "measurement." This is a concept that implies judgment according to some standard, with deliberate or careful choices, uniformity, dimensionality, and determination of extent, such as length, width, breadth, and capacity. Measurement also includes such ideas as: to apportion, to value, to allot or distribute, and to compare (*New Webster's Dictionary*). In research texts, measurement is frequently associated with numerical or quantitative instruments, such as the structured questionnaire, the physiological measure, and the projective test.

In qualitative research (and in the context of this chapter), measurement refers to the series of judgments made by the researcher about collected information in relation to its truthful representation of the desired content, its comparability with known information, and its verifiability across subjects and across situations, all of which meet the criteria for reliability and validity as set forth by both Selltiz et al. (1976, pp.160-197) and Kerlinger (1966, pp. 429-462; 1979, pp. 128-143).

Constant Measurement Error

Measurement errors in research can be either constant or random (Selltiz et al., 1976, pp. 168-169). Constant error affects the validity of the measurement or its ability to arrive at the true differences between and among subjects. Constant error affects measurement in the same way each time measurement is done, providing an incorrect measure of the variable that will be the same for all subjects. A quantitative example of a constant error is a weight scale that consistently weighs two kilograms over the actual weight. The measurement is consistent or reliable since repeated weights of the same object will result in the same scores. The measurement, however, will not be valid weight since it is always two kilograms over the actual weight of any item. A qualitative example of constant eror comes from a famous anthropologist (whose name is purposely withheld). He had spent a summer collecting ethnographic information on the Northwest Coast of North America, and on the last day, a going-away party was held for him. At that time, the tribe informed him that they had consistently lied to him the entire summer. They promised that if he returned the next summer, they would tell him the "truth." Constant error affects validity.

Types of Constant Error

According to Selltiz et al. (1976, p. 165), the two most stable and problematic sources of "constant error" in social science are: (a) social desirability in which research subjects respond with what they believe is the preferred social response whether or not it is true; and (b) acquiescent response set in which subjects consistently agree or disagree with the questions. Any questionnaire or interview that elicits agreement or disagreement with the interviewer is subject to this type of error. To avoid these sources of error, questions are constructed in such a way as to avoid a correct answer, or agreement/disagreement response modes are built into the design in such a way as to elicit what subjects believe to be the correct social response. Social desirability is a frequent problem in observational studies in which the subject attempts to look as good as possible to the observer, to behave and dress correctly or appropriately. To overcome this problem, observations are made more than once or are made over time. As subjects become more comfortable with being observed, they frequently forget the presence of the observer and eventually behave "normally," thus allowing the obsrver to see usual behavior. The longitudinal nature of qualitative research is an advantage and asset in observational studies.

Early experimental studies on attitudes were frequently plagued by these errors of "social desirability" and "acquiescent response set." Qualitative researchers rarely have difficulty with either of these sources of error. The reasons for the absence of these errors are: (a) qualitative studies are usually longitudinal, with the researcher interviewing the same subjects over time, which eventually elicits the subjects' true feelings (a built-in validity check not available in cross-sectional designs); (b) most qualitative studies are looking for the underlying cultural or social rules for behavior and are, therefore, directly seeking the "socially desirable" response from subjects; and, (c) the question formats used in qualitative studies, such as "grand tour" questions, contrast questions, and inclusive questions (Agar, 1980; Spradley, 1979, 1980; Spradley & McCurdy, 1972), generally avoid acquiescent response set. So these sources of error are simply not a major issue in qualitative designs as they are in experimental designs:

> Since we are unable to know directly an individual's "true position" on many of the variables that we [study], we judge the validity of the data by the extent to which its results are comparable with other evidence. Since there are differences in the type of evidence that is available to establish the validity of an instrument there are different levels and types of validation. (Brink & Wood, 1988, p. 164)

Other Types of Constant Errors

Intelligence and knowledge of the topic are prime examples of personal characteristics of informants that might influence their ability to understand and/or answer questions accurately. For example, in many early anthropological studies, the investigators and informants were both male. Yet, we have descriptions of the women's world as well as the men's world. Just how valid are those accounts? Can we accept them as men's accounts of the women's world? In other words, can an individual, occupying certain fixed social and cultural roles, ever be a true informant of the behavioral rules, beliefs, and attitudes of those who occupy totally different and contrasting positions? Can men speak for women, or parents for children? These are the sources of constant error with which qualitative researchers need to be concerned.

Sampling Issues as Validity Issues

Quantitative designs are based upon known populations from which to sample, so these designs rely upon probability samples drawn from some available list of the members of the population. Clear definitions of the "target population," followed by the rules for probability sampling techniques, are prerequisite to external validity (generalizability). Since qualitative studies seek to describe and explain phenomenon, the point of the research is not generalizability. So probability sampling techniques are not at issue because external validity is not the goal. In the same vein, quantitative studies make much of internal validity or "control over the independent variable." Internal validity is an issue in experimental designs. Qualitative research, by its very nature, is not experimental research and does not require manipulation of the independent variable. Therefore, internal validity is not a goal for qualitative research, nor is it an issue that needs to be "tended to."

Grounded theorists (Benoliel, 1970; Glaser & Strauss, 1967; Hutchinson, 1986) speak to the issue of "representativeness" in discussions on theoretical sampling. In grounded theory, the researcher deliberately selects a sample of individuals who are theoretically representative of the culture, role, or position needed for the study.

In other qualitative designs, sample selection is also "theoretically" representative. Qualitative studies are frequently conducted on populations for which no list is available (for frequently the population has never been studied before). The researcher must use his/her judgment, based uppon the best available evidence, that the sample does indeed possess the characteristics needed for the study (in other words, "represents" the population on some trait or variable). Because there is usually no list of the population, these samples are purposively selected, and in such cases, the judgment of the researcher may be based upon information gained from personal experience. Another method of selecting a sample is through the use of a panel of experts or a "judge panel." The judge panel helps to establish a theoretical or purposive sample for the study. If the research is carried out in unfamiliar environments with an unfamiliar group of people in an unfamiliar culture, a panel of experts is sought to assist with finding key informants to represent the group. The panel of experts is informed of the purposes of the study and the type of persons wanted in terms of their expertise in the content area under study. At the beginning of the study, when the investigator does not know the population, this judge panel is heavily relied upon to suggest informants. Later, as the researcher becomes more familiar with the target population, the selections of the judge panel can be reevaluated to see if they met the criteria for the study. Again, it is the longitudinal nature of qualitative research that enhances validity.

Establishing a judge panel at the outset of the study is itself problematic and depends upon the researcher's knowledge of the field situation. In nursing studies, for example, the nurse-researcher is very familiar with the clinical environment in which the research is to take place and knows which individuals in the situation could serve as a judge panel. These individuals, of course, do not become part of the sample. Even if a nurse studied a nursing situation in an unfamiliar environment, the individuals occupying certain roles would be known to be appropriate to serve as judges. It is when the researcher is a stranger that the establishment of a judge panel is a problem.

The person who provides entre into the field is the individual who will provide initial field contacts. Each of the recommended field contacts is then approached or contacted to begin the work of network or snowball sampling. As the center spokes for a network of contacts, these individuals serve as initial judges of who is an appropriate person to talk to and who is not. During these initial conversations with the judges, the investigator establishes why these particular individuals were chosen or recommended. Consequently, the judge panel provides information about cultural/social roles within the group, who is believed to be a "good" informant about that group, and on what basis that judgment was made. Some researchers maintain the same judge panel throughout the research. Others establish different judge panels over time or for different events/situations, while still others use the judge panel initially to provide the initial sample and later drop it.

Judge Panel Validity

Judge panels provide "self-evident validity" (Brink & Wood, 1988, p. 168), that is, to anyone in the culture group, it is obvious that the individuals selected as informants are knowledgeable about the content to be elicited. When the researcher is a stranger, nothing is "self-evident." It is only when one is familiar with the people and the culture that such validation is obvious. Again, the longitudinal design of most qualitative research studies provides verification of the choice of informants. The longer the researcher is in the field setting, the more familiar he/she becomes with the culture and its members, the better able he/she will be to self-evaluate the judgments of the original judge panel. In qualitative research, face and content validation procedures are, of necessity, "built into the design." In research texts today, authors are saying that these forms of validity testing are no longer necessary. Only when measurement is quantitative and based upon previously tested populations can self-evident validation testing be ignored. Even then, it can be skipped only because someone else has already gone through that step. In qualitative studies, this step remains important.

Pragmatic Validity

Another source of constant error is the initial lack of comparative data to assist the investigator to make judgments according to some standard. Establishing the standards against which data are compared is called pragmatic validation (Brink & Wood, 1988, pp. 169 171; Selltiz et al., 1976, pp. 171-172). In qualitative research, concurrent pragmatic validation is usually achieved through the use of multiple data collection methods and procedures on the same content (also known as "triangulation") over time. In this way, what is learned from one source is checked against one or more other sources. Information obtained through interview procedures is verified through observations, and vice versa. The information obtained from one expert informant is verified by asking one or more other "experts" about the same content. In this fashion, the standard, or the rules for establishing the standard, is developed against which information is compared. Concurrent validation is, perhaps, the most crucial validation procedure in qualitative research, establishing the standards or rules against which the data are verified as being "true" or "accurate." Although the term is used most frequently for quantitative research, its use in qualitative research is just as critical.

Another form of pragmatic validation frequently used in quantitative research, but which can be used effectively in qualitative studies, is the idea of predictive validity, in which, on the basis of concurrent validation procedures, one can predict the outcome of a situation. In this case, the qualitative researcher should be able to predict what will happen in a given situation, based upon information obtained from informants. Let us say that we have an "expert informant" attending an American football game with our "stranger researcher." The expert has already explained the game and its rules to the researcher. As they observe the game together, the "expert" predicts plays that will be made, based upon a knowledge of the game. If those predictions occur, the informant is an "accurate" predictor, and the rules upon which the predictions were made are accurate. If the predictions do not occur, the informant can be queried on why these plays did not occur. By the end of the game, the validity of the "expert" will have been established if the game went pretty much by the rules the expert had described (concurrent validity), if each play was based upon rules, and if the decisions made during the game did not invalidate the report but provided nuances to the data not otherwise obtained. Although each correct prediction validated certain bits of the information, it did not validate all the information. Again, interviewing coupled with observation concurrently validated the obtained data.

The strength of participant observation is pragmatic validation. Not only is interviewing validated by observations, but the use of written records, oral histories, kinship charts, and census are all used to validate each other bit of obtained information.

Establishing validity is a major challenge when a qualitative research project is based upon a single cross-sectional unstructured or semistructured interview or upon an unstructured single observation as the basis for data collection. How does the investigator make judgments about the validity of the data? When multiple methods are not built into the design, the investigator must rely on judge panel validity, must test for the reliability of the informants who provide the data, and must test the researcher's reliability in collecting and transcribing the data. The procedure depends, of course, on the data wanted. In 1970, while doing research on heroin addicts newly admitted to an inpatient psychiatric unit for detoxification, one of my concerns was the lack of information about this patient population (Brink, 1973). I addressed this concern by developing a semi-structured open-ended questionnaire to collect data from all the nurses on the unit about (a) their attitudes toward the addicts, and (b) information about addicts. The resultant data were very interesting. These data yielded a great deal of information about the nurses' attitudes toward addicts but nothing consistent about the addicts themselves (Brink, 1973). If I were to have planned nursing care based upon those data, I would have been in trouble. These nurses, the only sources of data about the nursing care of addicts, were assumed to be "expert informants." They provided, however, less than useful data based on the questions asked because the questionnaire did not have concurrent validity. The open-endedness of the questions provided free interpretation of what was wanted and offered no standardized answers to which to respond. Although I wanted standard answers, I got a possible universe of answers. In addition, the questions asked for information that not all of the nurses possessed, and assumed a knowledge base that the nurses did not have. With repeated information gathering, I could have obtained the information I wanted over time, but the single, one-shot questionnaire simply did not do what I had hoped it would. It was only when I compared the nurses' answers to other information I had collected from other sources that I found the nurses to be incorrect in several areas. For example, I had asked on what shift the addicts seemed to ask for more medication. Although the nurses rotated on all three shifts, they worked primarily one shift. Both day and evening shift thought the addicts demanded the most medication on their shifts, and the night shift was divided in their opinions. From a review of the medication record, I found that evenings were the time of highest medication consumption. Such cross-sectional qualitative data collection methods on unknown and unexplored territory require some type of concurrent validation procedures.

In reviewing other texts on qualitative research, the concept of validity is treated differently. For example, Lincoln and Guba (1985) use Cook and Campbell (1979) (a text on experimental designs) as their validity reference and speak only to *internal* and *external* validity. These concepts relate to control over the experimental variable (internal validity), which is not relevant in qualitative research, or to probability sampling techniques (external validity), which also is not relevant to most qualitative studies. Yet, no reference is made to such validation concepts as content validity, concurrent validity, or predictive validity. Since experimental designs were created to test causal relationships (cause/effect) in a positivist, linear, deductive rationalistic mode, one wonders why a qualitative researcher who uses different modes of inquiry would use the same methods of validation. Rather, why not use some of the validation procedures of other descriptive-deductive or inductive scientists to see if there is any "goodness of fit" of the concepts?

One problem of reviewing the qualitative methods literature is the proliferation of terms that have been developed to explain validity. Mehan and Wood (1975), in their work on ethnomethodology, use the term "reflexivity," and yet, they index the entire discussion (pp. 152-158) as a discussion of validity. In his text on ethnomethodology, Leiter (1980) does not mention validity, nor do Bogdan and Taylor (1975) in their introductory text on phenomenology. Garfinkel's (1967) ethnomethodology text does not have an index.

Validity is an issue in participant observation, field methods, and ethnography because these designs use a combination of unstructured, semistructured, and structured data collection methods. When unstructured interviews (or observations) are the major source of data collection and analysis, issues of validity and reliability are built into the design, rather than being treated as a separate issue of measurement.

Random Measurement Error

Random error, in contrast to constant error, is unpredictable error that varies from one moment to the next, even though the characteristic being measured has not changed (Selltiz et al., 1976, p. 169). Random errors result in unreliable and inconsistent data. If the same measurements are repeated on the same subjects, the results will not be the same. Random errors directly affect reliability, but because valid measures must also be reliable, random errors also affect the validity of the measurement technique. How much the results of qualitative research can be relied on depends upon the consistency, stability, and repeatability of data collection methods—in other words, its reliability.

Reliability

Reliability is concerned with the consistency, stability, and repeatability (Selltiz, et al., 1976, p. 182) of the informant's accounts as well as the investigator's ability to collect and record information accurately. The tests of reliability are:

1) stability over time is tested through repeating observations of the same events to look for similar occurrences or by asking informants identical questions of the same content to establish the consistency of the answers;

2) internal consistency is judged by the logical or explanatory rationale of ideas about the same topic within a single interview session; and

3) equivalence is tested by asking different kinds of questions within the single interview or questionnaire in order to establish the equivalence of the data elicited regardless of the form of question. For observation, all data equivalence is tested using two observers to observe the same event and compare the collected data.

When doing research, whether qualitative or quantitative, testing reliability is a first order of business, but because measurements differ, not all three forms of reliability can be used in every research project. For example, when using a stethoscope and sphygmomanometer as a highly structured quantitative measure, a test of stability is never used as a test of reliability. Everyone knows that if you pump up a blood pressure cuff several times in a row the blood pressure readings will differ on each reading as the previous reading changed the blood pressure. So when testing reliability in this case, a test of equivalence would be used; in other words, two persons should listen to the pulse and read the meter simultaneously. Since quantitative measures cannot always use all three methods of reliability testing, it seem spurious to require qualitative measures to do so. Yet quantitative researchers do. One example usually given by quantitative researchers of the unreliability of qualitative research is the use of the unstructured or open-ended clinical interview. Since the purpose of clinical interviews is to change something, "how," they ask, "can one test the reliability of that which changes over time?" The answer, is that qualitative researchers test reliability in "the same way reliability is tested in a quantitative study where the variable changes over time; another method of reliability testing is used such as equivalence." Therefore, the following discussion will speak to how these tests of reliability can be used in qualitative research projects.

When key informants are interviewed over time, their responses to the same questions on the same topic should be answered with essentially the same information (i.e., stability). To test the reliability and validity of the recorded data, the researcher uses content validity: the researcher tape records interviews, transcribes them, then presents the informants with literal transcriptions of the interviews. Frequently, these verification sessions will clarify the content as well as the verbatim terminology, expand on the information by clarifying unclear or incomplete materials, and essentially validate that this material is correct. Over time, this procedure is repeated with a number of informants, until by the end of the field work period, the material is considered both valid and reliable (see Brink & Wood, 1988, p. 178; Hammersley & Atkinson, 1983, pp. 195-200).

When the field researcher is interviewing an informant for a single time only, the reliability and validity of that particular interview is treated in exactly the same way as it would be in quantitative research. In the single interview situation, reliability of a particular informant is tested by the use of identical as well as alternate form questions within the interview itself (a form of equivalence), by transcribing notes during the interview, and/or by tape recording the interview for an alternate form (another form of equivalence) of data recording other than investigator memory. When triangulation is not used or multiple interviews are not conducted, verification of the accuracy or truth of the data is still necessary. Equivalence is the reliability check of choice.

Several methods are used in the field situation to establish the reliability of the investigator. When field researchers are alone and cannot use equivalence with another researcher (the preferred method of obtaining observational equivalence), equivalence is developed by working with informants. Early in the field work situation, when the investigator is a stranger and unfamiliar with the rules of behavior and the setting, establishing equivalence of observation of events is critical. The investigator usually takes along an informant, who also observes the occasion. The investigator then records the activity on the spot either taking field notes, taping a running documentary of the events, and/or photographing events in stills or films. (A written record along with photographic evidence has

concurrent validity.) Taking along an informant during these observations is critical to the field work as questions about the event can
be asked and answered at the time the event is being observed. In
this way, discrepancies between what is observed and what is
explained can be clarified. Also, the informant is more interested and
involved at the time of the activity and so is more willing to discuss
it. Also, the researcher does not have to rely on anyone's memory of
the events and thus avoids distortion caused by selective memory.
The written record is later reviewed with the informant for completeness and comprehensiveness of the coverage. Any conclusions or
inferences drawn are also verified with the informant. This is also an
excellent time for the informant to provide an explanation of what
has occurred and why, and this discussion/interview is, of course,
tape recorded.

When field researchers use multiple methods of data collection
and verify all data by triangulation, the validity of the final report is
often unquestioned. It is when a researcher uses a single data
collection instrument only once on single individuals, that questions
of reliability and validity arise.

Data Analysis

The concepts of reliability are usually dealt with in conjunction
with data collection procedures and data recording. The same concepts, however, can be applied to the process of data analysis
(Hammersley & Atkinson, 1983, chap. 8; Krippendorff, 1980; Miles
& Huberman, 1984).

Analysis in qualitative research refers to the categorization and
ordering of information in such a way as to make sense of the data
and to writing a final report that is true and accurate. Sometimes
analysis refers to condensation, extrapolation, and modeling. Judge-
ments are made by the researcher on what information represents
the body of data. That information may be verbatim, but frequently,
it must be some type of concatenation. How does the researcher go
about the process without losing the reality?

Following our original discussion on constant and random error,
the first constant error to be avoided is investigator bias, which is the
investigator's tendency to selectively observe and record certain data
at the expense of other data (Hunter & Foley, 1976, chap. 5). To avoid

such selective inattention, the data analysis procedures are exposed to a judge panel. The judge panel looks over the rules for data analysis prior to initiation of the analysis itself. The judge panel is selected on the basis of knowledge of content or knowledge of the research project. To assist the judge panel in its work, the investigator provides the answers to the following questions:

- What are the logical decisions that will be made in sifting through the data?
- Is the process of inclusion or exclusion of data consistent?
- Are the coding categories mutually exclusive?
- Do the coding categories cover the universe of the content?
- Are the categories major or minor headings?

Some of this type of categorization of content can be done by computer,[1] just as some of the original categorization could have been done with *Notebook* or *Ethnograph*. The actual categorization is not the issue here: it is the basic judgement upon which the categorization is made that is subject to criticism.[2]

The random errors that can occur deal with missing data, coding errors, misinterpretation of data, and miscoding due to judgement errors, unclear or illegible notes, poor transcriptions, and so on. If coders are hired, the PI (Principal Investigator) needs to check coding on a random basis after the initial training of coders is completed (alternate form). If the PI is the coder, the material should be allowed to sit, and then the investigator re-codes the material (test-retest) and compares the two sets of coded data (Lebar, 1973, pp. 715-716). In qualitative studies, these methods are amenable to computer manipulation, especially interview data or daily diaries.

These systems are not often useful in designs such as phenomenology, grounded theory, or Spradley's ethnographic interview (Spradley, 1979; Spradley & McCurdy, 1972). In these designs, data analysis occurs simultaneously with the data collection. In grounded theory (Glaser & Strauss, 1967; Hutchinson, 1986), for example, informants are interviewed and categories are filled until no further categories appear and the material becomes redundant. Validity and reliability are provided for by the use of the constant comparative method and the search for alternative hypothesis or negative cases (Hutchinson, 1986, pp. 116-117). Only when these have been explored can the researcher say that the series of decision rules (involved in the development of categories and their logical inter-relationships) and the resultant theory are a substantive representation of the data.

By virtue of the structure of the interview itself, Spradley's (1979) ethnographic interview actually categorizes data as it is collected. Spradley begins with the "Grand Tour Question," an opening question that attempts to put the informant into the cultural scene. He then has a series of questions constructed to categorize cultural information into relevant meaning. To do this, the investigator develops a taxonomy of terms based upon inclusiveness. Questions are constructed to provide meaning through inclusiveness and exclusiveness of content. Attribute questions, unlike structural questions, provide exclusions or contrasts. Other questions request definitions by labeling, defining, or pointing out an example. "Is a sugar maple a kind of something? Are there different kinds of sugar maples? Are there different kinds of maples?" (Spradley & McCurdy, 1972, p. 69). "Is a tree a kind of something? What kind of something is a tree (inclusiveness)? What is a tree? What is that over there? Show me a tree." The structure of the questions themselves provides ongoing analysis of the data so that the end point of such an interview is a definition of a tree, with all its component parts, its processes, its functions, or whatever else the investigator wants. Such analysis does not admit to coding errors because the informants are interviewed again and again, verifying previous material, clarifying, repeating, comparing the same information, and obtaining more.

Each of the qualitative designs has different issues involving reliability of data collection and each has "built in" tests of reliability. In grounded theory, for example, the use of theoretical sampling strategies and returning to the same subject over and over to verify the analysis and findings tends to eliminate any chance of the data being unreliable.

Grounded theorists who use the Glaser and Strauss methods follow a rigid protocol for data collection and analysis that essentially eliminates the problems of reliability. Since reliability refers to random error, the reinterviewing of subjects at different times and places tends to eliminate any random errors that might occur in both investigator and subject/informant performance.

When the investigator is following a phenomonological design, the subject is also approached over and over again to verify and validate all materials. As with grounded theory, this constant return to the subject all but eliminates any random error that can occur. In addition, however, in phenomenology, the investigator is attempting to elicit the subject's personal experience in order to describe that experience as accurately as possible. In order for these individuals to become subjects (or informants), they must have experienced the phenomenon themselves. Indeed, the researcher is also expected to have experienced the phenomenon under study. The goal is to produce a description of the experience that will represent what others having had the same experience will agree happened to them. Reliability is not an issue in this circumstance, only validity, and validity is established by readers saying, "Oh yes! That's exactly what happened to me!"

Lincoln and Guba (1985, p. 299) are the most widely quoted reference on qualitative research in nursing. They say that Kerlinger defines reliability as "consistency, stability, dependability, accuracy and predictability" (Kerlinger, 1973, pp. 422-423), but then, they go on to refute the stability portion of the definition, referring to reliability as a test-retest procedure. In fact, Kerlinger (1973, p. 542) is simply giving synonyms for reliability rather than a definition. A major problem with using Kerlinger as the basic referent for reliability is that Kerlinger deals with the measurement issues of reliability, giving a number of statistical tests for reliability of instruments. Selltiz et al. (1976), however, give the underlying rationale for reliability and validity. The rationale for these concepts, rather than the statistical tests, is the issue. For example, Lincoln and Guba do not make any reference to tests of equivalence as used in this chapter (again, based upon the work of Selltiz et al.) or by Goetz and LeCompte (1984). Indeed, Lincoln and Guba say that once we have established consistency "the reliability of the inquiry is indisputably established" (p. 299). Unfortunately, this is not true, Lincoln and Guba seem to have missed the point that reliability deals with elusive change, alterations in many things that frequently are not directly measurable; therefore, reliability requires many means for establishing that we can rely (or depend) on the findings as being true. A test-retest is not usable for a phenomenon that changes over time. This does not mean we cannot test for the reliability of informants' statements or of our data collection and procedures. We have other methods to do that (tests of equivalence). Also, Lincoln and Guba prefer to use the term "dependability" when referring to the reliability of data. The use of the word *dependability* instead of *reliability* to denote the difference between reliability in quantitative methods from dependability to qualitative methods would be useful if the process of establishing dependability were different from the process of establishing reliability. In reviewing the Lincoln and Guba methods and procedures, there seems to be a definite similarity in the two processes (see pp. 316-318) that do not appear to warrant the use of the terminology.

In a chapter entitled "Assessing Ethnographic Design," Goetz and Lecompte (1984) discuss issues of reliability in much the same way as has been discussed in this chapter, and they supply a full and complete discussion of how reliability of the data collection and analysis is accomplished given the caveat that no single piece of data can exactly replicate another.

In other qualitative methods texts, few describe or use the concept of reliability, preferring instead to discuss validity, if validity is discussed at all. Burgess (1984) is an example. He describes the process of collecting and analyzing field data, but he does not use reliability to describe the process. In *Designing Qualitative Research,* Marshall and Rossman (1989) merely mention "replicability," but they do not deal with the issue. In the text *Fieldnotes,* edited by Roger Sanjek (1990), there are only two chapters that mention reliability: the chapter by Johnson and Johnson (1990), which refers to reliability briefly and then only in relation to survey research methods; and the chapter by Sanjek (1990), titled "On Ethnographic Validity" (pp. 385-418). Still others do not even list reliability and validity in their index (Bogdan and Taylor, 1975; Garfinkel, 1967; Leiter, 1980), or if they do, they tend to exemplify rather than discuss reliability (Mehan & Wood, 1975).

Some qualitative research texts authored or edited by nurses do not discuss issues of reliability. The texts by Parse, Coyne, and Smith (1985) and Munhall and Oiler (1986) focus particularly upon phenomenology as method, so they provide no discussion on how reliability issues are dealt with. Field and Morse (1985), perhaps because they provide an overview of many qualitative designs, are an exception to this statement, and they use Lecompte and Goetz as their major reference source.

The primary references to reliability come in texts that deal with field methods, participant observation, and open-ended or semi-structured interviewing techniques, but rarely is reliability discussed in texts·dealing with phenomenology or grounded theory. In conclusion it appears that reliability and validity "issues," or the minimization of error and the control over the accuracy and veracity of the research process, are similar in both qualitative and quantitative research. What has been pointed out in this chapter, however, is that there are a number of other areas that need to be attended to, which affect any discussion of reliability and validity. These factors include: (a) the number and types of data collection methods and procedures used in the study; (b) the number of times data is collected on the same subject using the same method; (c) how often and over how long a period is data collected on the same and different informants; (d) the number of investigators collecting the same and different information on the same and different subjects; and (e) when and how data are analyzed.

Just as multiple methods validate one another (Miles & Huberman, 1984, p. 239), so do multiple investigators (judge panels) and multiple repetitions of measurements over time. For this reason, fieldwork teams in longitudinal designs provide the greatest validity checks. The type of research most at risk for validity and reliability criticisms is the single, one-shot, open-ended, semistructured questionnaire administered to a convenience sample. Researchers using this design need to build into their grant proposals tests of reliability and validity that are understandable to quantitative panels. The terminology used by quantitative researchers is translatable to qualitative studies and should be used in grant proposals. Studies using participant observation, multiple methods, phenomenology, or grounded theory need to provide information to review panels about how reliability and validity are ensured in these studies. Glaser and Strauss asked for clarity and precision in describing grounded theory procedures for data collection and analysis so that others can understand and critique what was actually done, and also to provide credibility so that readers can believe the results.

In my opinion, until qualitative researchers specify the means by which they deal with reliability and validity in their research, they cannot expect anyone to fund their proposals, nor believe their study findings enough to publish the research.

Notes

1. See Jacqueline Clinton's definition of ethnicity, 1982, in which a taxonomy of cultural content was constructed through the use of the IDEA Decision Tree.
2. Categorization is used here as an umbrella term to refer to themes, feelings, content, process, or whatever the unit of analysis desired.

References

Agar, M. H. (1980). *The professional stranger: An informal introduction to ethnography.* New York: Academic Press.

Bailey, K. D. (1987). *Methods of social research* (3rd ed.). New York: Free Press.

Benoliel, J. Q. (1970). The developing diabetic identity: A study of family influence. In M. Batey (Ed.). *Communicating nursing research; Methodological issues in research* (Vol. 3, pp. 14-32). Boulder, CO: WICHE/WCHEN.

Bogdan, R., & Taylor, S. J. (1975). *Introduction to qualitative research methods: A phenomenological approach to the social sciences.* New York: John Wiley.

Borzak, L. (Ed.). (1981). *Field study: A sourcebook for experiential learning.* Beverly Hills, CA: Sage.

Brinberg, D., & McGrath, J. E. (1985). *Validity and the research process.* Beverly Hills, CA: Sage.

Brink, P. J. (1973). Nurses' attitudes toward heroin addicts. *Journal of Psychiatric and Mental Health Nursing, 11*(2), 7-12.

Brink, P. J. (1987). On reliability and validity in qualitative research. *Western Journal of Nursing Research, 9*(2), 157-159.

Brink, P. J., & Wood, M. J. (1978). *Basic steps in planning nursing research: From question to proposal* (2nd ed.). North Scituate, MA: Duxbury Press.

Brink, P. J., & Wood, M. J. (1988). *Basic steps in planning nursing research: From question to proposal* (3rd ed.). Boston: Jones and Bartlett.

Burgess, R. G. (1984). *In the field: An introduction to field research.* London: George Allen & UNWIN.

Clinton, J. (1982). Ethnicity: The development of an empirical construct for cross-cultural health research. *Western Journal of Nursing Research, 4*(3), 281-300.

Fielding, N. G., & Fielding, J. L. (1986). *Linking data.* Newbury Park, CA: Sage.

Freeman, D. (1983). *Margaret Mead and Samoa: The making and unmaking of an anthropological myth.* Cambridge, MA: Harvard University Press.

Garfinkel, H. (1967), *Studies in ethnomethodology.* Englewood Cliffs, NJ: Prentice-Hall.

Glaser, B. G., & Strauss, A. L. (1967). *The discovery of grounded theory: Strategies for qualitative research.* Chicago: Aldine.

Goetz, J. P., & LeCompte, M. D. (1984). *Ethnography and qualitative design in educational research.* Toronto: Harcourt Brace Jovanovich.

Hammersley, M., & Atkinson, P. (1983). *Ethnography: Principles and practice.* New York: Tavistok.

Hunter, D. E., & Foley, M. B. (1976). *Doing anthropology: A student centered approach to cultural anthropology.* New York: Harper & Row.

Hutchinson, S. (1986). Grounded theory: The method. In P. L. Munhall & C. J. Oiler (Eds.). *Nursing research: A qualitative perspective* (pp. 116-117). New York: Appleton-Century-Crofts.

Johnson, A., & Johnson, O. R. (1990). Quality into quantity: On the measurement potential of ethnography fieldnotes. In R. Sanjek (Ed.). *Fieldnotes: The makings of anthropology* (pp. 161-186). Ithaca, NY: Cornell University Press.

Kerlinger, F. N. (1966). *Foundations of behavioral research.* New York: Holt, Rinehart & Winston.

Kerlinger, F. N. (1979). *Behavioral research: A conceptual approach.* New York: Holt, Rinehart & Winston.

Kirk, J., & Miller, M. L. (1986). *Reliability and validity in qualitative research.* Beverly Hills, CA: Sage.

Krippendorff, K. (1980). *Content analysis: An introduction to its methodology.* Beverly Hills, CA: Sage.

Lebar, F. M. (1973). Coding ethnographic materials. In R. Naroll & R. Cohen (Eds.). *A handbook of method in cultural anthropology* (pp. 707-720). New York: Columbia University Press.

LeCompte, M. D., & Goertz, J. P. (1982). Problems of reliability and validity in ethnographic research. *Review of Educational Research, 52*(1), 31-60.

Leiter, K. (1980). *A primer on ethnomethodology.* New York: Oxford University Press.

Lewis, O. (1951). *Life in a Mexican village: Tepoztlan revisited.* Urbana: University of Illinois Press.

Lincoln, Y. S., & Guba, E. G. (1985). *Naturalistic inquiry.* Beverly Hills, CA: Sage.

Marshall, C., & Rossman, G. B. (1989). *Designing qualitative research.* Newbury Park, CA: Sage.

McCall, G. J., & Simmons, J. L. (1969). *Issues in participant observation: A text and reader.* Reading, MA: Addison-Wesley.

Mead, M. (1928). *Coming of age in Samoa: A psychological study of primitive youth for western civilization.* New York: William Morrow.

Mehan, H., & Wood, H. (1975). *The reality of ethnomethodology.* New York: John Wiley.

Miles, M. B., & Huberman, A. M. (1984). *Qualitative data analysis: A sourcebook of new methods.* Beverly Hills, CA: Sage.

Munhall, P., & Oiler, C. (1986). *Nursing research: A qualitative perspective.* Norwalk, CT: Appleton-Century-Crofts.

Parse, R. R., Coyne, A. B., & Smith, M. J. (1985). *Nursing research: Qualitative methods.* Bowie, MD: Brady Communications.

Pelto, P. J. (1970). *Anthropological research: The structure of inquiry.* New York: Harper & Row.

Pelto, P. J., & Pelto, G. H. (1978). *Anthropological research: The structure of inquiry* (2nd ed.). Cambridge: Cambridge University Press.

PRO/TEM Software. (1985). *Notebook II: The database manager for unlimited text.* Stanford, CA: Author.

Redfield, R. (1930). *Tepoztlan—A Mexican village.* Chicago: University of Chicago Press.

Sanjek, R. (Ed.). (1990). *Fieldnotes: The makings of anthropology.* Ithaca, NY: Cornell University Press.

Seidel, J. V., & Kolseth, R. I. (1985). *The ethnograph.* Littleton, CO: Qualis Research Association.

Selltiz, C., Wrightsman, L. S., & Cook, S. W. (1976). *Research methods in social relations* (3rd ed.). New York: Holt, Rinehart & Winston.

Spradley, J. (1979). *The ethnographic interview.* New York: Holt, Rinehart & Winston.

Spradley, J. (1980). *Participant observation.* New York: Holt, Rinehart & Winston.

Spradley, J. P., & McCurdy, D. W. (1972). *The cultural experience: Ethnography in complex society.* Chicago: Science Research Associates.

van Maanen, J. (Ed.). (1983). *Qualitative methodology.* Beverly Hills, CA: Sage.

van Maanen, J., Dabbs, J. M., Jr., & Faulkner, R. R. (1982). *Varieties of qualitative research.* Beverly Hills, CA: Sage.

Whyte, W. F. (1984). *Learning from the field: A guide from experience.* Beverly Hills, CA: Sage.

Yin, R. K. (1984). *Case study research: Design and methods.* Beverly Hills, CA: Sage.

Dialogue

On Interviewing

LIPSON: I think it makes a difference whether you are interviewing people with whom you have a common experiential base or people with whom you don't have much of a common experiential base. And maybe one of our strains here is the difference between the researcher and the collaborator, the informant, or whoever that other person is.

MAY: I think that is a good point. I hadn't connected that before, but I had been struggling with my assignment of writing on "asking questions," and I kept bumping against the difficulty of doing work across so many experiential boundaries. Since I tend to do cross-gender work, I have got the frontier of gender boundaries pretty well mapped out—I haven't solved all the problems, but at least I know where I am likely to "fall in the pit"—and it's difficult for me to explain that process to another. It's as if I carry a man in my head, and I flip a switch, and then I enter a man's world and interact in a somewhat different fashion. And folks who have done work with immigrants say the same thing, and they adopt this "immigrant" in their heads. And I understand that when you speak of the "use of self." This "man" is a part of me, with blind spots, but I am unable to separate him out—the man exists while I am collecting data and while I am interpreting data—it is constant. It is not something that flakes out when I decide that my analysis is complete—it is what is there throughout.

LIPSON: Yes, but it takes time. It takes two or three years, at least, with your "man" or your "immigrants" before you can flip that switch and know how to act. It starts with empathy, I think.

TRIPP-REIMER: It's what some people describe as a cultural experience.

BARBEE: A cultural swinger!

187

11

Interview Techniques in Qualitative Research: Concerns and Challenges

KATHARYN ANTLE MAY

Interviewing is the predominant mode of data collection in qualitative research. Indeed, as a way of acquiring information, interviewing is an element so central to qualitative methodology that complexities and controversies associated with it are often overlooked. Assumptions about interviewing as a research process are widespread, that is, that everyone "knows" how to do it and that interview procedures vary little, regardless of the nature of the research question or approach. Further, despite its importance to most types of qualitative research, relatively little time and attention are paid to the number of challenging and/or controversial aspects of research interviewing which face investigators.

The purpose of this chapter is to highlight some particularly challenging aspects of qualitative research interviewing, which, to date, have received little attention in the methodological literature. Throughout this chapter, the rather generic term "qualitative research" will be used to refer to grounded theory, ethnomethodologic, ethnographic, ethnoscientific, and phenomenologic research, and important differences between these types will be noted when appropriate.

Challenges Associated with Interviewing in Qualitative Research

There are many aspects of qualitative research interviewing that are remarkably challenging, for example, the effective use of self to establish rapport and gain information from informants, coping with the unanticipated problems and rewards of interviewing in the field, and recording and managing the large volume of data generated by even relatively brief interviews. Since these aspects are central to effective research interviewing, most methods references (Chenitz & Swanson, 1986; Lofland & Lofland, 1984; Schatzman & Strauss, 1973) address these areas. However, there are other aspects of qualitative research interviewing that may be equally important to the success of a given study, but are seldom discussed in standard references. One such aspect is a precise description of interview procedures.

Precise Description of Interview Procedures

Precise description of data collection procedures is considered a hallmark of scientific work, and in the case of interview procedures in proposals as well as the final reports of qualitative research, this is challenging for several reasons. First, a variety of interview styles is likely to be used, but the terminology available to describe this variety is itself not uniformly precise. Second, in most qualitative studies, identity of informants, timing, structure, and even the content of interviews require adjustments by the investigator in response to ongoing data collection and analysis. So interview procedures used in a given study cannot be accurately described until after the fact, and even then, they may be difficult to present succinctly for publication purposes.

Interviews in a qualitative study may be formal, in that they are prearranged with informants for the purpose of detailed conversations, or they may be informal, in that they are unplanned encounters during periods of participant observation in a setting of importance to the study. Further, interviews may be done on a one-time basis or repeated over time, either in face-to-face encounters or by telephone follow-up. Interviews may also be done with one or more than one informant at a time (sometimes referred to as "solo" and "conjoint" interviews).

Each of these has its own particular strengths and limitations, depending on the nature of the research question. Clearly, one-time interviews may be best when access to informants is difficult or when the topic area can be covered readily in one contact and does not require substantial rapport and trust for exploration. Repeated contacts may be needed when change over time is of interest or when the interest area is best understood from a position of more familiarity and closer rapport with the informant. Even if only one interview may be needed, many experienced investigators build in provisions for later interviewing to allow for clarification on points that are unclear to the investigator, for validation as analysis proceeds, and for follow-up if the time period of the study must be extended.

Selection of the informant must also be determined initially by the research question and availability of informants and then modified as needed, based on experience gained in the field about who or what is the "natural unit" of analysis (Chenitz & Swanson, 1986; Schatzman & Strauss, 1973). Some phenomena are best understood through couple interviews, family interviews, or group interviews, while others demand solo interviews. While initial informant selection is based on natural groups (first-time mothers, residents in a certain community), subsequent informant selection is often guided by preliminary findings and is, therefore, impossible to specify in advance.

As a general statement, most phenomenologic studies in nursing appear to rely on formal interviews, often repeated over time, while ethnomethodologic, ethnographic, ethnoscientific, and grounded theory studies may include more participant observation (thus, more informal interviews) and one-time formal interviews (Munhall & Oiler, 1986). Many studies employ more than one style of interview; plans for who will be interviewed, when, about what, and in what level of detail are outlined at the proposal stage, but such decisions must be evaluated and changed as data are examined and analyzed. Thus, since so many elements of the pattern are dictated by the overall research perspective, the question or problem, and by preliminary findings, it is difficult to describe a "typical" pattern of research interviewing in qualitative research.

The Problem of Interview Structure

While timing, intensity, and informant selection for qualitative research interviewing may vary widely, there is considerable consistency in the overall approach to structure in research interviewing. Structured interviews (conducted using a predetermined and exclusive schedule of questions allowing maximum consistency and topic control) are frequently used in theory-testing and survey research, but they are rarely used in the types of qualitative research of interest here. Structured interviewing assumes that the investigator already knows the salient parameters of the topic under study, and this assumption is contrary to the underlying philosophy and the major goal of discovery implicit in most types of qualitative research. Qualitative studies typically employ unstructured or semistructured interviews. Unstructured interviews are defined as those that do not reflect preconceived ideas about content or flow and are done with little or no organization; and focused or semistructured interviews are defined as those organized around areas of particular interest, while still allowing considerable flexibility in scope and depth (Polit & Hungler, 1987).

While this terminology is widely accepted, it is not completely accurate for purposes of qualitative research. This terminology implies that an unstructured interview is conducted without utilizing any of the investigator's prior information, experience, or opinions in a particular area. Since human interaction is based on a culturally derived structure of meanings that is shared to some extent, it would be extremely difficult for the investigator to approach any interview as a completely neutral element. Investigators have some area of interest in mind at the outset, and their goal is to discover and understand the informant's perspective on that particular aspect of life.

In reality, the investigator's initial approach may be informed by previous knowledge, observations, and experience, but these sources of information are carefully subordinated to the process of discovering the informant's perspectives on the topic of interest. The informant's story then serves to "structure" the interview as it unfolds. This process is also apparent in the overall project: Early interviews are likely to be more unstructured, with increasing structure developing as analysis of informants' stories begins.

Adjusting the Interview Process

A common misconception is that qualitative studies involve unstructured interviews throughout the entire process of data collection. It is true that investigators begin with largely unstructured interviews, exerting only as much topic guidance as is necessary in the interview to elicit the informant's story. Since the salient parameters of the topic cannot be identified until several informants' stories are heard and analysis begins, active topic guidance or control early in the investigation is counterproductive. (The issue of appropriate topic guidance in this style of interviewing is a complex one and will be discussed in some detail later in this chapter.) Thus early interviews may look much more like "guided conversations" (Schatzman & Strauss, 1973) and may be appropriately called interactive interviews.

However, as a study proceeds, interviews often become more focused as the investigator uses more topic guidance to explore areas of special interest, begins to test preliminary findings, or begins to look for areas of commonality and difference in respondents' stories. Thus the distinction between "unstructured" and "focused or semi-structured" interviews for qualitative research has more to do with when in the process the interview takes place. Interviews that take place early in the study are more likely to be guided largely by the particular perspective of the informant being interviewed (unstructured interview), while later in the study, questions are likely to be suggested from preliminary findings generated to that point in the project (semistructured or focused interview). Also, there are times late in a study when the investigator may move back and forth in the same interview from a very unstructured approach, to see if "new" elements appear, to direct questions that test working hypotheses.

"Getting the Story": Balancing Flexibility and Consistency

Another challenge in adjusting interview procedures has to do with achieving and maintaining a balance between flexibility and consistency in data collection. Flexibility in topic selection and in questioning is essential for discovery and for eliciting the individual informant's story. However, some consistency is also essential in types of questions asked, depth of detail, and the amount of exploration versus confirmation covered in an interview in order for conclusions to be drawn. Thus an important challenge in qualitative research interviewing is maintaining enough flexibility to elicit individual stories, which are likely to vary a great deal (at least at first glance), while gathering information with enough consistency to allow for comparison between and among subjects.

When a study involves multiple interviewers, the problem of balancing between flexibility and consistency arises almost immediately. While exploration is essential, especially in early interviews, this may become unwieldy if two or more interviewers are involved, since each is likely to pursue different leads and levels of detail. This problem can be solved by having frequent team meetings in which team members use recordings and transcripts to hear one another's actual questions and the responses received. Team members can also highlight areas that can be kept in mind as interviews become more focused. Dividing up early data collection responsibilities into specific area assignments may allow team members to explore related, but separate aspects of the same study problem. This can be done using either different informants, follow-up interviews with the same informants, or further analysis of already collected data sets.

However, balancing between flexibility and consistency in interviews can be a challenge, even for a solo investigator, with consistency usually being more difficult to achieve. Consistency in qualitative research does not require that every informant be asked all the same questions; rather, the goal is to assure that questions, which appear to be important at a given point in the data collection phase, are asked of as many informants as possible, so that subsequent interviews can be informed by them. For example, individual stories can be so interesting that the investigator fails to follow up with questions generated by hunches from other interviews, or forgets to ask for background information that may be important in understanding an informant's responses. Informants may be so articulate and insightful that considerable depth is achieved very quickly; however, because they speak so readily about deeply emotional content, the investigator fails to ask about more factual aspects of the situation. Other informants may be more difficult to interview because they are unaccustomed to talking about their private lives, and in the process of trying to draw the informant out, the investigator spends most of the interview on the "facts" and runs out of time before any attention is paid to more sensitive aspects of the story. One strategy in dealing with the problem of consistency is systematic preparation for each interview, including review of field logs or previous interviews, making notes about questions that should be asked, and consciously "taking stock" at several points in an interview to see where additional questioning might be needed.

Consistency in a qualitative data set can be thought of as comparability, that is, having enough information about informants and enough detail in their stories that the investigator can compare their major elements. Some frequently used interview techniques employed by field researchers often build in some level of comparability between interviews. First, there is the fairly prevalent pattern of moving from rather general to more focused interviews as a study proceeds. Thus while early and late interviews may contain rather different kinds of information, interviews conducted at the same point in a study are likely to be similar, and in this way, comparisons can be made between data from individual informants. Second, skilled interviewers try to ensure that data, which may be missed in an interview, can be captured later, either by telephone or, if necessary, a brief interview. Often, permission for that type of follow-up is specifically sought at the time the informant is recruited for the study.

Investigators will frequently include specific types of questions that are designed to invite informants to compare themselves and their stories with those of others in their referent group. This kind of information is useful in understanding the informant's world view and for placing the informant's story in a meaningful context. Early in a study, such questions are often used to place the informant's story into some context; later, as analysis is proceeding, these same questions may be used to test a hypothesis under consideration (as in grounded theory research), to elicit "thick" descriptions (as in ethnography), to clarify components of the construct (as in ethnoscience), or to identify the limits of a norm (as in ethnomethodology).

Such techniques include the use of comparison questions, such as, "Some people say women shouldn't go back to work until their baby is a year old—how does that fit for you?" that will elicit explicit comparisons between self and imagined/real others. Generality questions, such as "People have a lot of adjusting to do when a baby is born—in what ways have you had to adjust your life?" help the investigator to validate an assumption about a range of shared experiences (adjusting); an informant's negative response may also indicate the assumption is invalid, or at least limited. Ubiquity questions, such as "When did you first feel like a mother?" explicitly assume the informant has had an experience that is widely shared, while acknowledging individual differences (in this case, timing).

The dynamic nature of qualitative research interviewing, that is, the need for ongoing adjustments in relative structure, timing, intensity, and selection of informants, and in balancing flexibility, consistency, depth, and breadth in data collection defies precise prediction. Such adjustments are based on experience and observation during early data collection and analysis, rather than on the investigator's knowledge and/or beliefs about a content area prior to entering the field. Often, the most precise description of interview procedures that can be done in the proposal is to describe initial plans for who will be interviewed and when, to give examples of questions to open topics of probable interest, and then to outline the types of adjustments that might be necessary in this plan and why.

Describing interview procedures does not necessarily get easier once the project is completed and findings are ready for dissemination. Detailed explanations about the various adjustments that were made in interview procedures may require more manuscript space than is available in a typical journal article. However, overly brief descriptions may give the appearance of slipshod work and become a source of confusion or concern about the credibility of the work.

Topic Interviewing as Interpersonal Communication

To risk stating the obvious, the success of interviewing as a research process is dependent to a very large extent on the investigator's skills in interpersonal communication. Unlike other forms of data collection, in which skills can be readily learned and independently evaluated, research interviewing tends to be a solo endeavor, characterized by "on the job training" with few well-recognized criteria against which competence can be judged. To compound the challenge, interpersonal communication is notoriously complex and influenced by personal, sociocultural, and environmental factors, many of which are quite subtle.

Essentially, skillful interviewing is characterized by the extent to which the investigator can establish rapport, elicit information without excessively controlling the nature or the flow of that information, and record it accurately; these elements are treated in some depth in the existing methodological literature in ethnographic and participant observation research. Since a widely recognized consequence of excessive control in research interviewing is the risk that preconceived ideas or other sources of investigator bias will actively shape data collection and, therefore, the subsequent analysis, the theme of avoiding excessive investigator control in the interview process receives considerable attention. However, the more subtle problem of inappropriate or unintentional topic control through choice of interview language would also seem to merit some attention.

The Issue of Topic Control in Interviewing

In most forms of qualitative research, as discussed earlier, there is an overall trend from unstructured to more focused interviewing as the investigator gains knowledge about the informant's world view. Thus as the investigator becomes increasingly familiar with the area and uses ongoing data collection and analysis to focus on new leads of particular promise, some topic control is utilized as the project unfolds.

However, at the beginning of every study, there is considerable trial and error in early interviews as the wording and ordering of questions in a particular area of interest are literally field-tested with informants. Since cultural differences and their influence on data collection and analysis tend to be quite obvious (Lipson & Meleis, 1989; Warren, 1988), investigators are particularly careful in this step if they are working outside their own cultural group.

Unfortunately, when research is done within the investigator's own cultural milieu, subtle factors, which nevertheless may have significant consequences in the process of interviewing, are sometimes not taken into account. For instance, while experienced interviewers know that it is possible to exert topic control through the wording of interview questions, novice interviewers may underestimate or be completely unaware of the influence of their own language.

At first, the skilled investigator typically "backs into" the area of interest by using rather nonspecific language and open-ended questions (such as, "Tell me about your life with diabetes,") and then framing subsequent questions using language that reflects the informant's language (for example, "What do you mean when you say 'out of control'?" "What does 'getting worse' mean?" "What do you do when you 'get worse'?") In this way the investigator seeks clarification and elaboration until he or she begins to understand the informant's meanings, which are separate and distinct from prior knowledge gained from the literature or previous experience.

On the other hand, an unskilled investigator will ask questions framed in language rooted in previous knowledge, for example, "How do you cope with stress related to your diabetes?" Sometimes the informant will not understand the investigator's language and will say so. However, if words have both popular and scientific use, such as "coping" or "stress," informants may be just as likely to pick up that language and use it in the popular sense, without either party recognizing that neither has explained precisely what they mean by these words. If the investigator does not back up and clarify the informant's meaning, the likelihood is that subsequent data collection and analysis will be colored by the unnoticed misunderstanding between the investigator and the informant. Indeed, the naive investigator may be pleased at how "good" the data are and how well they fit with the current scientific views. Unfortunately, the investigator may fail to recognize that these data simply reflect the received view "one step removed," that is, the informant's story encoded into and then analyzed using language offered by the investigator, rather than in language the informant would ordinarily use.

Techniques to avoid subtle topic control through language include: using open-ended questions in nonspecific language until the informant's terms can be identified and defined; consistently adopting and maintaining the stance of the learner in research interviews; field-testing interviews and submitting interview tapes to experienced field researchers for critical review and comment; and taking into account subtle sociocultural differences in verbal and nonverbal styles when planning and executing interviews (Lipson & Meleis, 1989). This problem of topic control through language selection is difficult, if not impossible, to detect without listening to audiotaped interviews or reading verbatim transcripts. Field notes can seldom be kept in sufficient detail to reflect how questions are worded. Often an experienced and skillful investigator can immediately pick up a question that has been worded in a way that tends to "lead" the informant, but without audiotape and verbatim transcripts, even the most experienced investigator may still miss subtle differences in the way words are used by the informants. Since one of the most consistent challenges to the credibility of qualitative research is the issue of systematic bias through investigator control of data collection and analysis, how interview data are recorded or logged becomes increasingly important.

Logging the Data

Given the dynamic nature of interviewing and the subtle problems of topic control and data interpretation, the procedures used to log data must be given considerable attention. Generally speaking, most studies involving formal interviews appear to rely to a large extent on audiotaping, while those involving participant observation and informal interviewing, for obvious reasons, tend to rely more on field notes as a way of logging data.

Since a major criticism of qualitative research methods is the issue of systematic bias during either data collection or interpretation, audiotaping of data sets is an appropriate step since it allows auditability of data collection procedures. Certainly, some studies do not lend themselves to this form of data recording because of the nature of the research question or the setting in which data must be collected. However, in most cases, studies involving formal interviews can benefit from the use of audiotaping, and the ease with which the investigator handles recording equipment can be a major factor in reducing its intrusiveness and increasing its acceptability to informants (Bozett, 1980).

Regardless of the method used to log data, the process of systematic collection and recording should continue over the entire period of contact with the informant. For instance, since especially interesting and valuable data "come up" as good-byes are being said, some investigators (Lipson & Meleis, 1989; M. Perkins, personal communications, October, 1987) have found that data logging should continue until after the investigator and informant have finally parted company. This may be true because the rapport established in the interview motivates the informant to make sure the investigator has the "whole story" before leaving, or because the informant has never discussed the topic in such depth and new insights have been stimulated during the interview. Capturing important information after the formal interview has ended can be accomplished by immediately making field notes or by committing an addendum to the audiotape after leaving the informant.

Ethical Issues in Interviewing

Ethical issues in relation to interviewing parallel those about human research in general, that is, they cluster around the need to balance the benefits of scientific discovery against the potential risks to the informant. Since interviewing is essentially a process of human interaction, all of the potential risks of interaction, such as embarrassment, anger, violation of privacy, misunderstandings, and conflicts in opinions and values are likely to arise at some point in a research project.

As is true in each step of the interviewing process, the investigator may be forced to make decisions about how to proceed with a particular informant, that will require some compromise between the goals of the project and the needs of the informant. Since interviewing may stimulate self-reflection, reappraisal or catharsis, and considerable self-disclosure, the investigator needs to take these possibilities into account and consider what provisions must be made for the informant's well-being.

These are standard elements of planning and implementing any research project, regardless of how data are collected. However, some interviewing situations may preset more complex decisions. For instance, if the investigator plans a one-shot interview format in an emotionally sensitive area, there should be some provision for "debriefing" the informant and, if necessary, for providing additional emotional support, either by the investigator or by referral to another source of assistance. When interviews are conducted over a long period of time, and there has been considerable self-disclosure and investment in the relationship, the investigator must provide for termination and closure.

However, more subtle and complex decisions face some investigators. Under what circumstances does an investigator decide to interview an informant because that individual "needs" to be interviewed, either to provide an opportunity for ventilation and supportive listening or simply to avoid being excluded when others in the social group have already been included? When the data are useless for scientific purposes, should an investigator prolong and direct an interview for the purpose of being helpful or even therapeutic? Should an investigator direct an interview away from areas likely to be "good" for an informant to discuss because that direction is unlikely to be useful for the forward progress of the overall study?

Answers to these questions are not straightforward. While scientists in some fields are not held to the principle of "doing good," and only adhere to the principle of "doing no harm," researchers from some of the practice disciplines feel an obligation to intervene, since interviewing can have the effect of "cheap therapy" for some informants. Others (Pat Munhall, personal communication, November, 1987) point out that volunteering for a research study is not a completely selfless act, that there are secondary gains to the informant, and they conclude that therapeutic intervention by the investigator at the expense of advancing the goals of the study is not expected, or even desirable. Ultimately, decisions involved in conducting qualitative research interviews and interpreting the subsequent data must be handled according to the individual investigator's previous experience, skill level, and judgment based on the surrounding circumstances.

Summary

This chapter addresses the subtle challenges of research interviewing that often creep into conversations between experienced fieldworkers. The challenges include accurate and precise description of interview procedures and the process of adjusting those procedures as a project unfolds, the delicate balance between flexibility and consistency, depth and breadth, and how to get the story and attend to the needs of the storytellers themselves. Interviewing is the "bread and butter" of most qualitative work, yet it is a skill in which students often get the least instruction and supervision and about which experienced investigators have few opportunities to compare notes. The process of asking others about their lives, and listening as carefully as one can, so that the story can be understood and retold is fascinating, exhausting, and stimulating; how well the processes of asking, listening, understanding, and retelling are done determines the quality of the research itself.

References

Bozett, F. (1980). Practical suggestions for the use of the audio cassette tape recorder in nursing research. *Western Journal of Nursing Research, 2*(3), 602-605.

Chenitz, W., & Swanson, J. (1986). *From practice to grounded theory: Qualitative research in nursing.* Menlo Park, CA: Addison-Wesley.

Lipson, J., & Meleis, A. (1989). Methodological issues in research with immigrants. *Medical Anthropology, 12,* 103-115.

Lofland, J., & Lofland, L. (1984). *Analyzing social settings* (2nd ed.). Belmont, CA: Wadsworth.

Munhall, P., & Oiler, C. (1986). *Nursing research: A qualitative perspective.* Norwalk, CT: Appleton-Century-Crofts.

Polit, D., & Hungler, B. (1987). *Nursing research: Strategies for a natural sociology* (3rd ed.). Philadelphia: J. B. Lippincott.

Schatzman, I., & Strauss, A. (1973). *Field research: Strategies for a natural sociology.* Englewood Cliffs, NJ: Prentice-Hall.

Warren, C. (1988). *Gender issues in field research.* Newbury Park, CA: Sage.

Dialogue

On the Relationship Between the Researcher and the Subject

STERN: Can I give you two quotes from Glaser and Strauss? Strauss said something like: "Everything is data, including everything that's happened in your life." And Glaser said: "The best way to approach a subject is to say to the person 'teach me' "—so they're co-investigators as well!

12

Conducting Qualitative Studies with Children and Adolescents

JANET A. DEATRICK
SANDRA A. FAUX

Researchers who primarily use qualitative methods value the first-hand accounts of those individuals involved with the phenomenon being studied. While the pediatric nursing research literature con tains many examples of studies based on these firsthand accounts, the majority of research literature generated both by nurses and researchers in other disciplines is generally not based upon children's and adolescents' accounts of the phenomenon being studied. Instead, an adult's (usually the mother's) view of the child's world is often substituted. This is reflective of two competing perspectives of researchers studying children and adolescents. The traditional socialization and developmental perspectives view children as being unable to describe and understand their world and life experiences due to developmental immaturity (cognitive and linguistic) and to a lack of socialization experiences (Speier, 1976). The other perspective is represented by researchers who view children as competent interpreters of their world. With the reseachers using a variety of appropriate qualitative techniques, children can provide a valid, meaningful description of the phenomenon being studied (Mandell, 1984).

In qualitative and quantitative studies in the pediatric nursing and family research areas where children or adolescents were used as primary informants, few researchers have documented how the children's developmental abilities may have affected the quality of the data. Yet, from theoretical and experiential perspectives, it is accepted that social, emotional, and cognitive development affect how informants of all ages approach the research situation. One notable recent exception is a study of family life conducted by Amato and Ochiltree (1987). The data analysis included assessing and comparing the quality of the data provided by a sample of 195 children (age 8-9 years) and 207 adolescents (age 15-16 years). Interviewers' ratings of children's behavior during the interview, the quantity of the missing data across interview items, and the percentage of agreements between parents and children on 10 objective questions concerning family characteristics were used as the three data sources. The quality of the data from adolescents was significantly higher than from primary school children across all three data sources. However, the quality of the data for primary school children was high in absolute terms. The authors optimistically conclude that "if researchers stick to the here-and-now, they can achieve articulate and informative responses from children about their families" (p. 674).

The purpose of this chapter is to explore various data gathering techniques that can be used in qualitative studies with children and adolescents and to describe related methodological considerations. Specific techniques selected from the literature appropriate for preschoolers, school age children, and adolescents will be used to explicate the variety of "qualitative techniques" available to nurse-researchers (see Table 12.1). Thus the primary emphasis will be on the developmental implications of various techniques.

The use of the term "qualitative techniques" will encompass techniques used by researchers to obtain data in an unstructured or semistructured manner while observing, interacting, and talking with children and adolescents. (It does not include, for example, observational techniques often used with children in which a preset, observational checklist may be used to rate a child's behavior.) The reader is also cautioned that these techniques are employed in different ways, depending on the nature of the research question and the specific qualitative approach. That is, these techniques will be used differently by the phenomenologist, ethnographer, grounded theorist, or researcher using a descriptive method.

The examples used are from the nursing research literature; no attempt is made to review the many examples available in the literature dealing with education, developmental psychology, and other disciplines. Due to their leadership in the area, many of the examples are from work done by Florence Erickson (1958) and

TABLE 12.1 Qualitative Techniques for Children and Adolescents

Developmental Stage	Selected Techniques
Preschool	Group and individual indirect observations
	Multiple interviews using variety of play and projective techniques
School age	Direct and indirect observations of individuals and groups
	Single or multiple interviews with individuals or groups which may be augmented by play
Adolescent	Individual and group single interviews
	Direct observations

the faculty and students at the University of Pittsburgh School of Nursing.

Selected Techniques and Methods

Preschool Children

Due to their limited cognitive, linguistic, and fine motor maturation, preschool children are usually studied by researchers using multiple qualitative techniques in an attempt to increase the accuracy, completeness, and understanding of the phenomenon being studied. Developmentally, this period is characterized by the child's efforts to gain increasing control over his/her environment, rather than being controlled by it. Although the preschool child is seeking ever-increasing independence, motor, cognitive, and linguistic abilities limit the child's ability to both control and be independent of his/her environment. Negativism, shyness, and separation anxiety characterize toddlers evolving into preschool children who are more confident of their abilities to interact and cope with the external world. Increasing linguistic ability and vocabulary permit preschool children to describe their world more clearly to adults. Cognitively, the preoperational child begins to use symbols to represent the outside world.

Two important developmental characteristics for the qualitative researcher are egocentrism and the dominant role of play and fantasy. Reality and fantasy are often interchangeable; however, the end of the preschool period is marked by an increasing ability to differentiate between pretending and reality. Observation, interviewing, and play are three qualitative approaches for data gathering most frequently cited in the literature. Since very few studies are reported concerning toddlers as they are defined developmentally, for this discussion, the toddler and preschool period will be combined in accordance with Fleming's (1986) definition.

Observation

Observational techniques are probably the most frequently used methods of gathering data in qualitative studies of preschool children. Repeated observations over extended time periods have been found to yield rich data in describing the experience of childhood.

In contrast to the traditional ethnographic situation, adult researchers observing children cannot assume that subjects have the status equivalent to their own (Fine & Glassner, 1979). The adult can never be a member of the preschool group due to the very different roles that are predetermined by age, cognitive development, and physical maturity. Thus the researcher can never be a complete participant (Gold, 1959; Schatzman & Strauss, 1982). Nonetheless, there are a variety of ways adult researchers may attain a limited degree of acceptance into the preschooler's world. Fine and Glassner define the degree of acceptance in participant observation situations with children as the extent of the positive contacts between the child and adult and the extent to which the adult has direct authority over the child. In this latter situation, four possible adult roles have been postulated: friend, observer, leader, and supervisor.

Due to the usual status role of the adult in relation to preschool children, the nurse-researcher studying this age group usually occupies one of two roles (observer and supervisor). The researcher may be the complete observer and remain entirely outside the preschool child's situation; this type of observation frequently takes place during nursing care, play, home, and nursery school situations, where the child is observed either individually or interacting with others in his environment (i.e., parents, peers, siblings, or caregivers). The researcher remains outside the situation and records the data, using field notes of the observations or videotapes. For example, using these methods, Carty (1980) observed three children's reactions to the pediatric intensive care unit, and Taylor (1983) observed the postoperative pain experienced by toddlers and preschool children. In Taylor's descriptive study, in particular, she observed 20 toddlers and preschool children in the recovery room during the first three postoperative hours, using field notes and extensive process recordings to record the data.

This role of complete observer does not allow the opportunity to collect data from the children's point of view, which is gained through direct interaction with them. When qualitative researchers directly interact with children in selected situations (e.g., play, school, or health care), they may be in the role of participant observer (Gold, 1958) or of supervisor (Fine & Glassner, 1979), roles that are common to nurses when providing care. Rubin and Erickson (1977) have emphasized this combination of roles for the caregiver/researcher when collecting clinically relevant qualitative data with this age group. This approach is also exemplified in the work of Aradine (1983), Dittemore (1973), and Seely (1973).

Interviewing

In the past, nurse-researchers have been somewhat reluctant to interview children directly, particularly children younger than six years of age. Although children are acknowledged to be the best describers/definers of their experiences, researchers have questioned data gathered from children in an age group that is characterized by a limited vocabulary and by extensive symbolism in their language (Yarrow, 1960). In contrast, researchers in early childhood education, developmental psychology, and other disciplines have used various techniques to elicit interview data from children as young as two years old. However, as demonstrated by Bluebond-Langner (1978) in her ethnographic study of 32 dying children ages three to nine years, where she combines interviews with observation, an increasing number of nurse-researchers are interviewing young children.

To an even greater extent than in interviews with adult subjects, the preschooler interview is dependent upon the interpersonal relationship established with the interviewer. Interviewers must be able to establish trust rapidly. They must also be flexible and be able to modify the interview constantly to meet the child's developmental requirements, language level, and physical needs, and have an ability to enter the child's world to some extent. This latter aspect is very difficult, since age alone prevents the interviewer from ever being completely able to do so.

As seen in Gellert's (1982) research of children's knowledge of body parts, by four years of age children usually have a vocabulary extensive enough to exchange information and describe events in a formal, direct interview situation. Researchers report informal interviews with children as young as two years old. No matter what the age, the most successful interviews take place informally and arise naturally from the situation in which the child and researcher are interacting (i.e., during play or the caregiving situation). A single interview, however, is rarely useful and productive with the preschool child due to their limited attention span, fatigue, and the time needed to build rapport and trust. Thus several short interviews (direct and indirect), conducted over a period of time and in a variety of situations, will yield rich data.

If the interviewer is already familiar with children in the research setting (e.g., has been observing children in the hospital playroom), the interviewing process will be enhanced. Certain strategies, such as play and projective techniques, also help facilitate interviewing with this age group. Simple play or drawing materials introduced at the beginning of the interview facilitate rapport and provide an opening to the interview (Bluebond-Langner, 1978). For instance, the interviewer may ask the child to draw a picture and to describe what the picture is about.

A major consideration is to prevent overdependence or over-identification with the interviewer. Young children, in particular, view adults as authority figures who control their world, and they can be so eager to please that they may tell the researcher what they think he/she wants to hear. Therefore interviews are usually combined with play and observation for children in this age group in order to generate a more complete and comprehensive understanding of the child's experience (Rumfelt, 1980).

Play

Fleming (1986) describes play, projective techniques, and drawings as the most valuable tools in obtaining data from preschool children. Three- to five-year-old children seem to be able to communicate most easily using the play interview, with its viability decreasing as the child enters the school age period. Children become socialized into the world through play because it serves to help them assimilate, comprehend, and master the experiences they encounter. Therefore it is an excellent medium to communicate the child's perspective. The play interview was first described by Erickson (1958). It has been used extensively since that time (Byers, 1972; David, 1973; Dittemore, 1973).

The play interview usually takes place with the child playing alone or interacting with the researcher in a relatively unstructured, informal situation with the child directing the interview. Play materials, including human figures and other developmentally appropriate toys, are presented to the child. In the hospital, health care equipment, such as syringes and empty intravenous bags, may be included. The researcher can either observe the child's play or interact with the child during the interview to obtain his/her point of view. The interviews can last from a few minutes to almost an hour, and as noted before, data gathered using this technique are most valuable when used in conjunction with observation and interviewing.

Children's drawings are a language, a way of symbolically communicating their thoughts, feelings, and experiences (DiLeo, 1970, 1983; Klepsch & Logie, 1982). For example, researchers have used this pictorial language as a research tool for exploring preschool children's hospitalization and illness experiences (Byers, 1972; Dittemore, 1973). The most essential aspect of this technique is the child-researcher interaction and explanation of the picture. The researcher can use either a directed or a nondirected approach. A directed approach may begin with an opening like "Would you draw me a picture of your family?" A nondirected approach may begin with merely providing the materials for spontaneous drawings or paintings.

School Age Children

The increasing cognitive, linguistic, social, and emotional maturity of the school age child (6-12 years of age) means that a broader range of data collection techniques is available to the qualitative researcher than to the researcher with preschool subjects. During this developmental phase, school age children are increasingly oriented to the world outside the home. The peer group is more important than during the preschool stage, with the same-sex group predominant in the later school age period. Moral development and rules are often rigid and inflexible. In contrast to the rebellious adolescent and in relation to their increasing independence, control, and self-esteem, school age children are usually comfortable speaking and working with adults. Cognitive abilities are characterized by their ability to mentally represent their perceptions and to view themselves and their actions objectively. The improved linguistic and cognitive abilities and positive adult relationships make school age children excellent research subjects for qualitative researchers. In discussing the qualitative techniques most often used with school age children, observations, interviewing, and play will be explored from the perspective of use with this particular age group.

Observation

All four roles previously mentioned are appropriate with school age subjects. The focus of the school age child's social world shifts from the primary roles of "friend" and "leader" to the same-sex peer group. As such, the adult researcher can partially enter the child's world when trusted as a "friend," as Kueffner (1975) did in her descriptive study of six burned children. In the leadership role, researchers are respected when they serve as experts and authority figures (e.g., coach of a Little League team). As with the preschool subjects, researchers can also use the observer and supervisory roles when in the caregiver role, as did Stoll (1969), in her descriptive study of three burned children, and Riddle (1972), in her descriptive study of five children who were experiencing binocular bandages. Both investigators combined observations and interviews during the hospitalization of the children. Although usually involving complex research situations, group observation of this age group is useful, and videotaping and observing school age children interacting with peers, family members, and others in their environment can generate insightful and interesting data. The researcher stance of either complete observer or participant in the group interaction is a viable data gathering modality.

Interviewing

Interviews have been used in nursing research studies of school age children to gain the children's descriptions of their experiences (Faux, 1984; Riddle, 1972; Taylor, 1980; Walsh, 1983). Cognitive and linguistic skills allow the school age child to be interviewed using more direct methods than those employed with preschool children. Fantasy and symbolic language have decreased with increasing age, making the interviewer's task somewhat less difficult. Research studies employing the single, individual interview in studying this age group are more common than the series of interviews required for the younger child. The many aspects to be considered when interviewing school age children individually have been covered extensively in other publications (Amato & Ochiltree, 1987; Faux, Walsh, & Deatrick, 1988; Rich, 1968; Yarrow, 1960). Faux et al. (1988) summarize the issues as gaining access and cooperation, constructing the interview guide, and conducting the interview. Methods that strengthen the credibility or overall quality of the data are discussed, using examples from three studies. Rather than relying on adult conceptions, the authors conclude that the interview method is an optimal way to study the child's world.

The group interview is another valuable source of qualitative interview data with this age group. Although group discussions have often been used for their therapeutic value, they can also serve to gain data concerning the experiences, values, and perceptions of school age and adolescent children (Amato & Ochiltree, 1987; Yarrow, 1960). For example, in her grounded theory study, Walsh (1983) uses group discussions to elicit school age children's descriptions of the experience of having asthma. Small groups (9 to 12 children) meet with the interviewer to discuss "Asthma and Me." The interviewer has a general topical outline and acts as a facilitator for the group; sessions are tape recorded, which enables Walsh to compare the individual and group responses to each child. Consistent descriptions (individual and group interviews) of the asthma experience are considered to be indicative of a more clear and complete picture of the child's experience and reality.

In addition to group size (small), careful consideration should be given to interview content, topic sensitivity, and group composition;

for example, what is meant by embarrassment and giggling during a discussion of menstruation. During the school age period, same-sex groups are most successful in data generation. Walsh notes that the sex of the group interviewer did not appear to influence the quality of data generated; school age boys indicated that the female interviewer "didn't count as a girl. You're like a mother." Group composition should be balanced, so that shy or anxious children are not overwhelmed by more aggressive members.

Play

Peer group play is characteristic of this age group. As noted, observations of group situations are extremely useful. Although doll play is far less effective with this age group, projective techniques, including sentence completion, games, and drawing are valuable data gathering tools. Rarely do these techniques provide adequate data bases in isolation, but they are a potential aid in observational and interview situations. Short games or having the child draw a picture can aid in establishing rapport and decreasing the anxiety engendered in the research situation. The child can be asked to draw himself, a friend, or his family; the researcher can then use the drawing as a point to start a conversation (Carson, 1986; Faux et al. 1988; Rich, 1968). Whether the drawings are to be considered data is decided by the researcher in relation to the study purpose. Pictures drawn by school age children have been used extensively in descriptive studies conducted by nurses (Aamodt, 1972; Barnes, 1975; Stoll, 1969). Stoll uses pictures collected serially over time to help interpret changes in the child's perception of the burn experience throughout hospitalization. Barnes combines drawings with interviews in her study of 13 children's perceptions of the PICU (Pediatric Intensive Care Unit) following open heart surgery. Aamodt uses pictures and sentence completion in her ethnographic study of Native American children's conceptions of health and healing.

The clinical method, which combines pictures prepared by the researcher with qualitative interviews, can also be an effective data gathering technique with school age children. Gellert (1982) pioneered this approach when studying preschool and school age children's understanding of their bodies and health/illness experiences. These techniques may help the qualitative researcher understand a vital aspect of the child's understanding and perceptions of the illness experience. Explanations given by the child about body parts and functions can lead to a discussion of what the child has thought, felt, seen, and experienced in relation to health and illness.

Adolescents

In his classic article on interviewing children, Yarrow (1960) concludes that, generally, the resistance that adolescents may have to adults probing their worlds may be counterbalanced by other characteristics, including developmental strides, intellectual curiosity, and idealism, which help the adolescent to be motivated to participate in research. The increasing capacities of the adolescent (13-18 years of age) allow for the use of the tremendous variety of data collection techniques that are also used with adults. That is, more traditional forms of participant observation and interviewing are options that can be used to gather data with adolescent subjects. (Play techniques are no longer viable options, other than the use of games and selected projective techniques.)

In order to be sensitive to these variations, it is common to conceptualize the early, middle, and late phases of adolescence and to consider the major social, emotional, and cognitive processes of each phase. Of special interest to the researcher who is using the adolescent as a research subject is the adolescent's progression from a child, who is reliant on parents and the same-sex peer group, to an emancipated, independent young adult. In early adolescence, a sense of belonging to, and approval from, the peer group is gained through conformity. (Self-absorption gradually evolves into interest in a special friend, who is usually of the same sex as the adolescent.) As adolescence continues, the struggle to gain independence intensifies, and parents and other authority figures become targets of reproach. Heterosexual relationships become more important, and emotional growth follows a related course, with the behavior in the midyears of adolescence usually being the most erratic.

From a cognitive perspective, even adolescents in the early phases may be capable of formal operations, which constitute Piaget and Inhelder's (1969) most sophisticated state of intellectual development, in which the developing adolescent is increasingly able to use logic in deductive and inductive reasoning without resorting to observation.

Observation

As with the school age subject, the researcher is able to employ all four types of roles with the adolescent. Due to authority issues, the observational roles of friend and observer may be most reliable, while roles of the leader and supervisor are least reliable. However, a balance must be obtained between building trust and over-friendliness because the latter will decrease both trust and rapport with this age group (Yarrow, 1960). Increasing cognitive and physical maturity means that the status of the observer and the adolescent become more equivalent, and the researcher is most likely to take advantage of these capacities and make direct observations. The sex of the observer in direct observation, however, can be an issue if the subject matter is sensitive, particularly if tied to sexual issues.

Participant observation and intensive interviewing were used by Deatrick (1982, 1984) in a descriptive field study, which examined how 24 chronically physically impaired adolescents defined and participated in events and relationships critical to their rehospitalization experience. Focal observational contacts were identified during a pilot project and outlined on a data flow chart, which included data collection, data processing, and data analysis. The chart allowed for rigorous comparison of data within and among contacts. Group observations were used as well, and the observation of the adolescents interacting verbally and nonverbally with other adolescent patients was a particularly rich data source. This technique could easily be explored and used in studies conducted in natural settings as well as in settings and in groups devised by the researcher.

Interviewing

As with adult subjects, direct, single interviews are commonly used with adolescents. Again, the many aspects to be considered when interviewing adolescent individually have been covered extensively in other publications (Amato & Ochiltree, 1987; Faux et al., 1988).

Multiple interviews with the same adolescent subjects can be used as a main in-depth source of data. In her ethnographic study, Aamodt (1986) conducted four or five interviews with seven adolescents who experienced alopecia due to cancer. Each was interviewed by a single interviewer in the ethnographic study. Communication and coordination among the interviewers was stressed by the investigator.

Group interviews can also be very productive with adolescents. The structure of the group is important. A small group will minimize distractions. The content of the discussion should be clearly under the control of the leader. The group can usually be composed of both sexes, so various perspectives can be described and compared. Of course, adolescents in the early and middle phases of their development may be more concerned about conformity with their peers, or their embarrassment concerning subject matter, than with truthfully discussing their perspectives. Therefore data must be analyzed carefully with these factors in mind. As with observations, the sex of the interviewer becomes crucial as the subject matter becomes more sensitive. If it is not possible to match the sex of the subjects, it is especially important for the leader to clearly define his/her purpose, role, and expectations. In the group setting, videotaping may be a particularly helpful adjunct to data collection as long as conditions are kept as "natural" as possible.

Methodological Considerations

Knafl and Howard (1984) suggest that the "minimal requirements" for the procedure subsection of a descriptive, qualitative study include "management of threats to the validity and reliability of the data" (p. 21). Threats are aspects of the method that potentially could weaken the reliability or validity of the data or analysis techniques. However many techniques and guidelines that are applicable to the generation and management of quantitative data simply cannot be used with qualitative data. Therefore the investigator is often at a loss when trying to identify, manage, and report threats to the reliability and validity of qualitative data collection and analysis techniques. These problems may be even more perplexing and complex with child and adolescent subjects.

While there is much literature on the reliability and validity of qualitative studies (Brink, 1987), the existing literature explores the issues from a very general "qualitative" perspective: from the perspectives of specific qualitative methods, such as grounded theory or ethnography (Kirk & Miller, 1986; LeCompte & Goetz, 1982), or from the combined perspectives of "credibility" (Lofland & Lofland,

1984). In qualitative research, reliability focuses on "identifying and documenting recurrent, accurate, and consistent (homogeneous) or inconsistent (heterogenous) features as patterns, themes, values, world views, experiences, or other phenomenon confirmed in similar or different contexts" (Leininger, 1985, p. 69). Validity in qualitative studies "refers to gaining knowledge and understanding of the true nature, essence, meaning, and characteristics of a particular phenomenon under study" (Leininger, 1985, p. 68). Specific methodological considerations include the reliability of the data and the analysis as well as the validity of the data gathering guides and the validity of the resulting data. Situational, personal, and administration factors and factors associated with the data gathering guides could theoretically enhance or detract from the reliability of the data.

Reliability

Specific strategies can be employed to minimize those factors that detract from the reliability of the data collected from children and adolescents (see Table 12.2). First, in order to enhance the consistency and stability of the situational factors, unless otherwise appropriate, all data gathered should be collected in an area that is "neutral territory" (LeCompte & Goetz, 1982). Noise can be particularly distracting to children, so it is optimal to have a closed area. A private area also helps reassure the child of confidentiality. This, in turn, increases the validity of the data as well as protecting the confidentiality of the child or adolescent.

Second, in regard to personal factors, fatigue and anxiety can alter data accuracy, particularly when working with young children who have relatively short attention spans. The researcher should attempt to note both the verbal and nonverbal signs of fatigue and anxiety in the child/adolescent or in himself/herself. The optimal strategy is to continue the data collection at another time. However this is not always feasible in terms of research resources or sample retention. An alternate strategy can be used, which involves modifying the remaining part of the data collection session to conclude as rapidly as possible. An adequate representation of the subjects' perceptions can be assured if all absolutely essential data are underlined or marked by an asterisk.

The third personal factor that can affect data reliability is an emotional reactions by the child/adolescent during the interview itself. Not only must researchers identify such reactions when they occur, but they must also anticipate what to do if they do occur. This and other phenomenon often make access to subjects by researcher difficult (Faux et al., 1988). For instance, Institutional Review Boards are particularly concerned that the researcher state on the consent form what resources are available to the child/adolescent if they have a severe emotional reaction to the data collection situation. When the reactions are noted, they should be validated with the child/adolescent in a developmentally appropriate manner, and their origins discussed: Is the behavior a reaction to the content of the interview or to the situation of the interview itself? A decision can then be made regarding whether to proceed with the interview. Usually, the intensity and duration of the reaction helps guide that decision. The next decision has more therapeutic implications. The researcher must decide whether to actively intervene with the person who is emotionally upset. The answer will again most likely be guided by the nature and severity of the reaction. Generally the researcher would attempt to comfort the child and refer him/her for additional help if the reaction is intense and prolonged and is connected with a serious issue discovered in the interview.

Fourth, the conditions for data collection are important in order to enhance the reliability of administration factors. Quantitative researchers emphasize the need for stable, similar conditions in administering instruments. The qualitative investigator has similar concerns, since using dissimilar administrative techniques with each child or adolescent will decrease data reliability and comparability. If multiple data collectors are used, training is especially crucial for all studies, particularly in those with children and adolescents. The interviewer must be completely familiar with the interview guide, know how and to what extent questions may be clarified, and understand which questions may be eliminated if it becomes necessary to shorten the discussion. A tape-recorded pilot interview can also be used in training multiple interviewers.

In the study itself, tape-recordings can be made of all formal interviews, while a systematic record can be made in field notes of observations made during each interview. The tape-recorded interviews provide a complete, accurate transcript of subject responses, and thus increase data reliability by preventing selective filtering of data due to investigator recall or summarization. In Faux's (1984) grounded theory study of sibling response to a chronically impaired

TABLE 12.2 Reliability Issues

Issue	Strategies
Situational factors	Interviews conducted in neutral, private area
Personal factors	Interviews rescheduled as necessary
	Interview shortened if necessary, questioned confined to essential areas
Administration factors	Experienced interviewers/observers
	Trained interviewers
	Tape recordings of all formal interviews
	Field notes of observations
Factors associated with interview guides	Clear wording
	Semistructured interview guide
Data Analysis	Expert consultants
	Investigators previous experience
	Recoding

brother or sister, there was no instance when the tape-recorder elicited a negative response. Most often the children were curious. In fact, in an increasingly technological society, tape-recorders are no longer the reactive stimulus once described (Webb, Campbell, Schwartz, Sechrest, & Grove, 1981). Allowing the child to insert the tape, turn on the tape-recorder, and listen to the tape at the completion of the interview are additional strategies to decrease any possible reactive effects of the device.

Fifth, factors associated with data collection guides could potentially influence data reliability. While flexible, semistructured guides are used in an effort to increase the comparability of interviews, the investigators should be aware that they may threaten reliability. In order to strengthen reliability, each item should be worded as clearly as possible to enhance understanding because child and adolescent subjects have varying cognitive levels (Faux et al., 1988). The pilot testing should be done to evaluate the questions, clarify wording, and sequence topics.

Another strategy to evaluate data validity is the use of triangulation to check the comparability of data collection. For instance, Faux (1984) used multiple sources of data on parental child-rearing strategies when she compared qualitative interview data with quantitative data obtained using the *Children's Report of Parental Behavior Inventory* (Schaeffer, 1962). Positive or negative parent-child relationships were usually confirmed by both data methods.

Validity

As in most qualitative research, threats to data validity or credibility are considered to be the most relevant validity concerns for the investigator (see Table 12.3). These threats include reactive effects, sources of distortion, and time sampling (Becker, 1958; Glaser & Strauss, 1966; McCall & Simmons, 1969).

Reactive effects are defined as the artificial conditions imposed on the respondents that affect validity of their data by virtue of the researcher's presence. In Deatrick's (1982, 1984) study, the researcher was well known to all of the staff in the setting and was integrated into the work environment. Her stance on nonclinical involvement with research subjects was known and had been in operation for a year-and-a-half prior to the study. An effort was also made to keep the environmental conditions during focal contacts similar to usual clinical conditions. Field notes described any incidents portraying evidence of reactive effects by any person being observed so that could be taken into consideration during data analysis (Blum, 1952; Douglas, 1976; Trice, 1957).

There are many potential sources of distortion that can lead to bias. In observational studies, the "researcher's status position" (Le-Compte & Goetz, 1982) can be one source of distortion. As was discussed, this is of particular concern in observational studies with children and adolescents, due to the obvious status and role differences between the subjects and the researcher. Professional socialization as nurses can be a further complication. These sources of bias or distortion cannot be eliminated. However, many of the credibility issues have two dimensions: that is, what is viewed as a source of bias can be reframed partially as a source of competence and expertise in the phenomenon under study. Strategies that can be used to

TABLE 12.3 Validity Issues

Issues	Strategies
Content validity	Expert consultants Pilot projects with resultant modifications Guides for informal interviews Comparable guides for parents, children, and adolescents
Threats to data validity or credibility	Topics derived from literature Triangulation Reactive effects Observer known to staff Similar environmental conditions during focal contacts Manipulation of tape recorder before interview by young subjects Field notes to document possible reactive effects
Sources of distortion	Experienced researcher Interviewer of same sex and race as respondent
Time sampling	Questions about time when not present Audit of charts and records Triangulation Data flow chart

control and/or account for bias include the use of field notes during data collection and the use of a second independent rater to evaluate coding categories and their application to the data during data analysis.

Finally, time sampling may threaten the credibility of the data. Deatrick (1982) uses a data flow chart to systematize contacts. The investigator obviously cannot be present at all times, so Deatrick relies on the adolescents themselves, the families, the staff, and other patients to provide data. Informal and formal interviews with parents and the patients contain questions concerning their perceptions of experiences during the absences of the researcher. Patients' charts are audited, and the researcher also attends team rounds, where staff share patient information from all three shifts.

Summary

While there will always be a gap between what is understood and what is questioned about the child's world, the use of a variety of qualitative strategies can enrich understanding. As the sophistication and complexity of a child's skills increase, the range of qualitative strategies available to the researcher increases. However, assessment of developmental abilities, as well as a flexible approach used by a trained, experienced researcher, are tremendous assets in any study of children and adolescents.

References

Aamodt, A. (1972). The child's view of health and healing. In M. V. Batey (Ed.). *Communicating nurse research* (Vol. 5, pp. 38-54). Boulder, Colorado: Western Interstate Commission on Higher Education.

Aamodt, A. (1986). Discovering the child's view of alopecia: Doing ethnography. In P. L. Munhall & C J. Oiler (Eds.). *Nursing research: A qualitative perspective* (pp. 163-172) Norwalk, CT: Appleton Century Crofts

Amato, P. R., & Ochiltree, G. (1987). Interviewing children about their families: A note on data quality. *Journal of Marriage and the Family, 49,* 669-675.

Aradine, C. (1983). Young children with long-term tracheostomies: Health and development. *Western Journal of Nursing Research, 5,* 115-124.

Barnes, C. (1975). Levels of consciousness indicated by responses of children to phenomena in the intensive care unit. *Maternal-Child Nursing Journal, 4,* 215-285.

Becker, H. S. (1958). Problems of inference and proof in participant observation. *American Sociological Review, 23,* 652-660.

Bluebond-Langner, M. (1978). *The private world of dying children.* Princeton, NJ: Princeton University Press.

Blum, F. H. (1952). Getting individuals to give information to the outsider. *Journal of Social Issues, 8*(3), 35-42.

Brink, P. (1987). Editorial: On reliability and validity in qualitative research. *Western Journal of Nursing Research, 9,* 157-159.

Byers, M. L. (1972). Play interviews with a five-year-old boy. *Maternal-Child Nursing Journal, 1,* 133-141.

Carson, T. R. (1986). Closing the gap between research and practice: Conversation as a mode of doing research. *Phenonmenology & Pedagogy, 4,* 73-85.

Carty, R. (1980). Observed behaviors of preschoolers in intensive care. *Pediatric Nursing, 6,*(4), 21-25.

David, N. (1973). Play: A nursing diagnostic tool. *Maternal-Child Nursing Journal, 2,* 49-56.

Deatrick, J. A. (1982). *Meaning of hospitalization and surgery to chronically disabled adolescents and their parents.* Unpublished doctoral dissertation, University of Illinois at the Medical Center, Chicago.

Deatrick, J. A. (1984). It's their decision now: Perspectives of chronically disabled adolescents concerning surgery. *Issues in Comprehensive Pediatric Nursing, 7,* 17-31.

DiLeo, J. H. (1970). *Young children and their drawings.* New York: Brunner/Mazel.

DiLeo, J. H. (1983). *Interpreting children's drawings.* New York: Bruner/Mazel.

Dittemore, I. (1973). Play utilized by a burned child. *Maternal-Child Nursing Journal, 2,* 202-214.

Douglas, J. D. (1976). *Investigative social research: Individual and team field research.* Beverly Hills, CA: Sage.

Erickson, F. (1958). Play interviews for four-year-old hospitalized children. *Monograph of the Society for Research in Child Development, 23*(3), 7-77.

Faux, S. A. (1984). *Sibling and maternal perceptions of having a child with a craniofacial or cardiac anomaly in the family.* Unpublished doctoral dissertation. University of Illinois, Chicago.

Faux, S. A., Walsh, M., & Deatrick, J. A. (1988). Intensive interviewing with children and adolescents. *Western Journal of Nursing Research, 10,* 180-194.

Fine, G., & Glassner, B. (1979). Participant observation with children: Promise and problems. *Urban Life, 8,* 153-174.

Fleming, J. (1986). Preschool children. In H. Werley, J. Fitzpatrick, & R. Taunton (Eds.). *Annual review of nursing research* (Vol. 4, pp. 21-54). New York: Springer.

Gellert, E. (1982). Children's conceptions of the content and functions of the human body. *Genetic Psychology Monographs, 293-411.*

Glaser, B. G., & Strauss, A. L. (1966). The purpose and credibility of qualitative research. *Nursing Research, 15,* 56-61.

Gold, R. L. (1958). Roles in sociological field observations. *Social Forces, 36,* 217-223.

Kirk, J., & Miller, M. (1986). *Reliability and validity in qualitative research.* Beverly Hills, CA: Sage.

Klepsch, M., & Logie, L. (1982). *Children draw and tell: An introduction to the projective uses of children's human figure drawings.* New York: Brunner/Mazel.

Knafl, K. A., & Howard, M. J. (1984). Interpreting and reporting qualitative research. *Research in Nursing and Health, 7,* 17-24.

Kueffner, M. (1975). Passage through hospitalization of severely burned, isolated school aged children. In M. V. Batey (Ed.). *Communicating nursing research* (Vol. 7, pp. 181-197). Boulder, CO: Western Interstate Commission on Higher Education.

LeCompte, M., & Goetz, J. (1982). Problems of reliability and validity in ethnographic research. *Review of Educational Research, 52,* 31-60.

Leininger, M. M. (1985). Ethnography and ethnonursing: Models and modes of qualitative data analysis. In M. M. Leininger (Ed.). *Qualitative research methods in nursing* (pp. 33-71). Orlando, FL: Grune & Stratton.

Lofland, J., & Lofland, L. (1984). *Analyzing social settings: A guide to qualitative observation and analysis* (2nd ed.). Belmont, CA: Wadsworth.

Mandell, N. (1984). Children's negotiation of meaning. *Symbolic Interaction, 7,* 191-211.

McCall, G., & Simmons, J. (1969). *Issues in participant observation: A text and reader.* Reading, MA: Addison-Wesley.

Piaget, J., & Inhelder, B. (1969). *The psychology of the child.* New York: Basic Books.

Rich, J. (1968). *Interviewing children and adolescents.* London: MacMillian-St. Martin's Press.

Riddle, I. I. (1972). Communicative behaviors of hospitalized school aged children with binocular bandages. *Maternal-Child Nursing Journal, 1,* 291-254.

Rubin, R., & Erickson, F. (1977). Research in clinical nursing. *Maternal-Child Nursing Journal, 6,* 151-164.

Rumfelt, J. (1980). How five-year-old children perceive the role of the nurse. *Maternal-Child Nursing Journal, 9,* 13-24.

Schaeffer, E. S. (1962). *Children's Report of Parental Behavior Inventory* (NIN-71). Washington, DC: Department of Health, Education and Welfare.

Schatzman, L., & Strauss, A. (1982). *Field research: Strategies for a natural sociology* (2nd ed.). Englewood Cliffs, NJ: Prentice-Hall.

Seely, E. (1973). Coping behavior of an immobilized eight year old. *Maternal-Child Nursing Journal, 2,* 15-21.

Speier, M. (1976). The adult viewpoint in studies of childhood. In A. Skolnic (Ed.). *Rethinking childhood perspectives on development and society* (pp. 168-186). Boston: Little Brown.

Stoll, C. (1969). Responses of three girls to burn injuries and hospitalization. *Nursing Clinics of North America, 4,* 77-87.

Taylor, P (1983). Post-operative pain in toddler and pre-school children. *Maternal-Child Nursing Journal, 12,* 35-50.

Taylor, S. C. (1980). The effect of chronic childhood illnesses upon well siblings. *Maternal-Child Nursing Journal, 9,* 109-116.

Trice, H. M. (1957). The "outsiders" role in a field study. *Sociology and Social Research, 41,* 27-32.

Walsh, M. (1983). *The experience of asthma in childhood.* Unpublished doctoral dissertation, University of Illinois, Chicago.

Webb, E. J., Campbell, D. T., Schwartz, R. D., Sechrest, L., & Grove, J. B. (1981). *Nonreactive measures in the social sciences* (2nd ed.). Boston: Houghton, Mifflin.

Yarrow, L. J. (1960). Interviewing children. In P. H. Mussen (Ed.). *Handbook of research in child development* (pp. 561-602). New York: John Wiley.

Dialogue

On Triangulation

KNAFL: I think triangulation is really a design issue [in qualitative research]. I don't think triangulation-as-multiple-operationalism is particularly salient to qualitative research.

TRIPP-REIMER: Unless you are trying to do some kind of concurrent validity with different instruments—probably not in this room!

MAY: That really is an issue, though. When you talk to my positivist friends about triangulation, they think it means that you accept as given the validity of an instrument, say a self-report instrument, and then you collect some soft qualitative data over here to prove the validity of the instrument. And they call that triangulation. And I call it bastardization of the qualitative side! If you don't do it right, don't do it! Do something else, but don't do that! I think it's worrisome because you can't do good grounded theoretical work if you have an a priori concept which is brought into your analysis. You will always find what you started out with.

TRIPP-REIMER: I see myself cited by people who write about triangulation as someone who does it—and I don't use the term—I talk about combining methods. And the reason I talk about combining methods rather than triangulation (and I don't think that's a bad word) is the fact that in combining methods you have to be careful not to combine methods that have different assumptions. So that an anthropologist from the outset may combine methods. They do archival work, they do interviews, they do participant observation, and they do a survey of the community to find out who lives in the household. And that's using multiple methods, but they don't come from different assumptions. Some pieces that I have seen presented as triangulation have combined phenomenological approaches with very positivistic approaches and used the same group of people, rather than two separate samples, so that they have a problem right at the beginning, so that their assumptions are in conflict, internally. So the caution that I have with the term triangulation is that you don't use it as a gloss, so that it just means putting anything together that you happen to get organized. It must be specific about using accurate data points that are consistent with each other.

MAY: I don't know how you could do that [use triangulation]. It seems to me that, even if you had separate teams, then they shouldn't talk to one another. Because one of the teams is going to drive the theory, and I'm real clear about which one is going to get driven! Also, how could you do it with grounded theory? How could you use an instrument to measure a concept when you don't know what the concept is yet? That's what triangulation means to me at a design level.

KNAFL: OK. But to me it means something different at a design level. It's not triangulation on a concept. It's triangulation on what I call a domain of interest. For example, understanding how families define and manage chronic illness isn't a concept, but there are multiple components or aspects of the problem that they may experience. And some of these aspects you may get at by talking to the family members, others you can get at using more structured measures. And that's how I was using this term in the second part of the paper.

MAY: I'll buy that! I have no difficulty with your explanation, but the rest of the world isn't explaining it in the same way! For example, you want to understand social support, and you take these measures, and then you do this fancy little qualitative bit on the side. That's what I really object to!

FAUX: That's a different purpose, and that's not a qualitative purpose.

KNAFL: But it is really interesting to note your comment that one or the other has to take precedence. I don't know if that always has to be, but in this study, the quantitative measures are really adjunct.

BERGUM: If triangulation is the going thing, and the way to get funding, I find that worrisome because I wonder what we are jeopardizing in the process. We have to be really clear on what the reason for triangulation is, and how it relates to the question. The other part of the problem is that it is very hard to do good phenomenological work. I don't know how one could do that and do something else at the same time. I don't know how you can do two things, and do them both well.

FAUX: Also, it assumes you are an expert in everything.

KNAFL: Yes, I think that is a legitimate concern, when it is presented as an end in itself.

13

Triangulation in Qualitative Research: Issues of Conceptual Clarity and Purpose

KATHLEEN A. KNAFL
BONNIE J. BREITMAYER

Inquiry is inquiry, regardless of methodology.

(Dzurec & Abraham, 1986)

The discipline of nursing needs methodological strategies that will enhance researchers' efforts to describe and conceptualize the multifaceted complexity of human response to illness and health care situations. In recognition of this need, there is a growing emphasis on combining qualitative and quantitative methods in a single study, a practice often referred to as triangulation (Dzurec & Abraham, 1986; Goodwin & Goodwin, 1984; Hinds & Young, 1987; Mitchell, 1986; Tripp-Reimer, 1985). For example, in their discussion of the complementarity between qualitative and quantitative methods, Goodwin and Goodwin conclude that "many studies could be enhanced considerably if a combined approach were taken" (p. 378). They note how a combined approach could strengthen the comprehensiveness and/or reliability and validity of a study.

Recognizing the potential merits of a triangulated approach, other authors have begun to identify guidelines for integrating qualitative and quantitative approaches (Myers & Haase, 1989). Nonetheless there has been relatively little discussion of the different ways in which the term "triangulation" has been used and the varying purposes triangulation can serve. Thus while it may be appropriate to admonish researchers to consider a combined approach, as Goodwin and Goodwin do, such considerations should be grounded in the context of the investigator's overall study purpose and in an explicit recognition of the goals to be achieved through triangulation. Triangulation is not an end in itself; rather, as Fielding and Fielding pointed out, there is a "need for rigor in establishing the linkage between the logic of the research design and the chosen methodology. It is impractical and unwise to list all available means of data collection and analysis and use as many as possible" (pp. 32-34). In this chapter, the authors discuss the origin, development, and application of the term triangulation. The aim is to clarify the different purposes and approaches encompassed by the term and to explicate the relevance for qualitative research of one approach to triangulation.

Origin and Development of Triangulation

Triangulation is a technical term used in surveying and navigation to describe a technique whereby two known or visible points are used to plot the location of a third point. It was first used metaphorically in the social sciences to characterize the use of multiple methods to measure a single construct (Campbell, 1956; Campbell & Fiske, 1959; Garner, 1954; Garner, Hake, & Eriksen, 1956), a practice also referred to as multiple operationism, convergent operationism, operational delineation, and convergent validation (Campbell & Fiske, 1959).

Growing out of work in the area of educational and psychological testing, this metaphorical use of the term triangulation focuses on the measurement of discrete variables or constructs. Campbell describes the approach by saying:

> In several instances in the present study, there has been achieved what might be called methodological triangulation, in that several different methodological approaches have been employed to get at the same variable, psychologically conceived. . . . The process is one of mutual confirmation among the various approaches. (pp. 73-74)

Other authors have developed and refined the theme of mutual confirmation through triangulation (Bouchard, 1976; Denzin, 1970;

Jick, 1983; Mitchell, 1986; Webb, Campbell, Schwartz, Sechrest, & Grove, 1981). Campbell and his associates (Webb et al., 1981) continue to equate triangulation with multiple operationism for the purpose of confirmation. Fielding and Fielding (1986), emphasizing that this use of triangulation constitutes more than a proliferation of methods, state, "The important feature of triangulation is not the simple combination of different kinds of data, but the attempt to relate them so as to counteract the threats to validity identified in each" (p. 31). Their position is consistent with that of Webb and his associates, who note:

> Once a proposition has been confirmed by two or more independent measurement processes, the uncertainty of its interpretation is greatly reduced. The most persuasive evidence comes through a triangulation of measurement processes. If a proposition can survive the onslaught of a series of imperfect measures, all with their irrelevant error, confidence should be placed in it. Of course this confidence is increased by minimizing error in each instrument and by a reasonable belief in different and divergent effects of the sources of error. (p. 35)

To use triangulation for the purpose of confirmation necessitates the identification of data collection instruments or techniques whose strengths and weaknesses are both known and counterbalancing with regard to threats to validity. For example, an investigator interested in the construct of "self-care agency" might combine data from the client's chart, open-ended interviews, and Kearney and Fleischer's (1979) structured instrument to measure self-care agency. Any claim to triangulation based on such an approach would have to be supported by a discussion of the complementary nature of the three approaches and evidence that the weaknesses of one were offset by the strengths of another.

Denzin (1970) introduced the notion of multiple strategies of triangulation as a way to confirm the accuracy of one's data set. Acknowledging Campbell and Fiske's contributions, Denzin states that "triangulation involves varieties of data, investigators, theories, and methodologies" (p. 301). Denzin extends the application of the triangulation metaphor from the measurement of discrete concepts to the level of research design, an approach he terms *multiple triangulation*. Denzin believes that the ultimate purpose of such an approach is "to overcome the intrinsic bias that comes from single-method, single-observer, single-theory studies" (p. 313). While Denzin extends the triangulation metaphor beyond a measurement focus, he supports the view that the fundamental purpose of triangulation is to confirm one's results and conclusions.

Other authors (Jick, 1983; Fielding & Fielding, 1986) identify additional purposes served by combining methodological strategies and retain the term triangulation to designate their approach. Jick delineates a completeness as well as a confirming function for triangulation: "Triangulation, however, can be something other than scaling, reliability, and convergent validation. It can also capture a more complete, holistic, and contextual portrayal of the unit(s) under study" (p. 138). According to Jick, triangulation can be used to achieve completeness by portraying the contextual elements of the phenomenon of interest.

In a similar vein, Fielding and Fielding advocate the combining of multiple theories and methods in a single study in order to add to the investigator's depth and breadth of understanding. They maintain that when triangulation is conceptualized as a means to achieve convergent validity, it has limited relevance for the qualitative researcher who seldom, if ever, is concerned with the measurement of a discrete concept. Following their view, triangulation is not limited to the methods used to measure a single concept. Jick (1983) and Fielding and Fielding (1986) link the term triangulation to the goal of completeness. Following this use of the term, multiple methods, sources, theories, and/or investigators are combined in order to reveal the varied dimensions of an area of interest. When using this form of triangulation, the investigator does not expect multiple sources of data to confirm one another; rather, the expectation is that each source will contribute an additional piece to the puzzle. Multiple strategies are selected and combined because of their unique contribution to addressing the research question and not because of their counterbalancing strengths and weaknesses. The metaphorical use of the term triangulation breaks down when the term is applied to a situation where completeness, and not convergence, is the goal.

It is important to recognize that the term *triangulation* has two distinct though complementary applications. While some researchers focus on the convergence function of a triangulated approach, other authors use the term to describe the multi-strategy approach they use to attain completeness. Unfortunately, these differing applications of the term have resulted in ambiguity regarding both the purpose of triangulation and the appropriate application of the term.

Triangulation and Nursing Research

Both approaches to triangulation described above have relevance for nursing research. The convergence function is especially salient for those researchers (Kearney & Fleischer, 1979; Laffrey, 1986) who are directing their efforts either to the development of instruments or to the measurement of discrete constructs, such as stressors associated with specific events (Carr & Powers, 1986) or mental status (Forman, 1987). This less often is the case with qualitative researchers, who typically seek to describe or conceptualize more encompassing areas of interest, such as substance abuse among nurses (Hutchinson, 1986) or the impact of technology on nursing practice (Strauss, Fagerhaugh, Suczek, & Weiner, 1985).

Regardless of their approach (e.g., grounded theory, ethnography, or phenomenology), qualitative researchers share a common focus on completeness. Leininger (1985), for example, describes the goal of qualitative research as the attempt "to document and interpret as fully as possible the totality of whatever is being studied" (p. 5). As previously discussed, triangulation can make an important contribution to this goal; and when the qualitative researcher adopts a triangulated approach, it is usually for the purpose of achieving completeness, as opposed to convergence, within the data set.

However, to achieve completeness through a triangulated approach, researchers must be clear as to their purpose and must be able to demonstrate how their approach to triangulation contributes to the completeness of the resulting data set. This need for an explicit clarification and justification of one's approach is especially crucial in view of the different applications of the term triangulation and the different literature supporting each application.

Triangulation in Qualitative Research:
An Example

In Table 13.1, a framework is presented for evaluating the completeness of a qualitative study that uses triangulation to achieve

TABLE 13.1 Framework for Evaluating the Completeness of a Qualitative Study Using Multiple Triangulation

Type of Triangulation	Approach	Purpose/Goal
1. Investigator	4 Member Team	Substantive, theoretical, and methodological diversity.
2. Data Sources	Person, Time, and Situation	Represent individual perspectives over time and across a variety of situations. Theoretical sample.
3. Methods	Intensive Interviews Child Behavior Checklist Harter Self-Perception Profile Profile of Mood States Child Attitude Toward Illness Scale Feetham Family Functioning Scale	Identify individual definitions and management behaviors. Explore outcomes of definitions and behaviors.
4. Unit of Analysis	Individual and Family	Conceptualize individual and family unit response.
5. Theory	Development and Application	Conceptualize family management style. Interpret individual and family unit response patterns.

completeness. The table includes five types of triangulation (investigator, source, method, unit of analysis, and theory), each of which is evaluated with regard to approach and purpose/goal. The examples presented in Table 13.1 are based on the authors' ongoing study of how families define and manage a child's chronic illness (Knafl, Breitmayer, Gallo, & Zoeller, 1987).

Investigators

Investigator triangulation entails assembling a research team or thesis/dissertation committee whose members have a shared interest in the topic under study as well as diverse perspectives and areas of expertise with regard to the topic. Myers and Haase (1989) suggest assembling a research team that includes "maximally conflicting points of view with provision for systematic and controlled confrontation" (p. 300). A diversity in intellectual and methodological backgrounds contributes greatly to a research team's ability to achieve the other types of triangulation described in the table.

As shown in Table 13.1, the study of family response to chronic illness is being conducted by a four-member team whose specific interests, theoretical expertise, and research backgrounds are purposely diverse. Team members' general interests in how families respond to a member's chronic illness are complemented by more focused interests in either parents, chronically ill children, or siblings. These more focused interests were especially valuable when drafting the separate interview guides that were used to interview parents, chronically ill children, and siblings.

Team members are knowledgeable about differing aspects of the literature on family response to chronic illness. While some have directed their reading to how individual family members respond to chronic illness, others have concentrated on understanding the response of the family unit as a whole. These varying areas of expertise are complementary and contributed to the development of interview guides, which addressed both the individual and familial level of response to chronic illness. Moreover, varying experiences with interviewing adults and children made it possible to develop interview guides and interviewing techniques which were sensitive to the diverse cognitive levels of the research subjects. Team members' theoretical backgrounds are grounded in sociology, human development, and education, and include expertise in grounded theory, family theory, and child development. Team members also vary with regard to whether their research training and experience has been predominantly qualitative or quantitative in nature. This diversity in the intellectual and methodological backgrounds of the team made it possible to design a study that triangulated on both method and theory. No single member of the research team had the breadth of methodological or theoretical expertise to achieve this. Finally, team members' diverse clinical backgrounds, which include pediatrics, child psychology, and family nursing, helped to assure that the study design would address questions and identify implications relevant to a broad spectrum of nursing practice concerns.

Data Source

When using the strategy of data source triangulation, the investigator explicitly attempts to maximize the range of data that might contribute to a more complete understanding of the topic being investigated. Denzin describes how one can triangulate data sources across the three dimensions of time, space, and person. For example, if studying the socialization experiences of student nurses, one would want to take into account what they were doing at various times of the day, on different days of the week, and in different settings. In order to vary data source by person, the investigator would need to consider not only the individuals involved in the socialization experiences of the nurses, but also the nature of the interaction between these individuals. Finally, it would also be necessary to compare certain collectivities or groups of individuals in order to determine the extent to which such groups (e.g., faculty, students) held shared or discrepant views of the socialization experience.

The triangulation of multiple data sources is essential for obtaining a complete view of family life. In the study summarized in Table 13.1, data are being obtained from the chronically ill child, the parents, and the sibling closest in age to the chronically ill child. The investigators have adopted a noncategorical approach to identifying chronic illnesses that qualify for inclusion in the study (Stein & Jessop, 1982). This approach deemphasizes viewing diseases as discrete diagnostic categories in favor of focusing on their social-psychological dimensions. Following a noncategorical approach, it was decided not to limit sample selection to certain disease entities; rather, in keeping with the purpose of the study, any disease situation that entailed a need for ongoing family management qualified for inclusion.

In an effort to expand further the types of situations studied, the decision was made to recruit families in which a child had been recently diagnosed, as well as families where the child's diagnosis was longstanding.

The study also entailed two major data collection sessions, which were 12 months apart. In between the major data collection sessions, families were called at three-month intervals. The purpose of these calls was both to maintain rapport and to gather information on changes in the family's situation. In this study, a triangulated approach to data sources made it possible to obtain longitudinal data reflecting the perspectives of both individual family members and family units confronting a variety of chronic illness situations over time.

Methods

Triangulation of methods involves using a variety of data collection techniques (e.g., structured instruments, observations, and intensive interviews), which have been selected because each taps a different aspect or dimension of the problem being studied. Jick (1983) provides an excellent example of mixing qualitative and quantitative methods in a study of employees' responses to an organizational merger. He describes a research "package" which included a questionnaire survey of a random sample of employees, intensive interviews with selected employees, archival data on turnover and absenteeism, and content analysis of rumors. Jick aptly describes the integration of such a diverse data set in the following way: "Overall, the triangulating investigator is left to search for a logical pattern in mixed-method results. . . . One begins to view the researcher as builder and creator, piecing together many pieces of a complex puzzle into a coherent whole" (p. 144).

Methodologically, the study of family response to chronic illness employed a combination of qualitative and quantitative data collection techniques. The primary qualitative technique was intensive interviewing, using a semistructured interview guide. In addition, structured tools were used to measure family functioning (Feetham, 1988), children's self-perception (Harter, 1985), parental mood (Mc-Nair, Lorr, & Droppleman, 1981), children's behavior (Achenbach & Edelbrock, 1983), and child attitude toward illness (Austin & Huberty, 1987). The qualitative interviews provide the basis for conceptualizing family management style and identifying and delimiting management styles used by the families in the study. The quantitative measures make possible an initial exploration of the relationships between family management style and individual and family unit functioning. In addition, the multiple data collection techniques contribute to the completeness function of triangulation by providing explanatory insights about data from varying sources. For example, interview data lead to a more contextual understanding of scores on structured measures of individual and family unit functioning (Breitmayer, Ayres, & Knafl, in review). Ultimately, a complete understanding of family response to chronic illness requires both knowledge about how families define and manage such situations and knowledge of the consequences of various management styles.

Unit of Analysis

Triangulation of unit of analysis relates to the person dimension of triangulation of data sources. If, for example, the investigator is obtaining data on individual behaviors and perceptions as well as interactions between individuals, it is likely that the analysis will take into account both the individual and interactional components of the data. Such a merging of levels of analysis contributes to a more complete understanding of the phenomenon being studied. The usefulness of incorporating more than one level of analysis is especially apparent in studies of families, organized groups, and communities.

Data analysis in the study of family response to chronic illness occurs at both the individual and family unit level. The completeness of any conceptualization of family response to a child's chronic illness is enhanced to the extent that it can address both levels of response. By incorporating two levels of analysis, the study takes into account both individual definitions of the situation and management behaviors as well as the way and extent to which individual family members' responses come together to form a coherent family management style. In their recent work on measurement issues in family research, Ranson, Fisher, Phillips, Kokes, and Weiss (1990) point to the importance of taking both family unit and individual variables into account. They conclude that "until we are able to describe the relationship of family patterns and individual response with more precision, that portion of the field of family research interested in health is not likely to move forward" (p. 63).

For example, preliminary analysis of data from mothers, fathers, and the chronically ill child indicate that family members hold shared definitions of the seriousness of the child's illness. On the other hand, individual family members sometimes have discrepant views of the extent to which the child's activities should be limited as a result of the illness. When focusing on the individual as the unit of analysis, the investigators direct their efforts to identifying themes that characterize a particular subject's interview (e.g., financial concerns, conflicts with external systems, and efforts to create a normal life for the child). When the focus of the analysis shifts to the family unit, efforts are directed to comparing the configuration of themes across family members and the extent to which these themes are shared, conflictual, or complementary. Eventually, based on the analysis of data from individual family members, we will be able to conceptualize how children with chronic illnesses, their parents, and siblings respond to chronic illness. In addition, we will be able to conceptualize how the family as a unit responds to this same situation.

Theory

Theoretical triangulation can occur in either theory testing or theory generating studies. Denzin (pp. 304-305), citing Westie (1957), describes how propositions related to a given area, but derived from competing theories, can be tested simultaneously in a given study. Explaining the advantages of such an approach, he says that "the procedure demands that all relevant propositions be considered and made explicit before the investigation begins, a structure that would lead researchers away from particularistic explanations of their data" (p. 306). In theory generating studies, theoretical triangulation typically occurs at the conclusion rather than the outset of the study. For example, Hutchinson (1986) concludes her presentation of a substantive grounded theory of the process by which nurses become chemically dependent, with a discussion of the relationship of her conceptualization to other theories of addiction.

Like Hutchinson's study, the study of family response to chronic illness is primarily theory generating in purpose. At the same time, however, the investigators are using existing theories of family and child development to interpret both the qualitative and quantitative results. The theoretically diverse backgrounds of the investigators contribute to efforts to both generate and apply theory.

Conclusion

Because the term triangulation has been applied to two distinct, although very legitimate and often complementary purposes, there continues to be confusion in how the term is used and how authors frame and justify their approach to triangulation. There is still a tendency to treat triangulation as an "inherent good." This tendency is most apparent in studies that include a limited qualitative or quantitative component, the purpose of which is never clearly delineated. Reports of such studies may indicate that the study was strengthened because a triangulated approach was used, but fail to provide evidence as to how the so-called triangulated approach contributed to either confirmation of certain aspects of the data, to the completeness with which the domain of interest was addressed, or to both purposes.

A second source of confusion in the presentation of a triangulated study entails the inappropriate framing of one's approach to triangulation. If one has adopted a triangulated approach to establish confirmation or the convergent validity of one's data set, it is inappropriate to justify the approach with literature that links triangulation to completeness. On the other hand, if one's purpose in triangulating is to achieve completeness, then it makes little sense to cite authors, such as Campbell, who equate the term triangulation with multiple operationism. The inappropriate framing of one's approach to triangulation makes it virtually impossible for the reader to discern the purpose in triangulating and to evaluate the adequacy of the approach.

It is important to reiterate that triangulation is not an end in itself. Rather, it is a research approach that can serve at least two rather distinct ends. In the measurement of discrete variables, triangulation contributes to the investigator's efforts to achieve confirmation or convergent validity. In studies that address more encompassing domains of interest, multiple triangulation contributes to the investigator's ability to achieve a complete understanding of that domain. Because multiple triangulation can enhance the completeness with which one addresses an area of research, it is a useful approach for qualitative researchers who typically are seeking a complete, contextually embedded understanding of an area of interest. At the same time, the confirmatory function of triangulation also can have relevance for qualitative studies. Investigators engaged in qualitative research will have increased confidence in the credibility of their results when multiple data collection methods yield consistent findings. The investigator maximizes the effectiveness of taking a triangulated approach by delineating both the purpose or goal in adopting a triangulated approach and the specific strategies of triangulation followed. Such an explicit delineation makes it possible to evaluate the extent to which a specific design achieves convergence across multiple data sources, a complete portrayal of a given domain of interest, or both. Explicitness as to one's purpose in triangulating may also provide insights into ways to more fully and efficiently achieve the methodological goals one has in mind.

References

Achenbach, T., & Edelbrock, C. (1983). *Manual for the child behavior checklist and revised child behavior profile.* Burlington, VT: Department of Psychiatry, University of Vermont.
Austin, J., & Huberty, T. (1987). *Child attitude toward impact of illness scale* (CATIS). (Available from Joan Austin, Indiana University, Indianapolis, IN).
Bouchard, T. (1976). Unobtrusive measures: An inventory of uses. *Sociological Research and Methods, 4,* 267-300.
Breitmayer, B., Ayres, L., & Knafl, K. (In review). *Triangulation in qualitative research: Evaluation of confirmation and completeness purposes.*
Campbell, D. T. (1956). *Leadership and its effects upon the group.* Columbus: The Ohio State University.
Campbell, D., & Fiske, D. (1959). Convergent and discriminent validation by the multitrait-multimethod matrix. *Psychological Bulletin, 56,* 81-104.
Carr, J., & Powers, M. (1986). Stressors associated with coronary bypass surgery. *Nursing Research, 35,* 243-246.
Denzin, N. (1970). *The research act: A theoretical introduction to sociological methods.* Chicago: Aldine.
Dzurec, L., & Abraham, I. (1986). Analogy between phenomenology and multivariate statistical analysis. In P. L. Chinn (Ed.). *Nursing research methodology: Issues and interpretation* (pp. 55-66). Rockville, MD: Aspen.
Feetham, S. (1988). *Feetham Family Functioning Scale* (FFFS). (Available from Suzanne Feetham, National Center for Nursing Research, Washington, DC).
Fielding, N., & Fielding, J. (1986). *Linking data.* Beverly Hills, CA: Sage.
Forman, M. (1987). Reliability and validity of mental status questionnaires in elderly hospitalized patients. *Nursing Research, 36,* 216-220.
Garner, W. R. (1954). Context effects and the validity of loudness scales. *Journal of Experimental Psychology, 48,* 218-224.

Garner, W. R., Hake, H. W., & Eriksen, C. W. (1956). Operationism and the concept of perception. *Psychological Review, 63,* 149-159.

Goodwin, L., & Goodwin, W. (1984). Qualitative vs. quantitative research or qualitative and quantitative research. *Nursing Research, 33,* 378-380.

Harter, S. (1985). *Manual for the self-perception profile for children.* Denver, CO: University of Denver.

Hinds, P., & Young, K. (1987). A triangulation of methods and paradigms to study nurse-given wellness care. *Nursing Research, 36,* 195-198.

Hutchinson, J. (1986). Chemically dependent nurses: The trajectory toward self-annihilation. *Nursing Research, 35,* 196-201.

Jick, T. (1983). Mixing qualitative and quantitative methods: Triangulation in action. In J. Van Manen (Ed.). *Qualitative methodology* (pp. 135-148). Beverly Hills, CA: Sage.

Kearney, B., & Fleischer, B. (1979). Development of an instrument to measure exercise of self-care agency. *Research in Nursing and Health, 2,* 25-34.

Knafl, K., Breitmayer, B., Gallo, A., & Zoeller, L. (1987). *How families define and manage a child's chronic illness.* Funded by The National Center for Nursing Research, Public Health Service (Grant #NRO 11594).

Laffrey, S. (1986). Development of a health conception scale. *Research in Nursing and Health, 9,* 107-114.

Leininger, M. M. (1985). Nature, rationale, and importance of qualitative research methods in nursing. In M. M. Leininger (Ed.). *Qualitative research methods in nursing* (pp. 1-25). Orlando, FL: Grune & Stratton.

McNair, D., Lorr, M., & Droppleman, L. (1981). *Profile of mood states.* San Diego, CA: Educational and Industrial Testing Service.

Mitchell, E. S. (1986). Multiple triangulation: A methodology for nursing science. *Advances in Nursing Science, 8*(3), 18-26.

Myers, S., & Haase, J. (1989). Guidelines for integration of quantitative and qualitative approaches. *Nursing Research, 38,* 299-301.

Ransom, D., Fisher, L., Phillips, S., Kokes, R., & Weiss, R. (1990). The logic measurement in family research. In T. Draper & A. Marcos (Eds.). *Family variables: Conceptualization, measurement, and use* (pp. 48-63). Newbury Park, CA: Sage.

Stein, R., & Jessop, D. (1982). A noncategorical approach to chronic childhood illness. *Public Health Reports, 97,* 354-362.

Strauss, A., Fagerhaugh, J., Suczek, B., & Weiner, C. (1985). *The social organization of medical work.* Chicago: University of Chicago Press.

Tripp-Reimer, T. (1985). Combining qualitative and quantitative methodologies. In M. M. Leininger (Ed.). *Qualitative research methods in nursing* (pp. 179-194). Orlando, FL: Grune and Stratton, Inc.

Webb, E. J., Campbell, D. T., Schwartz, R. D., Sechrest, L., & Grove, J. B. (1981). *Nonreactive measures in the social sciences* (2nd ed.). Boston: Houghton Mifflin.

Westie, F. (1957). Toward a closer relationship between theory and research: A procedure and an example. *American Sociological Review, 22,* 149-154.

Dialogue

The Granting Game

TRIPP-REIMER: It's important that your grant application has "nursing" in the title so that it can be appropriately directed within NIH [National Institutes of Health].

LIPSON: So it doesn't go to epidemiology. . . .

HUTCHINSON: Rhymes with ethnology, right?

And . . .

BRINK: Every time I write a grant proposal, they don't write and ask me about "auditability"—they ask me about reliability and validity, and why haven't I attended specifically to these, these, and these. . . . And if I can't use their words, I'm not going to get my grant funded. They don't want terms that they can't understand.

But Later . . .

BERGUM: I worry about funding agencies. I think rather than fitting our research into meeting their expectations, [we should] really say this is not valid in this research, or this is not an issue, and change the expectations.

ANDERSON: Yes, you are right! I am very reluctant to use the language of quantitative research in presenting my proposal because I feel we have to change the system, not feed into it. We need more qualitative reviewers on these committees!

BARBEE: The problem with those articles without criteria for reliability and validity of qualitative research is that they are written as though there was one type of qualitative research, and people use them as bibles. Then your article is reviewed using those criteria, whether they be appropriate or not, and if you don't do it exactly this way, it's not done right.

BRINK: The problem is that there are few qualitative researchers on these review boards to provide the explanations. That means our proposals have to be longer and include descriptions of method.

MORSE: But I have a moral problem with that, Pam. There is no way I would sit on a grant review board and review a proposal if I didn't understand it! How can they possibly pass judgement on a proposal and not be familiar with the method.

BRINK: They send them out for review to our peers, and frequently, they send them out to some of our better gatekeepers.

MAY: I can think of a related problem, though, that reflects dominant science. Its very easy for them to think, "Ah, ah! This person doesn't speak statistics" when I turn back an article unreviewed and say, "I don't understand this analytic plan." The fact that I don't understand it means that I don't know causal modeling and therefore can't evaluate it. I don't feel defensive about that. But there is a general assumption that everybody should be able to critique a quasi-experimental design—I mean, that's the dominant science—and they don't look it over and turn it upside-down to notice they don't know human beans about qualitative work and shouldn't be passing judgment on it.

STERN: I don't think there is a person in this room, who would disagree with what you are saying. But Pam has a really important point. The reviewers do try, and the only thing we can do is to make it easier for them. Jan, you're right, they shouldn't be passing judgment on it, but they do! And that's the reality of this social world!

BRINK: Another problem is that the differences between qualitative methods aren't recognized. And they say, "Well, we had a qualitative person on the committee." But what they have done is sent the phenomenological study to the grounded theorist, and the ethnography to the phenomenologist! It's just as bad as having a survey person look at an experimental design with all the intricacies of the design.

MAY: My colleague doesn't have to explicate causal modeling step-by-step. She explains it in a paragraph, gives reference, end of story—and they believe it! And if I submit an article to a research journal, write two nice paragraphs and cite Chenitz and Swanson, I get it back! What's good for the goose is not good for the gander, and so part of me says I don't want to play this game anymore if I have to spend two or three pages in a proposal on method or it doesn't get by.

MUNHALL: There is another problem, too. Have you read the article about why Socrates would never get a grant? It's because he would refuse to investigate anything he knew something about. And in a sense, that is the dilemma that we are in—we write that we don't know anything about the topic, so we are not considered qualified to conduct the study! Also, some say you cannot get a grant unless you know the outcome to your study. So essentially, that's what these institutional review boards want. They want hard evidence before you go in!

BRINK: I think the problem is that review boards consider qualitative research to be the pilot project. They ask you, "Where is the prior research on this?" There is none; so in their view, we are asking for money to do the pilot study. We don't want to go beyond the qualitative; yet they want us to enumerate and test. There is a major problem as a result because we want the money to do what they call the pilot—where do we get the money to do that?

MUNHALL: We're not coming in with a problem; they want the problem already identified. If they want the problem identified, they should pay for that! Heaven knows, that's the most important step! We've been coming up with solutions to the wrong problem for enough years! They've got to see the value of stepping back.

And later . . .

BARBEE: They [the granting agencies] advise you to do a pilot—which creates some problems for us. The pilot has to be smaller than the larger study, which means you either have to enlarge your study or do a teeny, teeny little pilot.

BRINK: A real teeny pilot—like one person! Because if we do any more, we finish the study!

AAMODT: A better idea may be to surround the idea—go to a different setting and see if it holds.

14

Funding Strategies for Qualitative Research

TONI TRIPP-REIMER
MARLENE ZICHI COHEN

In seeking research funding, qualitative researchers have not yet capitalized on that which we do best: understanding the norms, customs, and patterns of conduct considered appropriate by members of a target community. In this case, the populations of interest are funding agencies. This oversight is compounded by our good fortune that actual standards of review have been codified and are publicly available. Of course, as with all groups, there are also informal rules of behavior which merit at least as much attention as the formal rules.

In requesting grant funds, one needs to consider both the agency most appropriate for the project and the developmental stage of the investigator's research career. Figure 14.1 illustrates a potential configuration of an investigator's research trajectory. While this figure illustrates a range of funding sources, this chapter will focus primarily on those that have most salience for investigators at an early stage of their research career.

Funding Agencies

Funding agencies most amenable to junior investigators include the Sigma Theta Tau, the American Nurses' Foundation (ANF), the National Science Foundation (NSF), and the National Institutes of

AUTHORS' NOTE: The authors wish to acknowledge that illustrations in this chapter were drawn from grant #1 RO1 NR 01 813-01, funded by the National Center for Nursing Research to Principal Investigator Marlene Zichi Cohen.

Stages of Development

Ph. D Student	Postdoctoral	Career	Mid-Career Change
Predoctoral Training Support (F31)	Postdoctoral Training Support (F31)	American Nurses' Foundation Award Sigma Theta Tau Award National Science Foundation Grant Academic Research Enhancement Award (R15 Area Grant FIRST Award (R29) Research Project Grant (R01) Academic/Clinical Investigator Award (K07, K08)	NRSA Senior Fellowship (F32) RWJ Health Policy Fellowship Fulbright Scholar Program Kellogg Clinical Scholar Award RWJ Clinical Scholar Award

Figure 14.1 A Research Trajectory: Research Training & Development Support Sources

Health (NIH). While programs in each of these agencies will be outlined, major attention will be given to NIH because it remains the primary source of funding for nursing research.

Both Sigma Theta Tau and the American Nurses' Foundation offer small grants programs that have deadlines once each year. Applications to Sigma Theta Tau are due March 1, and those to ANF June 1. Budget for Sigma Theta Tau must be within $3,000; for ANF, the maximum award is $2,700. Additionally, these two agencies offer a joint Clinical Research Grant annually; this grant awards up to $6,500 and has an application deadline of June 1. Application forms and comprehensive guidelines for application may be obtained from the executive offices of each agency.[1,2]

The National Science Foundation (NSF) offers awards in the Division of Behavioral and Neural Sciences for both predoctoral and senior investigators. The maximum funding period is five years, although awards are generally for considerably less time. While there is no upper or lower limit specified, awards tend to average around $25,000/year. NSF submission dates for the Anthropology Program are the first of January and July. Other programs may have different deadlines. Proposals are sent out to external ad hoc reviewers (whose names the investigator may suggest), and the reviewers (generally 6-10) submit their reports to a National Panel, which makes recommendations based on the scientific merit of the project.[3]

Within the Public Health Service of the federal Health and Human Services agency, there are several broad agencies that fund qualitative nursing research. These broader agencies include the Alcohol, Drug Abuse and Mental Health Administration, which has the following component units: National Institute on Alcohol Abuse, National Institute of Drug Abuse, and the National Institute of Mental Health. However, clearly the most prominent funding agency for qualitative nursing research is the National Institutes of Health (NIH). Within NIH, there are 12 freestanding institutes, as well as the National Center for Nursing Research (NCNR). Institutes other than the NCNR that have funded qualitative nursing research include the National Institute on Aging, the National Cancer Institute, and the National Institute of Child Health and Human Development. Most (but not all) of these federal Public Health Service (PHS) agencies offer the same range of grant programs.

There are several mechanisms of support used by the PHS agencies. This chapter will describe those that are specifically offered through the National Center on Nursing Research. Fundable research proposals submitted to the NCNR will fall within one of three programs in the Division of Extramural Programs:

- Health Promotion/Disease Prevention,
- Acute and Chronic Illness, or
- Nursing Systems.

Investigators are encouraged to contact the staff of the specific program for advice prior to submission of a grant proposal. The following are the major program areas (NCNR, 1988):

1. *Predoctoral Fellowships (F31).* These National Service Awards (NRSA) support supervised doctoral research training in degree programs related to the mission of the NCNR. Applicants must have either a baccalaureate or master's degree in nursing.
2. *NRSA Postdoctoral Fellowships (F32).* These awards support postdoctoral research training for doctorally prepared individuals, including non-nurses, generally at an early stage of their research career.

3. *Academic Research Enhancement Award (AREA) (R15).* These grants are awarded to individuals at academic units not receiving Biomedical Research Seed Grant (BRSG) support. Favored here are small-scale projects, especially feasibility studies and other research projects of limited scope. Awards may be up to $75,000 for up to three years. The AREA program is two years old and has an annual deadline in June.

4. *First Independent Research Support and Transition Award (FIRST) (R29).* These grants support the first independent NIH-sponsored investigation and were established to aid transition to other NIH grants. These grants have a maximum budget of $350,000 over five years.

5. *Research Project Grants (RO1).* These traditional grants support discrete projects related to the investigator's interests and competence. Initial support may be up to five years.

6. *Academic or Clinical Investigator Awards (K07, K08).* These are awards either to junior faculty members or promising clinically trained nurses. Faculty applying for K07 are generally four to six years post-doctorate and have demonstrated research potential. These awards fund release time to allow establishment of research programs. Salary up to $40,000 per year and $20,000 in direct costs are awarded. Provisions for the K08 are essentially the same.

7. *NRSA Senior Fellowships (F33).* These awards fund doctorally prepared nurses and non-nurses who generally have at least seven subsequent years of relevant research or professional experience. This award allows the experienced scientists to make major changes in the direction of their career, to broaden their background, to acquire new research capabilities, and to enlarge their command of an allied research field.

Submitting a Competitive Proposal

In competing for funds, there is a need to convince the review panel that the proposal has more merit and should be selected over others that are submitted. This is what competitive funding is all about, and this is why these proposals differ from those for theses, dissertations, and projects of personal interest, which can simply consist of an interesting, do-able project.

The first step is to select the right funding agency for the project. As illustrated in the seven mechanisms of support through the NCNR described above, it is also important to select the appropriate program within an agency. While the same proposal may be submitted to multiple agencies, each will likely have a different format and may require tailoring for appropriate emphasis. Agency deadlines, topical restrictions, and investigator qualifications are important considerations. Special attention should be given to specific agency directions for preparation of proposals. For example, traditional NIH Research Project Grants (RO1) must be submitted on the 10/88 version of the Grant Application Form 398. These forms are available from the sponsored program office at most universities or from NIH. In addition there is a 20-page limitation for the portion of the application entitled "Research Plan," which includes specific aims, background/ significance, preliminary studies, and design and methods. If this page limitation is exceeded, the application will be returned without review.

Prior to submitting a proposal, local peer review is important to provide feedback on both content and logical composition. When a draft of the proposal is completed, it is advisable to ask knowledgeable people for a critique. Two types of reviewers are recommended: one who is familiar with the content area and a second who is unfamiliar with the content. The first can provide an evaluation based on scientific merit; the second can give feedback on style, clarity, and logical flow. Most review panels consist of persons who are experts in your area and others who know very little about your topic, but who will judge the proposal on the basis of logical arguments and precision of planning.

Reviewers for agencies follow specified formats. The critique format used for traditional research grants by all units of NIH will be discussed and illustrated with a proposal by Cohen, which was initially approved but not funded and subsequently resubmitted and funded. The NIH critique format examines five major areas: scientific merit, protection of human subjects, investigators and other personnel, resources and environment, and budget.

Scientific Merit

A proposal is first evaluated to determine the significance and originality of the proposed study in its scientific field, the validity of the hypotheses or research questions, the logic of the aims, and the feasibility and adequacy of the procedures for the proposed research. The likelihood of producing new data and concepts and whether alternate routes to the solution of the problem have been provided is assessed. The reviewers' critique of Cohen's proposal illustrates these evaluations. The reviewers stated:

> This proposal continues to have the potential to make a significant contribution to nursing science both substantively and methodologically. The lack of congruity between the patient's needs and the nurse's perceptions of the patient's needs is still a major deterrent to clinical effectiveness. Although this issue has been addressed by many nursing theorists, the principal investigator's approach to the problem is original and likely to yield new information on an old question.

NIH reviewers evaluate seven specific areas regarding scientific merit: aims, significance, variables, method, correspondence of method with aims, sampling, data collection methods, psychometric properties of any instruments, and plans for data analysis. Cohen's proposal illustrates the criteria for these areas and the ways these topics can be managed.

The first area concerns whether the aims are logical and appropriately conceptualized. Cohen's proposal dealt with issues pertinent only to phenomenological research. The specific aims section stated:

> The general aim of this research is to investigate and compare the concerns of postoperative patients and the nurses who cared for them. This investigation will extend a previous project which identified patient's perceived needs after surgery. The specific aims of this project are:

> 1. Obtain descriptions of patients' experiences of their hospitalization for surgery and the nursing care they received.
> 2. Obtain descriptions of nurses' perceptions of these same patients' experiences of their hospitalization for surgery and the nursing care they received.
> 3. Analyze and present these descriptions using phenomenological methods (Barritt, Beckman, Blecker, & Mulderij, 1983) and the constant comparative method (Glaser & Strauss, 1967).
> 4. Identify patients' perceived priority needs and concerns after surgery and how nurses were helpful or not helpful to them.
> 5. Identify nurses' priority concerns for these postoperative patients.
> 6. Compare patients' and nurses' priorities.

The critique says, "Aims are clearly described."

The objectives, or aims, are the essence of the proposal. They convey what is intended to be accomplished. The objectives describe what will be done, to whom, why, and where. An objective is an action to be attained. Each objective should be stated in a simple sentence and should be a statement of what will be accomplished. If a series of objectives is proposed, arrange them in logical order, either with the most important first or as they will sequentially be accomplished.

Orlich and Orlich (1977, p. 34) identified several common mistakes regarding objectives. The writer might state a problem or procedure rather than the objective. For example, conducting an interview is a procedure rather than an objective. Another problem may be that the objectives might never be stated explicitly. It is helpful to specifically state. "The objectives of this project are. . . ." Finally, too many objectives might be specified. The more objectives you have, the more likely that the reviewers will take issue with them.

The second area, evaluating the significance of the project in relation to the needs for research in this area, was addressed in the opening remarks of Cohen's critique. The problem statement explains why the proposed project should be funded, and it must convince the reviewers of the worthiness of the project.

A review of the literature is necessary when addressing this second area. It should include a review of relevant research and a critical analysis concerning why a qualitative approach is justified. Rationale for using qualitative methods may be that this is a new area of research and first needs exploration to generate hypotheses, or that this is an already well investigated area that can be fruitfully approached from a different perspective. Major studies should be cited and critically analyzed, noting how the proposed study builds, expands, or highlights areas that have previously been neglected or approached inadequately. This review will demonstrate evidence to support the worthiness of research questions or the need to investigate a previously unstudied area. The review should be contemporary, only citing dated resources when they have historical significance.

If you are investigating an area that has not been previously reported in the literature, you may build a case around the logic of "related studies." In this way, you can highlight the importance of the intended project and illustrate how it is different from the already existing body of knowledge.

The third area concerns whether variables are adequately defined. Although defining "variables" is clearly not appropriate to phenomenological research, extensive prior work was described in Cohen's proposal, which included an analysis of interviews with surgical patients who described their experiences of hospitalization, and an extensive review of what patients and professionals have said in the literature about these experiences.

The fourth area concerns an evaluation of whether the suggested methods are appropriate, adequate, and feasible. Cohen's proposal described methods in detail. Research for the proposal involved interviewing patients from four different hospitals. The rationale for maximizing the diversity of experiences to find common themes that emerge, despite differences in demographic details and surgical procedure, was explained. However, the proposal included the assurance that these details would be recorded to determine if they do indeed affect the experience. Details of the interview were described. Prior to submitting this proposal, the principal investigator and four research associates conducted pilot interviews. These research associates are staff nurses at the four hospitals who agreed to participate in the project. As they did in the pilot project, the research associates are conducting interviews with nurses and patients at hospitals other than the one in which they are employed, and as the main project progresses, they will jointly conduct analysis and co-author manuscripts.

Information from these pilot interviews was included in the proposal. Examples of probe questions were included since the phenomenological approach necessitates very broad initial questions. Conducting the pilot study and including these examples had several other benefits. Training of the interviewers and discussion of critical interviewing techniques could be illustrated. The pilot study also allowed two nurses to discover that this project would not be feasible for them, given their other responsibilities, and other nurses were identified to work on the project. Also, the pilot study demonstrated that the plan actually works in operation.

A time line was used in the proposal to illustrate the activities of the project. This time line continues to be useful to the project staff for making sure deadlines are met and to ensure that the research is completed in a timely fashion.

The fifth area questions whether sampling procedures are appropriate and feasible and whether the sample size is adequate. Cohen included evidence to justify the "sample" size. She cited other phenomenological studies and increased the number of informants to a number larger than had been used in these prior studies to assure the reviewers that there would be sufficient information to provide clear descriptions of the experiences.

The sixth area questions whether the investigator adequately addressed the psychometric properties of any instruments to be used in the project. While reliability and validity of instruments to be used are not germane to most qualitative projects, issues of accuracy are. The proposal stated that the principal investigator would listen to all tape-recorded interviews and discuss them with the interviewer prior to the next interview. Because examples from the pilot study showed interviewer bias, the principal investigator helped the interviewers identify their assumptions and leading statements. The reviewers noted that it was not initially specified that follow-up interviews would be tape-recorded. This tape-recording is, of course, essential for maximally accurate content analysis.

The question was also raised about the degree to which the research creates knowledge among informants. It was acknowledged that discussing an experience and "seeing" the words in print does indeed change the experience. However it was noted that follow-up interviews would be used primarily to clarify and elaborate on what was initially said. Furthermore nurses would be interviewed about only one patient.

Patients and nurses would be interviewed only after the patients were discharged from the hospital. This was important to reduce patients' fears about their interview affecting the care they received. This raised the question about retrospective bias. It was noted in the proposal that the importance of reducing patients' fears about their care and of ensuring that the interviews did not tax a person who was too sick to be interviewed outweighed what might be gained by interviewing patients in the hospital. It was also stated that the time between the interview and the patients' discharge would be as short as possible, which led the reviewers to comment that the interview is "not terribly retrospective."

A final area of concern addresses whether plans for data analysis are appropriate to the aims and methods. To aid in the evaluation of this issue in Cohen's proposal, an example of transcript data from the prior research was included to illustrate how analysis would be conducted.

In summary, investigators using qualitative methods should not attempt to ignore issues that will be raised by reviewers more familiar with proposals using quantitative methods. The issues should be addressed "head-on," without defensiveness. It is far more beneficial for qualitative researchers to personally identify the issues and state how these areas will be addressed in ways congruent with assumptions underlying qualitative research. Alternatively, qualitative researchers can acknowledge when an issue is a serious limitation to the study, while stressing that the overall importance of the project justifies funding.

The Protection of Human Subjects

Institutional review of the proposal was conducted by several of the hospitals involved in this project, and their approval was included in Cohen's proposal.

Investigators

Reviewers will judge the background of the investigator. Prior funded projects that resulted in research-based publications are the clearest measure of an investigator's qualifications. However, lacking prior funding, pilot data for the project under consideration is highly seductive. If a pilot project is not feasible, another option is to demonstrate how this study builds on your prior (perhaps dissertation) work. Similarly, it is prudent to show that initially proposed projects are part of a program of research efforts. Short-term or "one-shot" studies or projects are often not rated as highly as studies with longer duration, as these longer projects tend to establish the research career pattern of the investigator.

The review of Cohen's proposal included a statement about the principle investigator's doctoral education and publications in peer reviewed journals. The pilot interviews of patients and nurses were cited as "clearly demonstrating competence in the use of unstructured interview techniques." Finally, the reviewers noted that having a recognized, experienced qualitative researcher as consultant to the project was a strength.

Resources and Environment

Resources at The University of Iowa, Cohen's employer, were described in detail. Cooperation was elicited from each of the hospitals, and letters of cooperation were included. If these were not included, the review panel might have rightly questioned whether the investigator would be able to carry out the project.

Budget

The work schedule should be clearly specified, and it should be clear what personnel will be responsible for what areas. The budget should not be too high, asking the agency to carry normal institutional costs. The work schedule needs to be realistic in terms of time and money. Generally a carefully thought out project translates into specific amounts. A clearly described project and precise time schedule will be easily translated into budgetary terms. A vague proposal will generally require much guesswork to make the budget. If this happens the proposal may need to be reworked.

Additional Writing Suggestions

Since your proposal is strictly a one-way mode of communication, writing must be clear and explicit. All terms that are not common must be defined. Cohen was advised to avoid some existential terminology, which might be unfamiliar to the reviewers. The proposal, and especially the abstract, should be written so that it is intelligible to someone who is generally informed but not an expert in the area of the proposal. Honesty and clarity of purpose are the best avenues to successful writing.

Proposals fail for a variety of reasons. The problem must not be of limited significance. Project completion must be likely to yield results that provide new or useful information that is not of only local significance. Areas most prone to criticism in qualitative proposals are that jargon is used without explanation or that a description of methods is not sufficiently detailed and clear. It is generally inappropriate (and unfundable) for an investigator to simply identify that she/he has an interesting research question, is requesting $250,000, and should simply be trusted. The more detail that the investigator can provide regarding actual and potential methods, the greater the likelihood of funding. A bibliography at the end of this chapter provides additional resources for the new researcher.

Summary

Reading descriptions of the review process can seem overwhelming. However, both authors have successfully competed for small and large grants. Perhaps more important, both authors have unsuccessfully competed for small and large grants. Addressing critique comments and resubmitting a rejected or unfunded proposal are often required. Persistence is frequently the difference between success and failure. It is important to remember that the process is not unlike the task of gaining acceptance of a target community, a task familiar to qualitative investigators.

Notes

1. Nell Watts, Executive Officer, Sigma Theta Tau, International Honor Society for Nursing, 550 West North Street, Indianapolis, IN 46202.
2. Director, Center for Research, American Nurses' Foundation, Inc., 2420 Pershing Road, Kansas City, MO 64108.
3. NSF, 1800 G Street, NW, Washington, DC 20550.

Bibliography of Grant Writing

Allen, E. M. (1960). Why are research grant applications disapproved? *Science, 132,* 1532-1534.
Behling, J. (1980). *Guidelines for preparing the research proposal. Washington: The University Press of America.*
Berthold, J. S. (1973). Nursing research grant proposals: What influenced their approval or disapproval in two national granting agencies. *Nursing Research, 22,* 292-299.
Bloch, D., Gortner, S. R., & Sturdivant, L. W. (1978). The nursing research grants program of the Division of Nursing, United States Public Health Service. *Journal of Nursing Administration, 8,* 40-45.
Campos, R.G. (1976). Securing information on funding sources for nursing research. *Journal of Nursing Administration, 6,* 16-18, 54.
Catalogue of federal domestic assistance. Washington, DC: Government Printing Office.

Clinton, J. (1985). Couvade: Patterns, predictors, and nursing management: A research proposal submitted to the Division of Nursing. *Western Journal of Nursing Research, 7,* 220-243.

Cuca, J. M. (1983). NIH grant applications for clinical research: Reasons for poor ratings or disapproval. *Clinical Research, 31,* 453-461.

DeBakey, L. (1976). The persuasive proposal. *Journal of Technical Writing and Communication, 6,* 5-25.

DeBakey, L., & DeBakey, S. (1978), The art of persuasion: Logic and language in proposal writing. *Grants Magazine, 1,* 43-60.

Eaves, G. N. (1978). A successful grant application to the National Institutes of Health: Case history. *Grants Magazine, 1,* 263-268.

Eaves, G. N. (1972). Who reads your project-grant application in the National Institutes of Health? *Federation Proceedings, 31,* 2-9.

Eaves, G. N. (1984). Preparation of the research-grant application: Opportunities and pitfalls. *Grants Magazine, 7,* 151-157.

Fuller, E. O. (1982). The pink sheet syndrome. *Nursing Research, 31,* 185-186.

Gortner, S. R. (1971). Research grant applications: What they are not and should be. *Nursing Research, 20,* 292-295.

Gortner, S. R. Researchmanship (Columns). *Western Journal of Nursing Research.* (Note especially Vol. 2, No. 1 and 2; Vol. 3, No. 3; Vol. 4, No. 3).

Henley, C. (1977). Peer review of research grant applications at the National Institutes of Health. *Federation Proceedings, 36,* 2066-2068, 2186-2190, 2335-2338.

Kaiser, L. R. (1973). Grantsmanship in continuing education. *Journal of Nursing Education, 12,* 12-20.

Krathwohl, D. R. (1977). *How to prepare a research proposal* (2nd ed.). Syracuse, NY: Syracuse University Bookstore, 303 University Place, 13210.

Lauffer, A. (1983). *Grantsmanship* (2nd ed.). Beverly Hills, CA: Sage.

Lauffer, A. (1984). *Grantsmanship and fund raising.* Beverly Hills. CA: Sage.

Lindholm, K. J., Martin, G., & Lopez, R. E. (1982). *Proposal writing strategies.* Los Angeles: The Regents of the University of California.

Merritt, D. H., & Eaves, G. N. (1975). Site visits for the review of grant applications to the National Institutes of Health: Views of an applicant and a scientist administrator. *Federation Proceedings, 34,* 131-136.

Novello, A. C. (1985). The peer review process: How to prepare research grant applications to the NIH. *Mineral Electrolyte Metabolism, 11,* 281-286.

Phillips, T. P. (1975). What is the difference between a research grant and a research contract . . . ? *Nursing Research, 24,* 388-389.

Pike, J. M., & Bernard, S. C. (1978). The research grant budget: Preparation and justification in relation to the proposed research. *Grants Magazine, 1,* 175-176.

Reif-Lehrer, L. (1982). *Writing a successful grant application.* Boston: Science Books International.

Sexton, D. (1982). Developing skills in grant writing. *Nursing Outlook, 30* (1), 31-38.

The project-grant application of the National Institutes of Health. (1973). *Federation Proceeding, 32,* 1541-1550, Contents Include:
Eaves, G. N. Introduction
Eaves, G. N. The grant application: An exercise in scientific writing.
Rifkin, D. B. A beginning scientist's first project-grant application.

    Gee, H. H. Preparation of the project-grant application: Assistance from the ad-
        ministrator in charge of a study section.
    Malone, T. E. Preparation of the project-grant application: Assistance from the
        institutes and other awarding units.
    Ross, R. Participation of the administration of the grantee institution in the prep-
        aration and transmission of a project-grant application.
    Schimke, R. T. Preparation of the project-grant application: Assistance from the
        grantee institution's experienced investigators.
Tripp-Reimer, T. (1986). Health heritage project: A research proposal submitted to the
    Division of Nursing. *Western Journal of Nursing Research, 8,* 207-228.
U.S. Department of Health and Human Services, Public Health Service, National
    Institutes of Health (1979). *NIH Public Advisory Groups: Authority, Structure,
    Functions, Members.* Available from Committee Management Office, National
    Institutes of Health, Building 1, Room 300, Bethesda, MD 20892.
White, V. (1975). *Grants: How to find out about them and what to do next.* New York:
    Plenum Press.

References

Barritt, C., Beckman, A. J., Blecker, H., & Mulderij, K. (1983). *A handbook for
    phenomenological research in education.* Ann Arbor: The School of Education,
    University of Michigan.
Glaser, B. G., & Strauss, A. L. (1967). *The discovery of grounded theory: Strategies for
    qualitative research.* Chicago: Aldine.
National Center for Nursing Research, (1988). *Nursing science: Serving health through
    research.* Bethesda, MD: National Institutes of Health.
Orlich, D., & Orlich, P. (1977). *The art of writing successful R & D proposals.* Pleasant-
    ville, NY: Redgrave.

Dialogue

On Muddling Methods

BOYLE: But we are all in agreement that one should not muddle
           methods as we are beginning to see in the literature today.
           We take a very strong stand on this.
MORSE: Muddling includes everything. It includes the assumptions,
           the language, the methods. Phenomenological language be-
           longs to phenomenology.
MAY: And then there is the generic use of phenomenology. This
           stance is that "I'm only interested in the 'lived experience' "
           and everything else is ignored. And they use "grounded
           theory" to mean everything that "emerges from the data,"
           which the muddled often use to mean "I'm not sure how that
           happened."
HUTCHINSON: And then phenomenology can be grounded theory, and
           grounded theory can be phenomenology, and then they say,
           "And you guess what it is!" Because of all this confusion,
           people who write about this must be clear and specify what
           they are doing in every stage of the research.

15

Institutional Review of Qualitative Research Proposals: A Task of No Small Consequence

PATRICIA L. MUNHALL

Placing the Task in Context

A colleague of mine sent her research proposal to a large university hospital where the sample for her study was to be derived. She followed the format precisely and was somewhat surprised when she was asked to appear before the Institutional Review Board (IRB) of the hospital. When she arrived she was astonished to find 26 members of the Board present. They discussed the project with her for two hours, and engaged in what appeared to be an internal struggle over the design and conceptual framework of the study, before granting her permission to conduct the study.

My colleague's study was a traditional quantitative research project. Ironically, the study was not to be conducted within the institution itself; rather, the nurse-researcher wanted to do a follow-up mailing to all patients who had hip-replacement surgery. My purpose in this chapter is to place the review of qualitative research proposals in a perspective where this context can be understood. According to Noble (1985), IRBs often pose problems for researchers, *regardless* of their research method: "A frequent solution . . . is to engage in minimally clinical projects, such as research involving healthy, intelligent, middle-class clients . . ." (p. 293).

Using this solution, many researchers have looked for subjects outside of institutions. That is one alternative, but since many nurse-researchers are committed to research within institutions, the aim of this chapter will be to facilitate the IRB process, specifically with qualitative research proposals.

The Setting

In this chapter, the presentation of qualitative research methods to IRBs in institutional settings will be addressed. Similarities of IRB requirements for qualitative and quantitative research designs will be discussed. Departures and additions specific to qualitative research methods will be analyzed, with emphasis on the educational aspect of research proposals. Also, the idea of process consent will be examined, and the appearance of qualitative researchers before IRBs with research proposals will be discussed.

Institutional Review Boards are the conscience of an institution. They are deeply concerned with human rights and human dignity. The principles of patient autonomy and rights of privacy, confidentiality, anonymity, self-determination, and safety are critical components of the philosophical statements of IRBs.

The most important aspect of any research proposal is the education of our colleagues about qualitative methods and the assurance that we share the same concerns for the dignity and rights of our human subjects. A psychological principle pervades this need for education as most people are generally invested in the status quo, that is, the familiar. Individuals on IRBs are, for the most part, accustomed to the traditional quantitative research design and thus feel a certain amount of confidence when reviewing these proposals. Qualitative research designs within the traditional medical science setting present problems for these individuals and raise questions simply because the reviewers are unfamiliar with the more unstructured qualitative research methods. This leaves the qualitative nurse-researcher with a task of no small consequence.

The Challenges

Qualitative research in institutional settings presents different challenges from those of more traditional research methods. The three main challenges in receiving permission to conduct qualitative research in institutions are:

1. the IRBs unfamiliarity with the methods, language, and legitimacy of qualitative research;
2. the structural-functionalist perspective that pervades most institutions; and
3. the conscious or unconscious perception of the similarity of qualitative research methods with investigative type journalism.

Although these challenges ar interrelated, each one will be addressed separately.

The Unfamiliarity with Qualitative Research Methods

Most IRBs (and in fact, most grant review panels) have members who are unfamiliar with the aims and outcomes of qualitative research. Presently many IRBs are developing guidelines and are uncertain about the role they play in the institution. Their task is complex—so complex that a request for the release of names to do a follow-up mailing to individuals who are no longer patients (as previously described) resulted in a major meeting of the IRB. The receipt of a proposal with a method called "phenomenology" may also result in an invitation to provide further information.

Phenomenological studies aim at understanding phenomenon by studying the essences of a life experience with thoughtful attention, and they search for what it means to be human in the attempt to discover plausible insight. Many members of IRBs are not familiar with such language in a research proposal. They will ask, "What is phenomenology?" or "What is grounded theory?" Though these questions do not spell disaster for proposed qualitative research projects, they do complicate matters because these important questions are asked from the structural-functional perspective of institutions.

The Structural-Functional Approach of Institutions

The structural-functional perspective is often viewed as the sacrosanct way of organizing a bureaucratic institution. Roles are prescribed, functions are distributed, behavior and outcomes are predictable, and all should go well according to fixed rules and procedures. The values in our health care institutions seem removed or, at best, unrelated to qualitative research aims. For the most part, within our health care institutions, pragmatic goals prevail. There should be an action, an intervention, and a concrete observable task with a measurable outcome. Pragmatism in research is narrowly perceived, for example, the idea of testing something to solve some problem. The idea that understanding preceding experience or any lived experience has pragmatic value is not self-evident from the highly structured functional perspective. From this perspective, the search for "meaning" appears irrelevant. It is this search for meaning that creates confusion in some minds about the difference between qualitative research and investigative journalism.

Similarity of Qualitative Methods with Investigative Journalism

All research methods are essentially investigations, but perhaps, they are more threatening to individuals when unstructured interviews and the possibly threatening participant observation technique are part of the research design. Quantitative research designs are by nature more specific, the variables are already known, and the researcher searches for relationships between variables. On the other hand, discovery, the finding out about something otherwise not fully understood, is often the aim of qualitative research designs.

Within institutions, such studies may be perceived as threatening. Interviewing patients may cause staff to worry about negative information the patient may give, for example, complaints, reporting incidents, and so forth. If there is to be observation, who does not experience some anxiety about the idea of being observed? Fear, then, is an important feeling to consider, and one that cannot be summarily dismissed, for what if you do "discover" some "negative" findings that do not reflect well on the institution or staff?

These challenges must be addressed in any proposal that goes before an Institutional Review Board. The strategies for meeting these challenges include education and translation, establishing compatible values, and generating trust.

Meeting the Challenges

Education and Translation

Becoming sympathetic to the concerns and psychological dynamics of the individuals on Institutional Review Boards is the best place to start. In many cases, qualitative research proposals may not be understood by these individuals, may be contrary to the way they think, and may be threatening to them. In addressing these challenges, one should realize that the normal human response to change is resistance. Many qualitative nurse-researchers in institutions have reported that "resistance" was the only response to their research proposal and that they have had to change their proposal or move out of the institution. Although this is unfortunate, this situation can be avoided if qualitative nurse-researchers will educate their colleagues who sit on IRBs about the nature and philosophy of qualitative methods.

Most board members are thoroughly familiar with the methods associated with the Western Mind Set of objectivity, control, prediction, and so forth. No one needs to explain "ex-post facto," correlation, experimental designs, or statistical test, but phenomenology, grounded theory, ethnography, or whatever qualitative research method is going to be used must be explained. Not only must it be explained, but it must be presented in language that can be understood by individuals familiar with deductive, pragmatic, numerical ideologies.

There is a need to explain in concrete terms the primacy of perception, embodiment, and the philosophical concepts. All these ideas should be clearly stated in language that the reader will understand. For example, in submitting a proposal for a qualitative research project, which will examine the needs of patients who have had a mastectomy so that appropriate nursing interventions can be developed, language such as "the lived experience" of having a mastectomy, consciousness, and essences may be used but need to be explained. Is this a capitulation, a compromising of our principles? On the contrary, it is the recognition that it can take years to understand these concepts and that, in a proposal, there is a limited amount of time and space for explanation. So instead of a capitulation, it is actually a pragmatic action for a pragmatic setting. If the institution reflects a structural-functionalist approach, it is unrealistic to think that this perspective will not also be reflected in the process of an IRB review.

Compatible Values

In structural-functional bureaucracies, the reality is that the search for meaning, apprehending essential relationships among essences, thematic analysis of cultures, perceiving another's world, and discovering core variables are at odds with the predominant problem-task orientation. Helping patients find meaning does not rank high among institutional objectives. So this objective must be stated in the proposal in pragmatic terms, such as, this study will result in improved nursing care or act as the basis for developing nursing intervention. Also, the qualitative method must appear structured, even if there are fluidity and some flexibility in the design. As far as possible, research aims should be compatible with the aims of the institution. The members of the IRB must not think they are making an exception by accepting a qualitative research proposal, because it appears different from their value orientation. It is best, from any point of view, to *demonstrate the convergence of values* between the institution and the qualitative study by stating how the study's *quest for discovery is laying the groundwork for nursing intervention*.

Generating Trust

Developing trust and alleviating fear and/or anxiety within the institution is critical to a successful qualitative research proposal, and it is also one of the more awkward challenges. This difficulty arises from the perplexing situation in which the staff worry about the researcher having access to potentially damaging information or observing poor nursing care. They wonder what the researcher is going to do with possible "negative" findings.

This difficulty can be dealt with by pointing out that quantitative researchers in institutions may also witness and be part of the same environmental activities as qualitative researchers, and that the staff themselves are probably aware of whatever problems exist. Ideally, ethics committees or quality assurance programs address these problems, yet there is always the possibility that qualitative research may uncover some problems, and consequently, the staff may feel threatened.

The first step in dealing with this problem is to include a category for "unanticipated findings" in the proposal and to carefully spell out what channels the nurse-researcher will use to share such findings. If the members of the IRB understand that *findings that indicate problems are important to discover* so that they can then be solved, members and staff might be more assured. Again, education is important for achieving this perceptual shift. Traditionally, IRBs are familiar with research that attempts *to solve* problems. The value of research that may *identify problems* so that they too may be addressed need to be stressed, and stressed, and stressed. Indeed, it is critical to identify the right problem *before* testing solutions.

Sometimes this is difficult to do, such as when patients complain during interviews about poor nursing care. A good qualitative researcher looks at the larger context (before reporting such a result, ethics demands that the lens of the study must be widened) and finds that there is inadequate staffing. Although the administration may not be happy with that finding, the nurses on the unit will be glad to have such an important need substantiated. At other times the issue is thornier. Perhaps the poor nursing care is the result of an incompetent nurse. Although the nurse-researcher cannot be the only one to know of this, he/she is ethically obligated to report these findings through the channels that are established prior to starting the project (see the example in Field & Morse, 1985, pp. 48-49). While this is essentially "whistleblowing," with its attendant consequences, sometimes good, sometimes bad, this action embodies the belief that "the therapeutic imperative of nursing (advocacy) takes precedent over the research imperative (advancing knowledge) if conflict develops" (Munhall, 1988, p. 151).

These problems have fewer ramifications for researchers not researching in their home institution, and if possible, it may be wise not to conduct research in one's home institution (see Field, this volume). Also, IRBs have members who wish to protect their institution and/or their own reputation. This is a difficult problem that should be addressed in qualitative research proposals in positive, helpful terms and fully discussed with staff. They too need to be fully informed about the research project.

Similarities Between Qualitative
and Quantitative Proposals

There are many similar areas in qualitative and quantitative proposals that are of concern to Institutional Review Boards. More than likely, both type of methods will be using the same form, and the researcher will be asked to address the following areas:

1. Objective of study
2. Research methodology
3. Characteristics of group(s) involved
4. Special groups (children or compromised adults)
5. Type of content
6. Confidentiality of data
7. Possible risk involved
8. Nonbeneficial research

Although there may be other variables, ensuring that individual rights and human dignity are protected needs to be demonstrated and documented. Often, Institutional Review Boards have more elaborate requests than those listed above, and qualitative research proposals are often evaluated on adherence to traditional scientific method. Scientific legitimacy, then, is being evaluated rather than human subjects' protection. This may not be a problem 10 years from now, but today, proposals come back from IRBs with questions that indicate reluctance to approve the proposal because the Board does not understand the method and its concomitant language. As was previously suggested, educating members of IRBs about the scientific legitimacy of qualitative studies is an additional task for qualitative nurse-researchers. What follows are some distinguishing characteristics of qualitative research that need to be addressed in IRB proposals.

Departure and Additions
for Qualitative Research Proposals

Depending on the institution, a brief overview of the aim and purpose of qualitative research methodology may precede the proposal or, perhaps, be the introductory paragraph. This does not have to be a highly sophisticated discourse about world views and para-digms, with quotes from Husserl, Erasmus, or Speigelberg; rather, a simple paragraph explaining how qualitative research methodology seeks to discover new knowledge, uses narrative descriptions in the findings, involves interviews with individuals, and so forth, is all that is necessary. Stating that these aspects of the methodology can be used to build upon one another may be important. Nurse-researchers often get into difficulty by discussing intersubjectively, going "to the things themselves," living the question, and so on. Understandable language is critical.

Objective of the Study

As was previously discussed, the objective of the study should ultimately be stated in pragmatic language. Often the aim of qualita-tive research is stated in existential terms. Remember the setting and take the existential purpose one step further by showing how the study might, for example, (a) improve staff performance or (b) assist the patient in recovery.

This approach is appropriate because it is the qualitative research baseline that enables quantitative researchers to develop hypotheses for nursing intervention, staff performance, and assisting patients in their recovery. Stress the importance of the study in pragmatic terms.

Research Method

This is perhaps the most important part of the proposal and it offers the best opportunity for educating members of IRBs. Introduce the method, the rationale for choosing the method, and the outcome of this method. Take the reader through a step-by-step narrative in language that is familiar. This may mean taking the proposal that was written for nursing colleagues of a similar bent and translating it for individuals who may be puzzled over the use of the word "phenom-enon." For example, instead of saying "lived experience," just say "experience." In fact, someone once asked me what other kind of experience there is! Perhaps replacing the phrase "ontological com-mitment" with "it is my belief that" will also be helpful.

Although it may be human to want to impress one's colleagues with a high level of abstraction, it will probably be counterproduc-tive. In any case it seems paradoxical when qualitative research is actually very interested in the concrete. No one wants to feel inadequate, and it seems unwise to send out proposals loaded with unfamiliar language. Again, in order to achieve IRB approval, *members* must *be able to read* qualitative research proposals *without a dictionary*.

So qualitative researchers need to be clear and emphatic about their research methods. They need to teach about the method and its pragmatic usefulness to nursing sciences in language that will not distract the readers but keep them focused on the substance.

Consent

There is a debate in the literature as to whether informed consent is necessary when observations and discourse occur during nurses' routine work. (Noble, 1985; Oberst, 1985). Interviews have often been exempt from formal informed consent procedures if verbal consent by an individual is given. However, I fear we will be on a slippery slope if too many of these exceptions to the written consent process are allowed. Common sense needs to prevail.

Within institutions, qualitative researchers need to anticipate a request for informed consent. If more than one interview or observation is going to take place, the idea of a process consent seems to exemplify a negotiated view of not only the "phenomenon" but also the study itself (Munhall, 1988). All consents need to take into consideration the individual's capacity, full disclosure of the research activity, and voluntariness to enter and, of course, to withdraw freely. An inclusive consent can be found in Field and Morse's *Nursing research: The application of qualitative approaches* (1985). Additional ideas about consents can be found in Munhall and Oilers' *Nursing research: A qualitative perspective* (1986).

A proposal for process consent is suggested because an informed consent represents a past tense concept. Qualitative research is often an ongoing, dynamic, changing process. A process consent offers the opportunity to actualize a negotiated view and to change arrangements if necessary. A process consent encourages mutual participation and, perhaps, mutual affirmation for the participants and the researcher.

A process consent for qualitative nursing research should be developed with the research participants' input, ideas, and suggestions and reviewed at specific times if necessary. This approach is

TABLE 15.1 Process Consent

Researcher and Participant as Collaborators come to agree upon
     how you will enter the field
     how often, for how long
     how you will leave the field
     how you will prepare to leave
     how you will share the information
     how you will keep the information anonymous and confidential
     how you will assure an accurate portrayal
     what you will do if focus changes
     what you will do with "unanticipated findings"
     what you will do with secrets and confidential material
     what you will do with inclusion and exclusion of information
     where are the findings to go
Comments by participant
Comments by researcher
Dates reviewed and changes made
Signatures

Note: Each study would require a specific process consent depending on the substance of the study. This is in addition to the usual components of informed consent.

appropriate if the researcher is going to be doing observations or participant observations over a period of time. In addition to the informed consent, a process consent should also address some of the following processes (see Table 15.1).

It is probably wise to have information about self-disclosed secrets in the process consent. It should be stated that all data obtained will be part of the study. In other words, secrets should be discouraged if they cannot be included in the study. It is best to explain to the participants that some secrets pose a dilemma for researchers who are also concerned about the patient's well-being. The question of secrets and patients' confidentiality needs to be planned, and ethical dilemmas need to be considered before the proposal is written.

Confidentiality and Anonymity

The same guarantee of confidentiality of data and anonymity of participants that quantitative researchers give must be made a general principle of qualitative research. This is only a general principle because some institutions allow their identity to be known, especially if the study is going to reflect positively on them. Also, some individuals enjoy being identified in certain kinds of interviews or studies. However, the general principle is to maintain confidentiality and anonymity.

In qualitative research, can we promise confidentiality when we include precise quotations from the transcripts in our publications? The answer is "no," but we can provide anonymity by protecting the identity of the participant. Consequently, individuals and institutions will want assurances that only the researcher(s) will have access to the data and that there will be no identifying evidence, such as, names on cassettes, names on computer printouts, and so forth. They will also want information about how and where the data will be stored.

In this section of the proposal, it might be helpful to identify the lines of communication that have been established for reporting findings. Also, information concerning the plans for disseminating the findings (i.e., publication, presentation, and who will receive final reports) should be included and mutually agreed upon.

Possible Risks

Qualitative research is considered noninvasive, but in a sense, that is a limited perception of the word. While it is true that qualitative researchers do not physically alter the participants with an intervention, there is an invasion of their space and psyche. However, while this is often therapeutic, it can pose possible risks if certain precautions are not taken.

It is well substantiated that talking has therapeutic benefits. Patients in institutions, or staff for that matter, often find relief just "getting it out of their system" or "off their chest." Nursing intervention often speaks to the provision of opportunities for patients to ventilate their feelings, and interviews provide such an opportunity. Also, attention is usually viewed as a positive experience, and being important enough to study can be viewed positively. That someone's experience is worth studying can have a validating effect.

Are there risks in qualitative research? One reviewer from an IRB asked about "triggering" an emotional response within the informant. This cannot be lightly dismissed if the experiences under study are highly charged. Because of their training, nurse-researchers are usually able to intervene appropriately and make good assessments about how a patient is responding. It may be normal if a patient becomes upset during an interview, and the nurse-researcher must be supportive and manage the interview with good clinical judgment. Arrangements also should be made with the patient's primary caretaker to support the patient after leaving the field. Aamodt (1986) writes:

> In the Human Subject Consent Forms we had said there were no psychological or social risks. Because communication in response to client feelings is an expected nursing intervention, to ignore such a need could be classified as irresponsible. We planned that interviewers would not be the primary caretaker of the child, and when the situation demanded it, the child and parent were referred to the primary caretaker. (p. 167)

An inaccurate portrayal of participants or situations can also cause harm. A statement of how you intend to insure accurate description of participants and situations should also be included in this section of the proposal. Validation by the participants is respectful and necessary for authentic representation. The harm/benefit question is succinctly placed in context by Morse (1988) when she states:

> Are the risks to the participant any greater than the everyday risk from confiding in a friend? And the "friend" in this context is a registered nurse who is accustomed to handling confidential information, counseling the dying and the distressed, observing and listening. Yet, suddenly, because the information is obtained under the auspices of "research" (rather than practice), the activities of the nurse may be considered by the IRB as potentially harmful. We must learn to trust our colleagues. (p. 214)

Nonbeneficial Research

This section of the proposal addresses research that is devoid of therapeutic purpose for the participant. Again, the opportunity to verbalize and be appreciated for sharing often does have therapeutic effects. This section should not be problematic, particularly in light of what has previously been discussed.

Presenting to the IRB

When presenting to an IRB panel, anticipate as many questions as possible. Consider this a wonderful opportunity to discuss your study. However, educating IRB members about your research methods and translating them into clear, concrete, pragmatic terms should also be done in the verbal presentation. Know who the board members are and avoid answering questions in a philosophical or existential style. If there is a member of the clergy on the board, he/she might understand your answer, but the lawyer, the physician, the two laypeople, the banker, and the accountant might not, so keep your discussion clear and precise. Remember, the intentions of the IRB are the same as yours: to protect the patient.

In summary, writing clearly, especially philosophical translation, suggesting compatible values between the institution's goals and the research goals, developing trust, and establishing clear lines of communication are important areas to consider when submitting a qualitative research proposal to an Institutional Review Board.

References

Aamodt, A. (1986). Discovering the child's view of alopecia: Doing ethnography. In P. Munhall & C. Oiler (Eds.). *Nursing research: A qualitative perspective* (pp. 163-171). Norwalk, CT: Appleton-Century-Crofts.

Field, P., & Morse, J. (1985). *Nursing research: The application of qualitative approaches*. London: Croom Helm.

Morse, J. (1988). Commentaries on special issue. *Western Journal of Nursing Research, 10*(2), 213-216.

Munhall, P. (1988). Ethical considerations in qualitative research. *Western Journal of Nursing Research, 10*(2), 150-162.

Munhall, P., & Oiler, C. (1986). *Nursing Research: A qualitative perspective*. Norwalk, CT: Appleton-Century-Crofts.

Noble, M. (1985). Written informed consent: Closing the door to clinical research. *Nursing Outlook, 33*(6), 292-293.

Oberst, M. (1985). Another look at informed consent. *Nursing Outlook, 33*(6), 294-295.

Dialogue

On the Team Approach

BOYLE: I like to teach qualitative research by having students *do* something. I think you can talk about how to analyze data a lot, but until you actually send students out to interview and they sort of experience all of the problems, until they actually analyze the data and see how its done, they don't really *know* how to do it. That, I think is the best way to teach.

HUTCHINSON: What about the group approach?

BOYLE: Well, frankly, there are times when you think you're not coordinating science, you're coordinating a circus! But for a one-time quarter, for a one-shot deal, I can do that because the pay off is tremendous.

16

Field Research:
A Collaborative Model for
Practice and Research

JOYCEEN S. BOYLE

This chapter describes the development of a collaborative research model using ethnographic field methods and how the use of such models can solve problems in nursing practice. Hammersley and Atkinson (1983, p. 2) suggest that ethnography has two distinct characteristics: the first is a focus on understanding the perspective of the people under study; the second is observing their activities in everyday life, rather than relying solely on experimental simulations or personal accounts of this behavior. On the other hand, Agar (1986) notes that social researchers assume a "learning role" by trying to make sense out of their subjects' world firsthand (p. 12). As field research in nursing considers the whole patient in relationship to his or her environment, many problems in nursing practice might be clarified by this kind of explication. The knowledge gained by these methods is valued for the use it may have in the real world of nursing decisions, judgments, and human encounters. Wilson (1985) notes that given the characteristics of nursing field studies "research

AUTHOR'S NOTE: The author wishes to acknowledge the contributions of Candice Corrigan Turner in coteaching the Field Research Practicum and the Community Nursing Assessment; Susan Ely Ellerbee, a doctoral student enrolled in the Field Research Practicum, who conducted the preliminary literature review; Beanie Archer, Coordinator of Prenatal Services, Salt Lake City-County Health Department, who was instrumental in identifying key informants; Sandra Haak, whose expertise and knowledge of computer software were important for the success of this project; and Mark Marszolf, Media Director of the College of Nursing, University of Utah, who provided assistance with the figure shown in the text.

strategies originated by sociologists and anthropologists in their field studies have held considerable interest for nurse researchers" (p. 369).

Fagin (1986) observes that, traditionally, faculty interested in conducting nursing research focused on generation and dissemination of nursing knowledge, while practitioners have been primarily interested in the use of nursing knowledge. Recently, faculty at the University of Utah refined a model that uses field research methods in community nursing assessment and, at the same time, incorporates skills and expertise of researchers and practitioners. This model draws heavily on the early work of Glittenberg (1981) as well as previous research done by this author (Boyle & Counts, 1988; Counts & Boyle, 1987). Glittenberg (1981) named the original model GENESIS (General Ethnographic Nursing Evaluation Studies in the State), and at the present time, these research models are known as GENESIS projects. An example of the GENESIS model is seen in the work of Magilvy, McMahon, Bachman, Roark, and Evenson (1987).

The term "collaborative model" (as used in this chapter) refers to a field research experience that was initiated by the University of Utah nursing faculty and key members of the nursing administration at the Salt Lake City-County Health Department. This model incorporates the interests and skills of faculty, graduate students, and community health nurses in a field research experience that is designed to examine problems encountered in the care of clients. Rather than focus on the findings generated by the field research, this chapter describes the development of the collaborative model and the process used to implement the model during an academic quarter.

A major advantage of the collaborative model is the strong link between nursing education and practice; in addition, the model affords opportunities for the participants to learn field research methods and to become familiar with computer programs for storing and retrieving qualitative data. The ultimate goal of the model is to collect and analyze data in a way that helps solve clinical problems as well as raise other questions of interest to nurses. Diers (1979) indicates that "generating new questions, new ways to look at old phenomena or even new phenomena just discovered represents an important stage of inquiry and knowledge development for a practice profession" (p. 141).

What Is Ethnographic Research?

Over the past few years there has been a growth of interest in theoretical and practical ethnographic research among researchers in many different fields, and as could be predicted, there is considerable diversity in prescription and practice. Hammersley and Atkinson (1983) point out that "there is disagreement as to whether ethnography's distinctive feature is the elicitation of cultural knowledge, the detailed investigation of patterns of social interaction, or holistic analysis of societies" (p. 1).

Although ethnographic field research has long been used in anthropology, its use in nursing is relatively new. Leininger (1970) advocates this method in her book *Nursing and anthropology: Two worlds to blend*. Later, she defines the use of ethnography in nursing as "the systematic process of observing, detailing, describing, documenting, and analyzing the lifeways or particular patterns of a culture (or subculture) in order to grasp the lifeways or patterns of the people in their familiar environment" (p. 35). Presently, terms such as "ethnography," "field research," and "ethnographic methods" are used in different ways in nursing research and sometimes are associated with different terminology. For example, Wilson (1985, chap. 13) devotes a chapter in her text to field research strategies and provides a fine discussion of participant observation, a major technique of ethnography, but she does not mention ethnography or ethnographic methods as such. Diers (1979, p. 20) calls ethnographic research *factor searching* or *relation searching* studies. Leininger (1985, pp. 34-36) speaks of "maxi" and "mini" ethnographies in nursing: maxi studies are the more traditional ethnographies, usually seen in anthropology, where the researcher goes to another culture to study and learn about that culture over a long period of time; mini ethnographies are more commonly seen in other disciplines, such as nursing, but are also found in anthropology. Mini ethnographies are usually more specific, more time limited, and the investigation is more focused. Magilvy et al. (1987) use the term *focused ethnographic study* in a similar way to Leininger's use of mini ethnography. In a recent textbook, Burns and Grove (1987, chap. 4) include a section (pp. 89-94) on ethnographic research and cite Germain's (1979) work *The cancer unit: An ethnography* as an example of ethnographic research in nursing. Thus there are multiple terms used to describe ethnographic research, and as some of them are used in numerous ways, the effort by Morse in this text to clarify the types of ethnographic research in nursing seems particularly relevant and helpful. In this chapter the term *ethnographic field methods* is used to describe the research undertaken in the collaborative model.

According to Wilson (1985, p. 369), the emphasis on clinical nursing research prompted an interest in the research strategies of the social sciences. Also, answering questions about everyday practice or the "real world" of nursing decisions, judgments, and human encounters has increased nurses' interest in methods of field research. Agar (1986, p. 15) observes that even in anthropology ethnographies may differ because of the intended audience of an ethnographic report. And since understanding and/or clarifying clinical situations is a major emphasis in nursing, field studies investigating problems in nursing should be directed to nurses who are interested in solving problems related to clinical practice.

Ethnographic field research in nursing and other disciplines always involves face-to-face interviewing, with data collection and analysis taking place in the natural setting. Blumer (1969) observes that "the major goal of fieldwork is getting close to the people involved in it, seeing it in a variety of situations they meet, noting their problems, and observing how they handle them, being party to their conversations and watching their way of life as it flows along" (p. 37). Hammersley and Atkinson (1983) state that "the ethnographer participates, overtly or covertly, in people's daily lives for an extended period of time, watching what happens, listening to what is said, asking questions; in fact collecting whatever data are available to shed light on the issues with which he or she is concerned" (p. 2). They suggest that ethnography bears a close resemblance to the routine ways in which people make sense of the world in everyday life and point out that some critics regard this as its basic strength while others see it as a fundamental weakness.

Agar (1980, p. 114) suggests that the best term for ethnography is participant observation. The topic of participant observation has been extensively discussed in the literature, for example, see McCall and Simmons (1969), Agar (1986), Hammersley and Atkinson (1983), Whyte (1984), and Lofland and Lofland (1984). As early as 1969, Byerly described the use of participant observation in a nursing setting and discussed the advantages and contributions in a clinical context. Overall, the literature indicates that the bulk of participant observation data is usually gathered through informal interviews and supplemented by observation. Schatzman and Strauss (1973, p. 6) indicate that classic participant observation always involves the interweaving of looking and listening. The term *participant observation* suggests that the researcher is directly involved in the informant's life, observing and talking with people as he or she learns their view of reality. The end result is that participant observation allows the researcher to take a particular slice of behavior and interpret it by putting it into context. Immersion in the world of others, or "intimate familiarity," requires involvement over long periods of time and demands substantial investments of time and energy. Emerson (1987) believes that this traditional aspect of ethnography may be compromised in some present day studies as researchers' fieldwork activities are minimal, superficial, and short-term. He suggests that fieldwork would profit more by involvement over longer periods of time, more participatory styles, as well as periodic revisits to the field setting.

According to Wilson (1985, p. 370), field studies in nursing, whatever their location or goals, are characterized by certain features: (a) the researcher, through intensive interviews/participant observation, is the primary "instrument" for data collection; (b) data collection and analysis take place in the natural or research setting; (c) there is a sharp distinction between the context of discovery and the context of verification; and (d) a different set of ethical principles are confronted by field researchers.

In nursing, ethnographic studies can help discover new information about clients in various situations. The more nurses know about their clients and families and how they experience situations, the better able they will be to care for them (Diers, 1979, pp. 126-127). According to Whyte (1984, chap. 13), ethnographic field research facilitates the development of conceptual frameworks that help us understand and interpret behavior and situations across a wide range of social situations. Emerson (1987) emphasizes that research methods using participant observation are basically a form of socialization into other ways of knowing and doing. Thus, studies using participant observation may increase sensitivity to the ways in which clients understand, define, and categorize their worlds and may help nurses solve practical problems and assist them to make complex decisions in clinical situations. In addition, Diers (1979, p. 5) suggests that such studies may yield findings that will help nurses alter aspects of nursing care for particular clients; in other words, these studies involve "a difference that matters" in terms of consequences for improving care.

The Field Research Practicum
and Community Nursing Assessment

Before describing the process used to develop the collaborative model, a brief summary of the events leading to the use of the model will be presented. At the University of Utah's College of Nursing, doctoral students who wish to develop expertise in qualitative research may participate in a Field Research Practicum. The major objective of the practicum is to enable students to conduct field research using ethnographic methods.

At the same time, a continuing education course is offered for community health nurses. The title of this course is *Community Nursing Assessment;* potential students are informed that the course focuses on solving clinical problems encountered in community health nursing practice. Each group of students is assigned selected readings for discussion that are appropriate to their backgrounds and the course objectives. Reading lists included at the end of this chapter show reading assignments and the sequence of topics discussed in each of the courses. For purposes of clarity, the students enrolled in the continuing education course will be referred to as "the community health nurses"; the other students will be termed "doctoral students"; together the students in both classes and the faculty composed the "research team."

The Collaborative Model:
The Process of Development

Step 1: Identification of the Problem

The community health nurses assumed major responsibility for identification of the research problem. The process outlined by Diers (1979, pp. 10-27) was followed very closely. During the first class, the community health nurses were asked to describe some of the "problems" in their practice, what kinds of clients were "difficult," and why. They quickly identified teenage mothers as being the most problematic clients in their practice. From a community health nursing standpoint, the costs of teenage pregnancy are considerable, both for the teenager's family and society-at-large. Young mothers often experience high risk births, and in addition to other health concerns, more of their babies have low birth weights. These problems, coupled with a young mother's inability to emotionally or financially provide for her baby, detract from the family's quality of life. This situation has proved challenging for community health nurses who have many adolescent mothers among their clients.

In order to narrow down a broad community problem such as teenage mothers and their babies to a clinical nursing problem, Diers (1979, p. 12) suggests that the researcher describe a discrepancy in the nursing care of adolescent mothers and infants. For example, what is the nursing care really like? What should it be? The nurses felt that there must be ways to help teenage moms, yet they reported frustration in their efforts to provide care that might be helpful. Diers (1979, p. 12) observes that sometimes the discrepancy is expressed as a gripe; the community health nurses reported that when they receive a referral on an adolescent mother they anticipate difficulty because teenage moms are "hard to work with." Their first thoughts upon seeing the referral were: "Oh no, not again! Not another one!" While the nurses believed that there must be a better way to help adolescent mothers, they were not certain as to what works and what does not. Increasing their frustration is the fact that adolescent mothers and their new infants make up a large portion of the nurses' case assignments.

The discrepancy (or nursing problem) that the staff nurses described met the criteria which Diers (1979) lists as necessary for a potential research problem. These criteria are: (a) more knowledge about the problem might make a difference that matters, for example, additional knowledge would improve the care of clients and reduce nurses' frustration; (b) the potential for expanding nursing knowledge seems apparent; and (c) the staff nurses have access to and control over the phenomena in question (Diers, 1979, pp. 13-14).

Diers (1979, p. 15) suggests that once a problem has been tagged a "discrepancy that matters" and a conceptual relationship is identified with similar problems then the problem has to be turned into a form that will make it researchable. This task was the responsibility of the doctoral students. The nursing problems surrounding the care of adolescent mothers and their infants were described to them, and together with the community nurses, they analyzed the clinical problem. Many of the doctoral students and faculty could recall caring for teenage mothers and were able to evaluate how the discrepancy applied to their own experiences. The faculty served as the link between the two groups of students to enhance cooperation and the sharing of information.

Diers's (1979, p. 16) *Guide for Analysis of Clinical Problems* was used to convert the clinical problem into a research problem. Diers (1979, p. 24) suggests that there are two categories of resources for analyzing clinical problems: the experiences of others (usually reported in the literature) and one's own experience of nursing. Because of their experience with providing care to young mothers and their babies, the research team relied on the community health nurses' expertise for conceptualizing and analyzing the problem. The research team also relied on their own clinical knowledge to decide what was interesting and relevant to the study.

The professional literature on teenage mothers did not appear to address their perspectives or their daily life experiences with the new baby. There was a general feeling that if community health nurses knew more about adolescent mothers, their experiences, their problems, and how they solved them, care could be provided that would more adequately meet their needs. Diers (1979) describes this type of study as a relation searching study that answers the question "What's happening here?" She states that "in general, the purpose behind such studies is to understand better a situation so as to know how to intervene in it, or how to form one's prescriptions for care more accurately or acutely" (p. 126).

Step 2: Development of the Interview Schedule and Locating Key Informants

All members of the research team had equal input into the design of the interview schedule. The information solicited by the schedule included: a description of the place of the interview; the age and birthdate of the mother; marital status and the age of father; birthdate of the baby; educational status of the mother; religion; and a brief description of financial status. The Guide for Interview Questions included:

1. It seems to me that a lot of young girls are having babies . . . can you help me understand some of the reasons why this is happening?
2. Tell me how your life has changed since the baby arrived. How do you feel about these changes?
3. Tell me what an ordinary day is like for you. For example, tell me about the last 24 hours. Was that a usual day? How would you like it to be?
4. Tell me who helps you with all that you have to do. What things do they help you with? . . . I'm interested in how you manage. What has been most helpful? Least helpful?
5. What kind of help do you think that you need?
6. Who do you talk to about your baby? Why?
7. How did you learn how to take care of your baby? What did you learn in the hospital? From your mother? From others? We've been talking about how things are now. What kind of goals and plans do you have for the future?

Often the community health nurses suggested an area of inquiry, and the doctoral students phrased the questions in appropriate ways, although on occasion just the opposite occurred. Decisions were made about the demographic information to be collected from all informants, about taping the initial interview, and about obtaining a signed consent from each informant. Once these steps were taken, a modified institutional Review Board (IRB) proposal was submitted to the appropriate university committee for review, a process that took approximately one week for approval to be granted. An original IRB approval for a Community Assessment/GENESIS Project had remained current thus necessitating only modifications that described the focus and population of the Adolescent Mothers' study.

The value of a collaborative model was reinforced during the process of locating key informants. The community health nurses suggested young mothers from their case loads who they thought would be willing to participate in the study, and four informants were selected in this manner. The remainder of the key informants came from the clients using prenatal clinic services at the City-County Health Department. All informants were contacted first by telephone and asked if they would be willing to participate in the study. A total of 16 adolescent mothers agreed to participate in the study. Demographic characteristics of the key informants, such as marital status, living arrangements, educational status, and income, were varied.

Because of the cooperation and assistance of the nursing staff from the health department, it took only one and one-half weeks to locate the informants and obtain their consent for interview. Each member of the research team was given a name, address, and telephone number of an informant and asked to make individual arrangements for the interview and modified participant observation experiences. Two weeks were scheduled for interviewing and transcribing of taped interviews.

Step 3: Preparation for Field Research, Interviewing, Recording, and Ethical Issues

During the time that key informants were being recruited into the study, the research team continued to meet as separate groups to read, discuss, and solve problems related to the research experience. Practice sessions were held with tape recorders, and problems were anticipated and solutions proposed. Ethical issues related to field research were also discussed. The research team decided that any feedback about community health nurses or the health department, whether negative or positive, would be shared immediately with the community health nurses. Also, the decision was made to tell informants that the interviewer was a nurse and that the data were being collected for a nursing study. The research team also thought that informants should be given a copy of their transcribed interview for their personal keeping.

Step 4: Field Immersion: Data Collection and Modified Participant Observation Experiences

The key informants were told that they were being asked about the everyday life experiences of motherhood. The informants came from a wide variety of circumstances. One new unmarried mother lived in a group home and was attending an alternate high school; another was married and lived comfortably with her new husband and baby in their own home. Others lived with parents, friends, and boyfriends. Two of the informants, whose infants were under one year of age, were pregnant for the second time.

Members of the research team used the interview schedule as a guide to maintain a proper balance of structure and openness. Interviews were conducted during various times of the day and

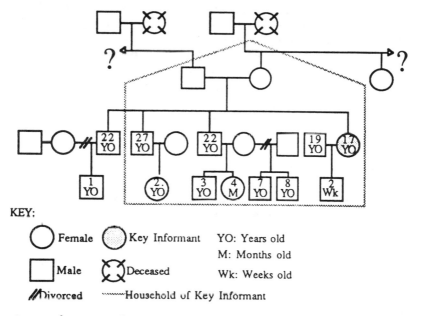

KEY:

○ Female   ◉ Key Informant   YO: Years old
                                M: Months old
□ Male   ⊗ Deceased   Wk: Weeks old
⫫ Divorced   ⁓⁓⁓Household of Key Informant

Figure 16.1 A Sample Genogram

week; the interviewers recorded participant observation data immediately after they had left the home of the informant. Some members
of the research team recorded these data on tape, while others made
extensive hand written notes about their observations and experiences during the interview. These data included an overview of
the home environment, observations of daily living activities, and
notes about other persons in the home while the interview was
conducted.

Genograms, as described by Wright and Leahey (1984, pp. 30-31),
were collected for each informant. The genogram is basically a
diagram of the family constellation that shows the structure of intergenerational relationships. Information for a genogram is easily
solicited, and it requires only a piece of paper and a pencil to record
the data. Figure 16.1, A Sample Genogram, provides an example of
the kinds of data collected.

Genograms were used in this project as some of the doctoral
students argued very strongly that organizing data in this way would
be helpful in placing young mothers in a family perspective. They

also thought that genograms would yield information about backgrounds and circumstances that would help interpret and explain the
experience of adolescent mothers.

Some members of the research team followed the interview schedule very closely in terms of sequence of questions; others were more
comfortable in varying the sequence and asking additional probing
questions. Issues surrounding reliability and validity, sampling procedures, and the "good informant" were noted, but not completely
resolved.

The research team noted that a number of the key informants were
quite articulate in responding to the questions and were comfortable
with a high degree of disclosure. A few of them, however, did
experience some difficulty in expressing their views of motherhood.
The interviewers sometimes found the language used by the key
informants rather baffling, for example, the word *stuff* occurs over
100 times in the 16 transcribed interviews. It seems a common word
that teenage mothers use as they struggle to express their views and
perceptions of reality. For example, in explaining why she became
pregnant, one informant said, "We spent a lot of time together and
stuff." Or, when asked to describe daily activities, another said, "I
bathe the baby and stuff." Still another informant described her
relationship with her husband by saying, "We do stuff together." One
member of the research team suggested that we call this study "The
Stuff of Motherhood."

Immediately after the interview, the community health nurses
dropped their tapes off for transcription directly onto the computer.
The doctoral students transcribed their own tapes, and this experience reinforced the understanding that the effort, time, and potential
expenses involved in qualitative research are considerable.

The transcribed interviews were returned immediately to the interviewer who scheduled another appointment with the key informant or contacted her by telephone. The major purpose of this second
interview was to review the transcription for accuracy and completeness. The changes made by the informants for the most part were
minimal; when the corrections were completed (a process facilitated
by the computer), a copy of the transcribed interview was given to
the mother.

In order to enhance the learning experiences of the students, data
collection and analysis were somewhat artificially separated. These
two steps often occur simultaneously, and their complete separation

is not possible in this kind of research. Even during the interview process, analytic listening and reflection allows the informant's unique perspective to emerge. As soon as all of the tapes were transcribed, the more formal procedures related to data analysis were initiated.

Step 5: Data Management and First Level Analysis

Coding the Data

As soon as each taped interview was transcribed, the author listened to the tape while reading the transcript. This exercise permitted (a) familiarity with the interview data to be gained and (b) the identifications of any errors in transcription or portions of the interview that were unclear or incomplete. Specific concerns about these problems were addressed prior to coding the data. Although the community health nurses participated in weekly sessions where the categories and coding procedures were discussed, they chose not to participate in the actual coding of the data. (In this chapter, the terms codes and categories will be used synonymously.) During this weekly interchange and dialogue, the clinical orientation and insights of the practitioners enabled them to raise issues and questions that otherwise might not have been addressed by the research team.

The doctoral students reviewed the transcripts and developed major categories for more detailed coding. These categories were:

1. reasons why young girls have babies
2. changes in life since the baby arrived
3. daily activities
4. assistance with the baby
5. learning about the baby
6. plans for the future

Wilson (1985, p. 408) states that one of the basic techniques for a content analysis is developing a set of categories. The researcher can set up categories in advance and then carefully read through the data, code them into the existing categories, and, ultimately, describe the responses that appear in the various categories. Obviously, if the researcher discovers in the course of coding the data that statements or responses fall outside of the pre-established categories, other categories must be devised that are based on the themes appearing in the data. The categories should be sufficiently detailed and mutually exclusive to allow for coding of all data from the informants. According to Wilson (1985, p. 408), another basic step in content analysis is developing a rationale and illustrations to guide the coding of data into categories. This requires that the researcher make a judgment on the right category for every response or unit of analysis, and it is important to define each category as fully and clearly as possible.

The process of coding the data from the Adolescent Mothers study can probably best be described by what Wilson (1985, pp. 410-411) calls the "Unfolding Tributary" method of evolving categories. This method extracts categories from the data rather than borrowing them from existing theories, and it proceeds systematically from broad categories to more specific ones. An example of this process of extracting categories from the data is shown below.

Reasons young girls are having babies.
ME:
    I wanted a baby.
      love kids, always wanted some
      wanted a baby like my friends
      when I moved away from home
      to force the issue of marriage
      didn't want to go to school
    I couldn't have an abortion.
    I had the baby to straighten him out (the baby's father).
    It's good to have babies when you are young.
    I switched contraceptive pills.
    I had to get away from my stepfather.
    I was in love.
    I didn't think it could happen to me.
    My mother
      didn't tell me anything about birth control
      didn't understand what my life was like.
OTHER GIRLS:
    It was an accident.
    To maintain a serious relation
    They wanted to have a baby.
    They lack information.

They don't know about birth control.
They can't ask their parents anything.
There is no information in the school.
They have family problems and want to get away.
There is pressure from the boyfriend.
There are more choices today, having a baby is one of them.
They don't care enough to be careful.
They don't know how hard it is going to be.
Their parents won't allow them to use birth control.
It's always the girl's problem.

In order to code the data from the broad categories to the more specific ones, the doctoral students and faculty divided into three small groups composed of three or four members each. One class period was devoted to discussion of coding, and with consultation and input from their colleagues, everyone had an opportunity to practice coding the data.

At this point, the coding groups were ready to use *The Ethnograph* (Seidel & Clark, 1983), a computer program that provides the researcher with a convenient means of coding and sorting text data that are collected in qualitative research. Swanson-Kauffman (1986) states that this program in no way substitutes for the rigor or analytic creativity of the researcher. Swanson-Kauffman (1986) probably gives the best available description of *The Ethnograph* when she says that "in truth *The Ethnograph* serves as little more than the traditional qualitative researcher's index cards, scissors, pot of glue, and a very messy living room floor" (p. 62).

The first step in the computer data analysis was to instruct the computer to format the transcribed files down to lines that were 36 characters in length and sequentially numbered. Copies of these sequentially numbered transcripts were then ready for hand coding and marking of categories, a process that involves writing in the codes on the blank right-hand side of the page. At this point, the coding groups met separately to code preassigned portions of the data into categories. Table 16.1 shows selected lines from *The Ethnograph*, with hand coded entries shown in italics on the right hand.

After the coding groups had completed their task, the hand codes were entered into the computer. The coding session was held in the College of Nursing Microcomputer Laboratory under the direction of one of the doctoral students in the course who was knowledgeable about computers and their use.

288

TABLE 16.1

Tell me how your life has changed since you had the baby?	49 50	*CHANGES*
It's a lot harder now. There's so many things I have to do for her.	51 52	*more responsibility*
Sometimes I wish I would've waited longer. Most of the time I'm glad I I have her but I don't know. It's a	53 54 55	*ambivalence*
lot of work. I don't like to get up until noon but I can't now because I have to feed her and stuff.	56 57 58	*interferes*

The next step of *The Ethnograph* was directing the computer to sort through each transcript for every occurrence of any given code. For example, each time one of the informants discussed her plans for the future (coded as "Future"), the segment was retrieved and printed out on the informant's sort page. Table 16.2 is a facsimile of Informant 5's sort page showing the code "Reason."

Lines 14-23 and 29-31 contain data about the reasons Informant 5 reported for having a baby. "Reasons why young girls become pregnant" was a broad category developed after reading through the transcriptions. During the actual coding process, this category was broken down into more specific ones. The facsimile shows some of these specific categories (*Parents, *Love, *Marriage) retrieved from the data provided by Informant 5.

Preliminary Analysis

By the end of the academic quarter, the research team had examined the major categories and could make some *preliminary* statements about the data that had implications for clinical practice. While the tentative nature of the findings must be stressed, the collective statements and descriptions of events are indications of the informants' reality and unique perspectives on teenage motherhood. For example, although the reasons for wanting to become pregnant differed by individual informant, one of the early findings was that

TABLE 16.2

INFORMANT: 5		
SV: REASON		
I: —Can you help me understand some of the reasons this is happening?		#Reason
IN-5: The reason that it happened to me	14	*Parents
is because my stepfather, he	15	
wouldn't let me go out or anything	16	
and, I guess I got snotty or	17	
something. But I did love the guy I	18	
married and that's why it happened.	19	
It's really not because my stepfather	20	
pushed it, but it really was because we	21	*Love
were in love and that's why it	22	
happened.	23	
I: Uh huh. Did you feel that by having a baby then that would force the issue.		
IN-5: Yeah, it did force it. Cause we	29	*Marriage
were going get married, but not that	30	
soon.	31	

15 out of the 16 young mothers reported that they had wanted to have a baby. In addition, young motherhood was viewed very positively by the majority of the key informants. This was surprising to members of the research team, most of whom had assumed that teenage girls do not want to become pregnant and that if pregnancy occurs it is unintended. Agar (1986) calls this lack of fit between the view of the researcher and the informant a *breakdown,* and this happens when "something does not make sense; one's assumption of perfect coherence is violated" (p. 20). Moving from *breakdown* as the starting point, to *resolution* (the process it initiates, to what Agar (1986, pp. 20-25) then calls *coherence,* produces ethnographic meaning and understanding of the informants' reality. To develop a more coherent view of young motherhood, more data are needed from the key informants. However, the preliminary analysis indicates that positive cultural values related to motherhood are very strong

in Utah, and young girls are encouraged at an early age to prepare themselves for this role. These values must be considered in any attempt to solve problems posed by teenage pregnancies or when providing nursing care to adolescent mothers and their babies.

Reflections on the Collaborative Model

As a Teaching Method

A collaborative model such as the one described here allows practitioners and researchers an "immersion" experience in field research. The actual process of identifying a clinical problem with colleagues who may have differing perspectives, designing an interview schedule, and conducting the research project is an extremely valuable experience as it provides team members with exposure to both the problems and the challenges of field research. When tape recorder batteries fail in the middle of an interview, an indelible impression is made upon the researcher. The frustrations of locating informants, of transcribing data, and obtaining inter-rater reliability for coding can be best understood through first-hand experience. The experience of coding data in small groups was a valuable learning experience because it was quickly evident how a team member might code a segment of data in a different manner than a colleague. The questions raised by the community health nurses in relation to the coding procedures were thoughtful and stimulating. Sometimes input from one of the nurses prompted major rethinking about the data and how it was interpreted. After participation in the field research experience, doctoral students were able to more realistically plan their dissertation projects because they had a grasp of the timing, energy, and expense involved in field research. Some students, of course, will never engage in field studies or qualitative research again; however, they developed skills in understanding and evaluating qualitative research designs as well as an appreciation of the contributions that qualitative studies make to nursing theory and practice.

One of the major attractions of this course (as far as the doctoral students were concerned) was the opportunity to learn *The Ethnograph* in a nonthreatening manner. One of the suggestions at the end of the course was that more time with the computer program would have been helpful. Consequently, the files were made available in the computer laboratory for any student who wished to access them either for review of the procedures used or for additional learning experiences.

A major goal of the collaborative model was to provide opportunities for researchers and practitioners to work together to solve clinical problems. An appreciation of each other's views and contributions emerged during implementation of the model. The skills the community health nurses exhibited in the design of the interview schedule and in terms of the actual interviewing were impressive. One of the early interviews was completed by a staff nurse, and that taped interview was used later in other courses to illustrate appropriate methods and skills in interviewing. The ease and familiarity of staff nurses in making home visits, meeting strangers, and asking thoughtful questions were apparent. At the same time, they reported being somewhat uncomfortable in the learning role of the field researcher. *Listening* versus *intervention* was a growth experience for them that was not always easy. Future field practicums will attempt to bring the two groups (doctoral students and staff nurses) together on a regular basis; perhaps, every third class could be held jointly as closer collaboration between the two groups throughout the experience seems worthwhile.

Many of the difficulties involved in the use of a collaborative model in teaching and research are not unique. Such an undertaking requires an extraordinary amount of time and coordination. Faculty who have good relationships with their colleagues in clinical agencies are obviously in a more advantageous position to initiate collaborative models. The possibility of not obtaining adequate numbers of key informants at the exact time when the research team is ready to begin interviewing is always a concern. The most difficult and challenging aspect of this collaborative model, at least for the faculty, was attempting to meet the separate goals of each group of students. For example, the doctoral students wanted to learn *The Ethnograph;* the community health nurses wanted information about adolescent mothers that would help them in providing care. At the end of the quarter, the doctoral students indicated that they needed still more time to learn the computer program, and the staff nurses were somewhat frustrated that specific answers to all the problems of their practice were not readily forthcoming.

As Field Research

A major advantage of the collaborative model is that it facilitates the collection of data from a number of informants over a short period of time, providing real experiences with people and data. The use of *The Ethnograph* greatly enhanced the research team's ability to leave a clearly marked decision trail in the analysis stage as well as providing a central location for the storage and sorting of data. At the same time, the concerns regarding the number of interviewers and the issues that this presents in regards to inter-rater reliability must be taken into account. In addition, obtaining only one interview per informant limits both the quality and amount of data. Issues related to construct validity (interpreting the experience of adolescent motherhood) are problematic as complex social phenomena cannot be explained on the basis of one interview.

On the other hand, members of the research team emerged from this experience with what Lofland and Lofland (1984) describe as "better developed and sharpened powers to analyze and synthesize—the intellectual skills that are applicable to far more than just social analysis" (pp. 155-156). This collaborative model does elicit data that has relevance to clinical problems, and nurses can base decisions about initial patient care on this information. The community health nurses reported that the fieldwork experience inherent in the collaborative model helped them modify their interactions with teenage mothers in light of the new information they possessed. The nurses have become spokespersons for the use of qualitative studies in clinical research as the use of clinical expertise in designing and conducting studies has the potential for improving practice. As Diers (1979) has stated, "the closer the relationship between nursing practice and nursing research, the better the research and the better the practice" (p. 5).

The collaborative model has attracted considerable interest in community health agencies as the nurses talked about and shared their experiences. As a result, members of the research team have been asked to serve on advisory boards, panels, and task forces because of their participation in the collaborative model and their interest in teenage mothers and their infants. This has increased nursing's visibility, input, and influence on issues that are of concern to the profession. In the final analysis, perhaps the final product of the collaborative model (i.e., the research report) is not as important as the process and the individual growth that accompanied it.

Towards "Doing Ethnography"

The collaborative model discussed in this chapter has been termed "field research with ethnographic methods." The importance of a community-based study using semi-focused interviews, genograms, and limited participant observation has been described. Currently several members of the research team are exploring other ethnographic methods that would enhance further data gathering techniques, moving towards a focused ethnographic study. Four members of the research team (including faculty, students, and community health nurses) are continuing the research project. Some of the informants are being deleted from the study, and others are being added to enrich the data base. Data will be collected on an ongoing basis over a period of time, with concurrent analysis taking place. Outside funding is being sought, and as several of the staff nurses are enthusiastic and supportive of the project and indicate an interest in continuing to facilitate a collaborative model, ties to the health department remain strong.

In continuing to expand the model, the need for spending more time with informants seems crucial. A fieldwork experience in one's own culture does not pose the problems of learning another language and of ordering reality; nevertheless, long-term and intimate involvement in the routine, everyday world of others is a methodological *sine qua non* (Emerson, 1987). In many nursing ethnographies, we can "return to the field" periodically, especially in community-based projects such as this collaborative model. Nurses can benefit from understanding experiences of teenage mothers over a time span of several years rather than at one certain point in time. This will add a historical dimension to the study that should yield greater explanatory power.

In addition, the research team is considering the use of less conventional fieldwork roles, including more "insider" or participatory styles. Adler, Adler, and Rochford (1986) suggest that immersion and familiarity are not matters of how much time is spent but also the manner in which that time is spent. In clinical nursing research, where nurses are a part of the clinical reality, the notion of field research by insiders is intriguing, especially with participatory field roles. Such research has potential for *data producing encounters;* a critical look at these encounters may enable us to more carefully examine the interactional processes in the nurse-client relationship. Emerson (1987) says that "the encounter between researcher and researched, then, is not simply one in which a reality is merely observed and noted: It is also an occasion in which reality is created" (p. 78). The use of a collaborative model suggests that nurse researchers can push beyond the stereotypes of past research in the social sciences and, especially, in nursing. Although we have not attained a clear sense of the contributions of field research or ethnography to nursing, we have attained a clearer sense of the possibilities we can exploit for the benefit of both nursing theory and practice.

DISCUSSION GUIDE AND READING LIST

Community Nursing Assessment

• Week 1
Introduction to a collaborative model of research-based practice
Introduction to community assessment of high-risk groups
Identification of the clinical nursing problem via field research
  Bohannan, L. (1980, pp. 44-48)
  Diers, D. (1979, pp. 10-60)
  Roberson, M. H. B., & Boyle, J. S. (1984, pp. 43-49)

• Week 2
Planning the project, entering the field, field relations, observation methods, field notes, studying one's own culture, researcher versus practitioners role
Development of the interview schedule.
  Counts, M. M., & Boyle, J. S. (1987, pp. 12-23)
  Diers, D. (1979, pp. 100-143)
  Geertz, C. (1973, pp. 3-30, 412-453)
  Mishler, E. G. (1979, pp. 1-19)

• Week 3
Refinement of the Interview Schedule
Participant observation, non-participant observation
Field notes
  Patton, M. Q. (1980, pp. 195-255)
  Spradley, J. P. (1979, pp. 78-93)

• Week 4 & 5
Interviewing, life histories, decision frames, key informants
   Agar, M. H. (1980, pp. 83-117)
   Spradley, J. P. (1979, pp. 55-96)
   Whyte, W. F. (1984, pp. 97-111)

• Week 6
Recording and indexing data
   Patton, M. Q. (1980, pp. 121-194)

• Week 7
Ethics, privacy, consent, strategies for confidentiality
   Diers, D. (1979, pp. 264-271)
   Whyte, W. F. (1984, pp. 193-223)

• Week 8
Data gathering

• Week 9
Data management and first level analysis

• Week 10
Preliminary draft of research project

DISCUSSION GUIDE AND READING LIST

Field Research Practicum

• Week 1
Introductions to the field, the history of ethnographic research in social
science and nursing, plan of the course, identifying a research problem,
quantitative and qualitative types of data, applied studies, nature of
current research in nursing
   Berreman, G. (1962, pp. 3-24)
   Counts, M. M., & Boyle, J. S. (1987, pp. 12-23)
   Roberson, M. H. B., & Boyle, J. S. (1984, pp. 43-49)

• Week 2
Planning the project, entering the field, entree, field relations,
observational methods, field notes, studying one's own culture (society),
researcher's role, rapport with informants
   Agar, M. H. (1980, pp. 1-81, 175-204)
   Edgerton, R. B., & Langness, L. L. (1974, pp. 20-26)
   Geertz, C. (1973, pp. 3-30, 412-453)
   Hsu, F. L. K. (1969, pp. 33-34)

Kimball, S. T., & Partridge, W. R. (1979, pp. 19-50)
Mead, M. (1977, pp. 100-149)
Spindler, G. D., & Spindler, L. (1970, pp. 273-282)
van Willigen, J., & DeWalt, B. R. (1985, pp. 1-4, 12-35)
Whyte, W. F. (1984, pp. 65-81)

• Week 3
Participant observation, non-participant observation
Agar, M. H. (1980, pp. 83-117)
Byerly, E. L. (1969, pp. 230-236)
Geer, B. (1969, pp. 144-162)
Miller, S. M. (1969, pp. 87-89)
Mishler, E. G. (1979, pp. 1-19)
Schwartz, M. S., & Schwartz, C. G. (1969, pp. 89-105)
van Willigen, J., & DeWalt, B. R. (1985, pp. 46-49)
Whyte, W. F. (1984, pp. 23-33)

• Week 4
Interviewing, life histories, decision frames, event analysis and other
techniques, informants (key and others)
Agar, M. H. (1980, pp. 119-173)
Agar, M. H. (1986, pp. 68-77)
Bohannan, L. (1980, pp. 44-49)
Crane, J., & Angrosino, M. V. (1974, pp. 42-50)
Frake, C. O. (1969, pp. 28-41)
Spradley, J. P., & DeWalt (1979, pp. 25-39, 45-68)
van Willigen, J., & DeWalt, B. R. (1985, pp. 36-72)
Whyte, W. F. (1984, pp. 97-112)
Young, J. C. (1978, pp. 81-97)
Young, J. C. (1980, pp. 106-131)

• Week 5
Recording and indexing data
Spradley, J. P. (1979, pp. 107-203)
Whyte, W. F. (1984, pp. 113-127)

• Week 6
Ethics, privacy, consent, strategies for confidentiality
Bowen, E. S. (1964, pp. 251-263)
Jordan, B. (1981, pp. 181-216)
Langness, L. L., & Frank, G. (1981, pp. 117-155)
Punch, M. (1986, pp. 70-84)
van Willigen, J., & DeWalt, B. R. (1985, pp. 5-11)
Whyte, W. F. (1984, pp. 193-223)

- Week 7
Writing the Report
  Knafl, K. A., & Howard, M. J. (1984, pp. 17-24)
  Sandelowski, M. (1986, pp. 27-37)
  Smith, J. K., & Heshusius, L. (1986, pp. 4-12)
  Spradley, J. P. (1979, pp. 204-216)

- Week 8
Data gathering

- Week 9
Data management and first level analysis

- Week 10
Preliminary draft

References

Adler, P. A., Adler, P. V., & Rochford, E. B., Jr. (1986). The politics of participation in field research. *Urban Life, 14*(4), 363-376.

Agar, M. H. (1980). *The professional stranger: An informal introduction to ethnography*. New York: Academic Press.

Agar, M. H. (1986). *Speaking of ethnography*. Beverly Hills: Sage.

Berreman, G. D. (1962). *Behind many masks: Ethnography and impression management in a Himalayan village* (Society For Applied Anthropology Monograph No. 4). Lexington: University of Kentucky.

Blumer, H. (1969). *Symbolic interactionism: Perspective and method*. Englewood Cliffs, NJ: Prentice-Hall.

Bohannan, L. (1980). Shakespeare in the bush. *Annual editions: Anthropology 80/81* (pp. 44-49). Guilford, Ct: Dushkin.

Bowen, E. S. (1964). *Return to laughter: An anthropological novel*. Garden City, NJ: Doubleday.

Boyle, J. S., & Counts, M. M. (1988). Towards healthy aging: A theory for community health nursing. *Public Health Nursing, 5*(1), 45-51.

Burns, N., & Grove, S. K. (1987). *The practice of nursing research: Conduct, critique and utilization*. Philadelphia: W. B. Saunders.

Byerly, E. L. (1969). The nurse researcher as a participant-observer in a nursing setting. *Nursing Research, 18*(3), 230-236.

Counts, M. M., & Boyle, J. S. (1987). Nursing, health and policy within a community context. *Advances in Nursing Science, 9*(3), 12-23.

Crane, J., & Angrosino, M. V. (1974). *Field projects in anthropology: A student handbook*. Morristown: General Learning Press.

Diers, D. (1979). *Research in nursing practice*. Philadelphia: J. B. Lippincott.

QUALITATIVE NURSING RESEARCH

Edgerton, R. B., & Langness, L. L. (1974). *Methods and styles in the study of culture.* San Francisco: Chandler & Sharp.

Emerson, R. M. (1987). Four ways to improve the craft of fieldwork. *Journal of Contemporary Ethnography, 16*(1), 69-89.

Fagin, C. M. (1986). Institutionalizing faculty practice. *Nursing Outlook, 34,* 140-144.

Frake, C. O. (1969). The ethnographic study of cognitive systems. In S. A. Tyler (Eds.), *Cognitive anthropology* (pp. 28-41). New York: Holt, Rinehart & Winston.

Geer, B. (1969). First days in the field: A chronicle of research in progress. In G. J. McCall & J. L. Simmons (Eds.), *Issues in participant observation* (pp. 144-162), Reading, MA: Addison-Wesley.

Geertz, C. (1973). *The interpretation of culture.* New York: Basic Books.

Germain, C. P. H. (1979). *The cancer unit: An ethnography.* Wakefield, MA: Nursing Resources.

Glittenberg, J. E. (1981). An ethnographic approach to the problem of health assessment. In P. Morley (Ed.), *Developing, teaching and practicing transcultural nursing: Proceedings of the Sixth National Transcultural Nursing Conference* (pp. 143-153). Salt Lake City: The University of Utah College of Nursing and the Transcultural Nursing Society.

Hammersley, M., & Atkinson, P. (1983). *Ethnography: Principles in practice.* New York: Tavistock.

Hsu, F. L. K. (1969). *The study of literate civilizations.* New York: Holt, Rinehart & Winston.

Jordan, B. (1981). Studying childbirth: The experience and methods of a woman anthropologist. In S. Romalis (Ed.), *Alternatives to medical control* (pp. 181-216). Austin: University of Texas.

Kimball, S. T., & Partridge, W. L. (1979). *The craft of community study: Fieldwork dialogues* (Social Sciences Monograph No. 65). Gainesville: University of Florida.

Knafl, K. A., & Howard, M. J. (1984). Interpreting and reporting qualitative research. *Research in Nursing and Health, 7,* 17-24

Langness, L. L. V., & Frank, G. (1981). *Lives: An anthropological approach to biography.* Novato: Chandler & Sharp.

Leininger, M. M. (1970). *Nursing and anthropology: Two worlds to blend.* New York: John Wiley.

Leininger, M. M. (1985). *Qualitative research methods in nursing.* Orlando, FL: Grune & Stratton.

Lofland, J., & Lofland, L. H. (1984). *Analyzing social settings: A guide to qualitative observation and analysis.* Belmont, CA: Wadsworth.

Magilvy, J. K., McMahon, M., Bachman, M., Roark, S., & Evenson, C. (1987). The health of teenagers: A focused ethnographic study. *Public Health Nursing, 4*(1), 35-42.

McCall, G. J., & Simmons, J. L. (Eds.). (1969). *Issues in participant observation: A text and reader.* Mass.: Addison Wesley.

Mead, M. (1977). *Letters from the field 1925-1975.* New York: Harper.

Miller, S. M. (1969). The participant observer and over-rapport. In G. J. McCall and J. L. Simmons (Eds.), *Issues in participant observation: A text and reader* (pp. 87-88). Reading, MA: Addison-Wesley.

Mishler, E. G. (1979). Meaning in context: Is there any other kind? *Harvard Educational Review, 49*(1), 1-19.

Patton, M. Q. (1980). *Qualitative evaluation methods*. Beverly Hills: Sage.

Punch, M. (1986). *The politics and ethics of fieldwork*. Beverly Hills: Sage.

Roberson, M. H. B., & Boyle, J. S. (1984). Ethnography: Contributions to nursing research. *Journal of Advanced Nursing, 9,* 43-49.

Sandelowski, M. (1986). The problem of rigor in qualitative research. *Advances in Nursing Science, 8*(3), 27-37.

Schatzman, L., & Strauss, A. L. (1973). *Field research: Strategies for a natural sociology.* Englewood Cliffs, NJ: Prentice-Hall.

Schwartz, M. S., & Schwartz, C. G. (1969). Problems in participant observation. In G. J. McCall & J. L. Simmons (Eds.), *Issues in participant observation: A text and reader* (pp. 89 104). Reading, MA: Addison-Wesley.

Seidel, J. V., & Clark, J. (1983). *The ethnograph: A user's guide.* Boulder: University of Colorado Computer Center.

Smith, J. K., & Heshusius, L. (1986). Closing down the conversation: The end of the quantitative-qualitative debate among educational inquirers. *Educational Researcher, 151,* 4-12.

Spindler, G., & Spindler, L. (1970). Fieldwork among the Menomini. In G. Spindler (Ed.), *Being an anthropologist: Fieldwork in eleven cultures* (pp. 273-282). New York: Holt, Rinehart & Winston.

Spradley, J. P. (1979). *The ethnographic interview.* New York: Holt, Rinehart & Winston.

Swanson-Kauffman, K. M. (1986). A combined qualitative methodology for nursing research. *Advances in Nursing Science, 8*(3), 58-69.

van Willigen, J., & DeWalt, B. R. (1985). *Training manual in policy ethnography* (Special Publication No. 19). Washington, DC: American Anthropological Association.

Whyte, W. F. (1984). *Learning from the field: A guide from experience.* Beverly Hills: Sage.

Wilson, H. S. (1985). *Research in nursing.* Menlo Park, CA: Addison-Wesley.

Wright, L. M., & Leahey, M. (1984). *Nurses and families: A guide to family assessment and intervention.* Philadelphia: F. A. Davis.

Young, J. C. (1978). Illness categories and action strategies in a Tarascan town. *American Ethnologist, 5,* 81-97.

Young, J. C. (1980). A model of illness treatment decisions in a Tarascan town. *American ethnologist, 7,* 106-131.

Dialogue

On Teaching Qualitative Methods

BRINK: I find it much more difficult to teach qualitative methods than it is to teach quantitative. It's *very* difficult to teach qualitative.

HUTCHINSON: I think it is. But why do you say that?

BRINK: There are a lot of students out there who cannot think creatively. They are so concrete! They don't have that incredible flight of fantasy that is needed to be a good qualitative researcher. They don't have the ability to make connections. When they see two pieces of data, they say, "Oh, well, I've got two pieces of data! I've got that, and I've got that, and now what do I do?" It takes a truly creative person to make those incredible connections and to come up with theory.

MUNHALL: And nurses are often rewarded for being concrete thinkers! We expect them to do nursing!

17

Teaching Qualitative Research:
Perennial Problems and Possible Solutions

SALLY A. HUTCHINSON
RODMAN B. WEBB

If we take in our hand any volume . . . let us ask, does it contain
any abstract reasoning concerning quantity or number? Does it
contain any experimental reasoning concerning matter-of-fact in
existence? No. Commit it then to the flames: for it can contain
nothing but sophistry and delusion!

(Hume, 1777/1977)

Since David Hume wrote this in 1777, we have learned that it is not
always useful to reduce the social universe to numbers and that
human behavior does not always yield gracefully to postivistic ex-
perimentation. Sometimes we must employ qualitative rather than
quantitative research methods to study human behavior and social
reality. Nevertheless, there is still wisdom in Hume's dictum. The
worth of social research—whether it be qualitative or quantitative—
is still dependent on the quality of the abstract reasoning used to
make sense of research findings. Learning how to make sense of data
is perhaps the most challenging problem facing a student of qualitative research methods.

Bronowski (1956) asserts that all science, including social science,
is an effort to discover unity in the "wild variety of nature" (p. 16).
The goal, in Bronowski's view (1978), is to "take parts of the universe
that have not been connected hitherto and . . . show . . . them to be

connected" (p. 110). The discovery of order, of connection is difficult because the order hides itself in the apparent disarray of nature. "If it can be said to be there at all," Bronowski warns, "it is not there for the mere looking. There is no way of pointing a finger or camera at it; order must be discovered and, in a deep sense, it must be created" (p. 14). The construction of order is, in part, an act of what Bronowski (1956, p. 16) calls disciplined imagination, what Hume calls reason, and what Dewey (1939, p. 255) calls "speculative audacity." Ultimately, of course, the order that researchers construct and the connections they discover must square with and make sense of the reality under investigation. But, as has been said elsewhere, "It is through connection and order that predictability and intelligibility are discovered" (Ashton & Webb, 1986, p. 14).

This chapter discusses the difficulties encountered when teaching qualitative research courses to graduate students. One of the authors teaches in a college of nursing, and the other teaches in a college of education. The examples, however, will be limited to nursing.

The difficulties teachers of qualitative research methods face generally fall into three categories. The first set of problems has to do with research method: teaching students to gather data and begin analysis. The second set of problems has to do with the reasoning needed to analyze data: helping students to make sense of the information they have gathered or, to use Bronowski's language, how to find unity in variety. The third set of problems has to do with writing: helping students present their findings in a clear and logical manner. Data gathering, data analysis, and writing are all part of a single process in qualitative research, so the problems discussed separately in this chapter are in fact inseparable.

As teachers, we have sometimes felt the urge to follow Hume's advice and commit our students' work to the flames. Where reason should have prevailed, we sometimes have found only "sophistry and delusion." Lest our students read this and become discouraged, let us quickly add that often we have had the same pyrotechnic urges with our own work. We guard ourselves against delusion by submitting our research to others for review. We guard our students against delusion by monitoring their work at every stage of the research process. We spell out each step of a research method, offer examples from the work of others, share our own errors, and fill the air with cautionary tales.

We are hopeful that this chapter will begin a conversation among teachers and students of qualitative research methods courses about the problems we all encounter and the strategies we employ to overcome those problems. The clear identification of difficulties can make professors more helpful to their students and more effective in the classroom.

Data Gathering: Matters of Method

Teaching a Qualitative Research Methods Class

Doctoral students in the College of Nursing at the University of Florida are required to take one three-credit course in qualitative methods, though some take more. Master's degree students do not have the same requirements, but some students elect to take the qualitative methods course in preparation for their thesis work. The course meets one day a week for 16 weeks, and generally between 10 and 16 students register for the class. Students planning to do qualitative dissertations or theses are encouraged to do pilot studies in the class.

Seminar

The only requirement for the course is that each student complete a qualitative study by the end of the semester. The class is run as a seminar, but we do some didactic teaching, especially in the early stages of the course. Gradually, as students become involved in their own research, we do less teaching. Students present problems, and the class attempts to solve those problems through discussion. We believe the role of the teacher in a seminar is to be first among equals, guiding the discussion, raising salient issues, and helping students explore the logic of their work and overcome the research difficulties they encounter. The give-and-take of a seminar is vital and cannot be hurried. Students become remarkably helpful to one another; they offer multiple perspectives, prevent tunnel vision, and enhance creativity. Most students are refreshingly open about the dilemmas they face. They appreciate the help they get from their classmates and are relieved to know that the problems they confront and the anxieties they feel are experienced by others.

A successful seminar is not a quiz session, or a bull session, or a lecture in disguise. We try to make each seminar a disciplined exploration of the problems commonly faced in qualitative research. The class is designed to be an example of the very thing it tries to teach, reasoned inquiry. Students who have not had much seminar experience are sometimes uncomfortable in the seminar setting. They miss the security of lectures and are reluctant to participate. We work to lessen the anxiety of these students and to bring them into the conversation.

Seminar Topics

Each week the class examines another phase of the research process, and students are encouraged to discuss the research problems they are encountering in the field. The first few classes focus on developing a research interest, finding a site, gaining access and entry, dealing with role conflict and ethical issues, and getting the approval of the university's human subjects committee. The theoretical underpinnings of qualitative inquiry are introduced in the first week or two, but these issues are revisited again and again throughout the course. We spend two or three weeks discussing data gathering, qualitative sampling, how to take field notes, what typed protocols (finished field notes) look like, and how to conduct ethnographic interviews. Later classes deal with coding and domaining and how to use initial findings to direct further interviews and observations. We go on to discuss triangulation, questions of validity and reliability, taxonomic analysis, and how to look for cultural themes. Toward the end of the course, we discuss the criteria for evaluating qualitative research and writing a final report.

Course Sequence

We believe that a qualitative methods course should involve students in a research project and that most projects worth doing cannot be completed easily in one semester. Though we would like the methods class to be a two-semester course, we have not yet been able to squeeze another three-credit course into the graduate program of most nursing students. Therefore we occasionally give incompletes to students who are interested in doing a more thorough job. Because the amount of work required to understand, initiate, and execute a qualitative study is great, in 1990, the College of Nursing mandated a three-hour "Philosophical Foundations in Qualitative Research" course for doctoral students and for master's students doing a qualitative thesis. The methods course follows this philosophy course, and it is in the methods course that data collection and analysis are carried out. Students doing qualitative thesis/dissertations or those interested in "getting a feel" for qualitative research take the methods course. Continuing seminars are also offered to students who are working on their thesis/dissertations.

Some Perennial Issues

Class Size

Certain issues have arisen over the years, some of which we have answered for ourselves, and some of which we continue to ponder. For example, there is the issue of class size. Our experience is that we cannot teach effectively when there are more than 10 students in the class. When classes grow larger, we cannot carefully read the students' weekly accumulation of field notes. Without studying field notes, we do not lead class discussions as well and are not as effective in helping students learn to solve their research problems. Also, when the class is large, students worry about taking more than their share of class time, and discussion is stifled.

What Research Method or Methods Should be Taught?

Initially, we taught grounded theory in the course. Recently, however, we have introduced students to Spradley's ethnographic method because his textbooks (1979, 1980) offer a step-by-step method that our pupils find helpful. Students who are new to qualitative research or who have difficulty finding an order in the chaos are particularly drawn to Spradley's methods. The text brings students through the research process and allows them to do analytical or descriptive ethnographies. Those students doing theses or dissertations and those good at conceptualization often combine the two approaches, beginning with Spradley's domains and working into grounded theory coding and theory development (see Grieve, 1986; Wrigley & Hutchinson, 1990). Students interested in other qualitative approaches (e.g., phenomenological, historical, biographical, or philosophical inquiry) are referred to other professors or courses (Sherman & Webb, 1988).

Ongoing Assessment

Because of the cyclical nature of the qualitative research process, problems that occur at one phase of the inquiry inevitably affect other phases as well. For example, if students have irrelevant or unclear interview questions, their data will be unclear and their study badly flawed. Therefore we think it necessary to monitor each student's work at every stage of its development. We accomplish this task by requiring that students hand in their field notes and coding sheets each week and by encouraging them to discuss their work in class. Students are also assigned days on which they can bring material to class for discussion. Each student is required to bring a problem that the class can work on together and to supply material (e.g., short excerpts from field notes or interviews) the class will need in order to work on that problem (see Strauss, 1987, 1988).

Overcoming Student Resistance

Some students fall into a qualitative research course by accident and are surprised to learn how much work it entails. We try to counsel such students out of the class in the first week. Such students seldom benefit from the course and may make it less productive and enjoyable for others. Sometimes, however, we are late in discovering that a student is not involved in the course. Such students employ delaying and avoidance tactics that are not obvious at first. They may change and rechange the focus of their research, report difficulty getting into the setting, and suggest shortcuts. A month or two may pass without much evidence of progress. In the end, such students usually request an incomplete for the course, which they fail to make up.

Some students are quite involved in their research, but resist guidance from the instructor or fellow students. We do not insist that students take our advice, believing that pupils learn as much from mistakes as they do from successes. However, we try not to let students make errors of such magnitude that the success of their projects is threatened.

Length Requirements

We assiduously avoid quantitative requirements and do not assign a specific number of fieldnote pages, a specific number of observation hours, or a specific length for the final report. However, providing a few guidelines helps students understand how much time and effort qualitative research requires. We now suggest that in-depth interviews last an hour; that complete transcripts be required for each interview; that at least 10 informants be interviewed in the course of a semester; that, when appropriate, interviews should be augmented by observations; and that 75% of the final paper should be devoted to data analysis. Concrete requirements decrease ambiguity and make the grading process easier.

Problems at Various Stages in the Research Cycle

Problems crop up at various stages of the research cycle that plague students and seasoned researchers alike. We think it is a teacher's responsibility to alert students to the problems common at each phase of the research and to help pupils overcome these difficulties so they can move on to the next phase in the research process.

Unclear Questions

Students who choose a poor setting and/or a poor topic invariably produce poor research. We have learned that time spent at the start of the course helping students choose a good site and an interesting question saves headaches later on. Some students want to study questions that are not appropriate for qualitative inquiry (i.e., "Is drug X or drug Y more effective in bringing down the temperature of postoperative patients?"); others ask questions that are too ambitious for a one-semester study (i.e., "How are Veterans Administration Hospitals different from for-profit hospitals?"); and still others ask questions that are too vague (i.e., "What are the qualities of a good nurse?"). We have come to the conclusion that it is unfair to let students work long and hard on a project that has little chance of amounting to much at the end. Some examples of clear questions that resulted in good reports include: "How do young male spinal-cord injury patients cope with their disabilities?", "What are a mother's experiences in having a premature baby in the neonatal intensive care unit?", and "What are the stages in the foster-parenting of abused children?"

Bias and Role Conflict

Students sometimes want to study an area in which they have a strong emotional investment. Such an investment may increase student motivation, but it can also lead to bias. We have found that other students sometimes recognize the signs of over-commitment and role conflict as fast or faster than we do. If given the opportunity, students will guide classmates away from subjects or sites an individual cannot study objectively. The professor who fails to detect role conflict must spend a great deal of time, in and out of class, helping students first to recognize and then to compensate for their biases. Steering such students away from problem topics early in the semester provides more time to help them with other aspects of their research.

Role conflicts can be avoided if the class thinks through the research problem of each student early in the semester. Sometimes it helps if a student is given a chance to experience role conflict for him- or herself. For example, a student who worked in the coronary care unit (CCU) wanted to study families' experiences in the CCU waiting room. He planned to finish his shift and then enter the waiting room to observe and interview families. The instructor and the class foresaw problems with role conflict, but the student was adamant. The instructor suggested a quick feasibility study. During his first hour in the waiting room, he was approached by a patient's husband, who complained about another nurse and about the care his wife was receiving. The student, feeling overwhelmed and in a bind, recognized the problem of role conflict and decided to conduct his study at another hospital.

Sometimes, what the research students propose has great relevance to them, but it has little relevance to the people being studied. For example, a student wanted to study how patients feel while undergoing radiation therapy. Several interviews revealed that the patients in her sample were coping with the larger problem of cancer; the experience of radiation therapy, by itself, was not particularly significant. In cases like this, students are advised to try different interview strategies to see whether another approach or different questions might elicit richer information from informants. When that fails, we suggest that students pursue the patient's concerns and, if necessary, adjust the focus of their research.

Researcher bias is often revealed by the tenacity with which a student holds on to a research interest that elicits thin data. For example, one student wanted to investigate how nurses felt about helping patients with what she called "their spiritual needs." The topic was promising, and the class helped generate a list of interview questions. Respondents answered the questions readily, but their answers did not square with what the student thought they should be saying. She continually rewrote her questions and resisted her classmates' contention that she was getting rich data because it was not what she wanted to hear. Frustrated, the student finally switched to another topic.

Reviewing the Literature

Because qualitative research may be used to generate substantive theory, it is not always possible or appropriate to use an existing theory to guide each phase of the research. Of course, some studies lend themselves to an existing theory. In such cases, students are directed to the appropriate literature early in the course and advised to read widely. This practice presents a number of problems, however, the greatest being time. The course is already demanding, and additional assignments make a taxing class even more difficult.

Students who plan a qualitative thesis or dissertation understand they eventually need to complete a thorough literature review for their proposals, and therefore, they encourage us to spend class time discussing the elements of a good literature review. We will not repeat that discussion here, but a few points are worth noting. Students read and evaluate good literature reviews. In class discussions, we dispel the misconception that a literature review is merely a listing of every study ever done on a particular subject. A good literature review is critical; it makes sense of the literature and organizes that literature in a way that clarifies the problem the student plans to study. The student must make clear the relevance of the problem, what is presently known about the problem, and what waits to be discovered.

During the end of the data analysis phase, students read literature relevant to their findings, and this literature is often different from that described in the proposal. In the writing-up phase, literature is integrated with the findings. Occasionally, findings are compatible (or contradictory) with existing theories, and presenting this correspondence is essential to a good study. One student (Grieve, 1986) studied how nurses cope with caring for nonviable patients in an intensive care unit (ICU). She reviewed literature on stress in ICUs, nurse coping strategies, cognitive dissonance, defense mechanisms, and the social construction of reality. Her data analysis produced a model that explained what nurses did in the setting under study. Nurses experienced dissonance which led to *Pretending* (acting as if the patients were not going to die) and, later, to *Separating* (mentally withdrawing from the nonviable patient), *Creating a New Reality* (restricting their work to give it meaning and purpose), and *Setting New Attainable Goals*. She began her study with a broad literature review, set out her own model, supported it with data from her research, and related the model to the theories discussed in the literature review. Of course, weaving together complex theoretical literature and study findings in a way that is clear and compelling is difficult. We will discuss the problems of writing presently.

Sampling

Sampling raises pithy issues, especially if students are doing participant observation studies. Students should consider the group being investigated and question the extent to which it is representative of a larger population. If one wants to study how nurses in a hospital evaluate a particular program, it makes sense to interview all the nurses in the hospital. If that is impossible, it makes sense to interview a representative sample of the total population (see Morse, this volume). Purposive samples require the researcher to make decisions in choosing informants who have knowledge relevant to the research question, are willing to talk, and represent the variety of people in the setting, for example, old and young nurses, white and black nurses, new and experienced nurses, and nurses with different levels of education. Sampling approaches should be discussed in class. However, even after due care is taken, most qualitative studies do not report statistically representative findings, nor are they designed to do so. Their aim is to make meaning (understanding) of the phenomena under study. Qualitative studies can be very useful, but they should not pretend to be what they are not. Students must clearly spell out the limitations of their work and not obfuscate those limitations behind a barrage of meaningless numbers, as some researchers do when they report demographic information in order to leave the impression that their findings are generalizable to a larger group (e.g., "There were 15 participants in my study; 5 are black, 9 are white, 1 is Hispanic. They range in age from 20 to 50 and have X and Y levels of education.") Demographic information is interesting, even useful, but it should not be provided under the pretense of statistical sampling.

We impress upon students that qualitative research is not a substitute for quantitative inquiry; the two modes of research are not in competition. The research method a student chooses should be governed by the question under study. Some questions will yield to quantitative inquiry, some to qualitative inquiry. Sometimes the two can be combined. One great strength of qualitative work is that it produces grounded hypotheses that then can be studied quantitatively. Students doing qualitative research need not imitate the rituals of quantitative inquiry and should not pretend that their findings provide the last word on the subject under study.

Data Recording

Data recording problems are easily discovered during a weekly review of field notes. Therefore, at the start of each class, we ask students to hand in a photocopy of work completed during the week. We require that protocols be typed, that codes be substituted for names, and that appropriate information be coded at the top of the first page of each protocol. A four-inch left-hand margin gives students space for notes and us a place to write comments.

Interviewing

Generating useful interview questions with appropriate content and structure takes time and thought. Students find it helpful to think through and try out questions in class. Demonstrating the correspondence between the research questions and the purpose of the research is vital. We have learned to give a lot of attention to interview questions because, occasionally, we have received papers in which interview questions were peripheral to the research question, and as a consequence, the findings were irrelevant.

The phrasing and wording of all questions must be examined to ensure that they are nonjudgmental, unbiased, and open-ended. It is also useful to look at the questions as a group and ask: Do they move from general to specific? Do questions follow a logical sequence? Are there too many or too few questions? Do they cover the topic thoroughly?

It is difficult to teach students to be good listeners, to probe, and to adjust questions to fit the situation at hand. Role playing is often helpful. Good interviewers can demonstrate their interviewing technique, and students can try out their questions on other students before venturing into the field. After one or two field interviews, we ask students to examine what questions were best and why, and what questions did not work and why they failed. The exercise helps students come up with new and better questions. For example, one student was studying why women did not get prenatal care. She discovered that although the women she interviewed did not receive the medical/nursing community's idea of prenatal care, they were receiving other forms of care. In her initial interview schedule, she asked about medical care, and respondents were unresponsive and somewhat defensive. But when she changed her first question to read, "Tell me about the kinds of care you get while you are pregnant," respondents provided a rich store of information. The student found that the women she interviewed, though uninformed in some areas, were not unmotivated, lazy, or uninvolved in their own pregnancies. Instead, each mother committed much thought and energy to caring for herself and her unborn child.

Participant Observation

Because of time limitations in the course, most students choose to do interview studies. Students doing dissertation work, however, are more likely to do participant observation studies. The problems of gaining access, becoming familiar with the scene, getting to know the roles being played and the people who play them, sorting out what to ignore and what to investigate, finding key informants, overcoming feelings of uncertainty, dealing with role conflict, and the myriad of other problems take a great deal of time and skill. One student spent time in a group residence for the elderly and suffered tremendous anxiety as she struggled to understand what was going on before her. The facility was part of a complex organization, many residents were confused or withdrawn, and the staff members were busy and reluctant to talk. Learning how to observe, when to talk, whom to talk to, and when to leave was a complex and time-consuming undertaking. Therefore we suggest that students doing one-semester studies enter somewhat familiar settings, that they set aside the time needed to complete the study, and that their foreshadowed questions be clear and relatively narrow.

Document Analysis

Documents offer additional "slices of data" (Glaser, 1978) that researchers may find invaluable. Students decide what documents, if any, are appropriate to their study question. Examples may include patient records, organizational charts, and incident reports. One student, studying pregnant teenagers, read diaries the girls offered to her. Document analysis may confirm, extend, or contradict other findings.

Anxiety

Qualitative research produces anxiety in students at every step in the process. Students are anxious about finding a problem and gaining entry. Once they have a problem and a research site, they are anxious about interviewing and taking field notes. No sooner do they begin to get comfortable in these activities than they must face the anxiety of data analysis. And, at the end, they must produce a paper spelling out their findings. Students who have become comfortable in the field often become fascinated by what they are doing and resist moving on to the next stage of research. No one wants to trade a hard-won sense of security for a new round of anxiety. Yet, students must do just that if they are to master the methods of qualitative research. At each stage in the process, they must let go of security and, once again, set out into the unknown.

We have not discovered a way to free students from anxiety, nor have we found a way to free ourselves from those feelings in our own research. Uncertainty comes with the qualitative territory. Nevertheless, students need to talk about their anxieties because class discussions help them understand they are not the only ones experiencing uncertainty. Such discussions also keep students aware of their accomplishments. When students say they are not sure that they are able to do a rigorous analysis of data, we remind them that a few weeks earlier they were not sure they could find a question, choose a site, do interviews, or produce useful field notes.

Data Analysis: Nurturing Imagination

The imagination, being not tied to the laws of matter, may at
pleasure join that which nature hath severed and sever that which
nature hath joined, and so make unlawful matches and divorces of
things.

(Bacon, 1605/1975)

Spradley (1979, 1980) clearly spells out the steps in data analysis, as do Chenitz and Swanson (1986), Field and Morse (1985), Glaser (1978), Munhall and Oiler (1986), Strauss (1987), and numerous others. Their methods are complex and varied and cannot be detailed here. However, for the purposes of this chapter, we are less interested in the details of method than in the imagination needed to apply the method and make sense of the data or, to return to Bronowski's (1978) sentiment, to find order in its chaos.

Bronowski (1956) claims science progresses when unity is found in variety. But the search for unity entails a disciplined use of imagination. He points out that Newton made a daring imaginative leap when he hypothesized the dropping of an apple and the flight of the moon around the earth were "two expressions of a single concept, gravitation. Faraday did [the same] when he closed the link between electricity and magnetism. Clark Maxwell did [a similar leap] when he linked both with light" (p. 15). Science is made possible by the workings of the human imagination. Of course, Bacon had good reason to warn against unbounded imagination. People can, and often do, impose unity where, in fact, none exists.

But Bronowski's point is that imagination is merely the gateway to science, not science itself. Imagination allows us to hypothesize connections that must then be tested against available data. What made Newton, Faraday, and Maxwell spectacular scientists was their ability to propose imaginative insights and then, through reason, find ways to test them.

We discuss the importance of imagination because students often believe that connections and unities mysteriously "emerge from qualitative data"; that the data somehow speak for themselves. Data do nothing of the sort. We must go looking for unity and organize our data so that patterns are easier to see. Continually working with the data helps us speculate about possible connections and then put our speculations to the test. We go through the steps of analysis not because the steps "produce" findings but because they help us imagine what the findings might be. The analysis process helps us to have hunches and to take those hunches back to the data to see whether they hold up.

We are not sure that we can teach people to be imaginative or to reason carefully, but we can encourage students to work with speculative audacity and, using reason, to test their imaginative insights against the data. The analysis process entails working with the data. That process is dialectical and imaginative, not linear or mechanical. Students find it helpful to bring a few pages of field notes to class where the group can work together on coding and analysis. Of course, the class can only begin the analysis process. but the experience of working together can start students off in the right direction or help them over a difficult stumbling block.

Many students find that reading books and articles is another way to spark the imagination. For example, a student who was studying rescue workers spent her free time reading novels and newspaper stories and watching TV shows about medics and rescue squads. A student studying pregnant teenagers read magazine stories, romanic novels, and teenagers' diaries that dealt with the topic. Another student, who was studying the use of humor in hospital settings, copied the cartoons nurses hung on the walls of their offices and work areas. Such documents offer ideas and insights and spark the student's imagination. The use of collateral materials by Goffman (1959, 1961) reveals his creative connections. Reading his footnotes is a delightful excursion into his thinking.

Writing the Report

Matters of Perspective, Focus, and Organization

We have come to the conclusion that, in most cases, unclear writing reveals unclear thinking. Thus whenever problems go undetected in the early stages of a student's research, we can be sure that the difficulties will reveal themselves again in the final report as bad writing. Thus when we work to help students form good research topics, produce rich data, and do a careful analysis, we are doing a lot to help them write a clear and coherent final report. Nevertheless, certain problems plague all beginning researchers.

Determining the Kind of Report to be Written

One-semester courses make it difficult for any student to come away from a site with a complete understanding of what is going on there. Therefore students need to determine the kind of report they will write before they start writing. Their decision should be based on the data they have collected and the extent of their analysis. Some students produce descriptive studies, in which they discuss the patterns they found in human behavior. Others, usually doctoral students, generate conceptual models. Unusual students may produce full ethnographies (those that provide a cultural analysis and have explanatory power), especially if they continue working with their data after the semester has ended. In any case, students benefit from discussing the kind of ethnography they plan to produce before they sit down to write.

Perspective

Many students lose track of whose perspectives they are studying. For example, a student may investigate children's experience of long-term hospitalization and, in the course of the study, interview young patients, their parents, and hospital nurses. However, in the process of analysis the student may make the mistake of treating all data as if they accurately depicted the perspectives of children. Parents' comments and nurses' reports may be coded as if they are children's descriptions of their own experiences. Such problems are difficult for the instructor to detect, and for that reason, we encourage students to hand in some of their preliminary coding sheets. If we miss the problem at that point, it is likely to show itself in the final report. When students lose track of the perspective they are reporting, their writing becomes disorganized, and the experiences of one group are tangled into a discussion of other groups.

Focus

Writing also becomes tangled when there is little continuity between the research question and reported analysis of data. For example, one student said early in the course that he was studying nurse-physician interaction, and he began his paper with reference to that issue. However, the paper really focused on administrative policy and nurses' beliefs about how medical decisions were affected by administrative policies. The problem of lost focus occurs most often when we do not closely monitor every step of the process.

Naming the Codes, Domains, and Themes

Naming categories of data is tricky and requires close attention to detail. Students who have a broad knowledge of relevant literature are sometimes at an advantage. However, there is a tendency in beginning students not to call things what they are (suffering, copping out) and to inappropriately import language from nursing and the social sciences (defensive avoidance, dogmatism). When good categories of data are misnamed, students find it difficult to write clearly. Some students recognize that their writing is confused and repeatedly attempt to rewrite their work. The problem, however, does not reside in the writing, but in the naming of categories. Our role as instructors is to bring students back to the data and to remind them that the best words and the best codes are those that describe what is actually going on. We also remind students that speaking the professional dialect of social science does not make them social scientists and that often social science jargon adds more clutter than clarity.

Once a code is named, it must be described, but students sometimes fail to adequately define their terms and describe their codes. We spend a good deal of class time discussing codes and looking at examples of code descriptions. Some students are able to go beyond description and tie their codes or categories to the theoretical literature. Everything we have said about codes also pertains to the concepts that are used to connect codes and give the ethnography its unity and theme.

Good code and category descriptions are usually followed by illustrative vignettes from the data. Such examples not only stand as evidence for the claim being made but help clarify the claim and lend interest to the ethnography. Choosing relevant illustrative examples takes time and thought. Irrelevant and unclear examples are all too common. Students must continually ask themselves, "Does this example best illustrate this code?" The examples should illustrate the specific code or concept under discussion and usually should not be cluttered with data relevant to other domains or themes.

Levels of Analysis

Students often confuse levels of analysis, and that confusion shows up in their final reports. We suggest that students move from micro-codes up to macro-concepts because the macro-theories derive from micro-data. Students benefit greatly from a critical analysis of good and poor qualitative research, but unfortunately, the course does not provide the time needed for such an examination.

Students need help analyzing the levels of codes and distinguishing between those that are descriptive and those that are theoretical. If different coding levels are used, the researcher needs to make this clear to the reader. One student studied "home schoolers" (children who are taught by their mothers at home) and used the theoretical code "dissonance" to describe why parents withdrew their children from public school. A major descriptive domain was "advantages of home schooling." The student treated the descriptive code as if it were theoretical and, in the process, confused her readers. When the class members pointed out their confusion, the student was able to rework the paper and make it clearer.

Tone and Style

Occasionally, students write reports in the terse, minimalist language characteristic of (but not always appropriate for) quantitative research. They forget that they are dealing with human situations that demand description and elaboration, and, consequently, their reports are flat and do not allow the reader to understand the people studied or their motives. To combat this problem, we encourage students to make good use of quotes and data from field notes. In most instances, such data will make points more successfully than anything the student may write.

Some students make the mistake of merely stating their conclusions without elaboration, sufficient use of data, or evidence of analysis. These reports appear erroneous, simplistic, and boring. These writers need a lot of help thinking through ideas. Even with help, however, an occasional student does not get the message and turns in an eight-page paper or writes short lists under categories and fails to expand ideas in a descriptive narrative.

Providing Direction for the Reader

Two major difficulties during the write-up phase include absence of road maps and lack of appropriate subheadings. By "road maps" we mean the effort to let the reader know from the start where the paper is going. Of course, students who are not sure where they are going cannot provide such road maps. A good paper tells the reader what is being studied and how it will be presented . The reader also needs to be signaled when the paper changes direction, new topics are being introduced, and connections are being drawn between data from two parts of the paper. Generally, a few well placed sentences work miracles; "X is a phase of a multi-phenomenon we call Y. The phases in Y are interactive and do not always follow in the order presented here. After a discussion of each phase, its salient properties will be discussed."

We advise students to use vignettes from their data. However, they must make clear what point the vignette is meant to illustrate. It is also necessary to be sure the reader has the background information needed to make sense of the vignette. For example, "The following excerpt from field notes provides a number of examples of denial behavior among drug-using nurses. The nurses quoted below were taking part in a drug rehabilitation program and were all recovering abusers. The topic of denial was introduced by Betty, a 27-year-old nurse who was, and still is, working in an intensive care unit."

Headings and Subheadings

Students do not always make good use of headings and sub-headings. The reason for this is probably that they do not write from an outline and do not go back over what they have written with the express purpose of providing headings and subheadings. Separate headings are a useful practice in defining categories or theoretical constructs. They orient the reader and give order to an often-complex narrative. We suggest that there should be a heading or subheading every few pages in the final report. When inserting headings, it is useful if students ask themselves. "What is this? What is an example of it? How does it fit? Where is it going?" Subheadings aid the conceptualization process and serve to emphasize major points. They also serve as signposts, orient the readers, and remind them of the paper's road map. Having students draw and redraw road maps helps in the data analysis and in generating headings and subheadings.

Conclusions

We have discussed both the problems students face in doing qualitative studies and the steps we take to help students overcome those problems. It is through an analysis of the "problems" that we are able to alter our teaching strategies in an attempt to generate "solutions." By focusing on problems, we may have left the impression that students in our classes are reluctant learners, that they do not enjoy qualitative inquiry, that they cannot manage all that is asked of them, and that they do not produce impressive research. Nothing could be further from the truth. We are continually thrilled by and amazed at the quality of student work. We are energized by our students' enthusiasm and by the indefatigable effort they put into their studies.

We have discussed some concrete teaching methods we employ in our classes and have described what we have done to help students solve common problems encountered in the course of qualitative inquiry. Implicit in our discussion are the criteria we hold for judging the quality of qualitative research. Of course, other criteria of quality would suggest other teaching methods. We make no claim that our methods are best or that our criteria are complete.

However, the continued discussion of these matters should help all of us improve what we offer students.

References

Ashton, P., & Webb, R. (1986). *Making a difference: Teachers' sense of efficacy and student achievement.* New York: Longman.

Bacon, F. (1975). *Advancement of learning.* Atlantic Highlands, NJ: Humanities Press.

Bronowski, J. (1956). *Science and human values.* New York: Harper & Row.

Bronowski, J. (1978). *The origin of knowledge and imagination.* New Haven, CT: Yale University Press.

Chenitz, W., & Swanson, J. (1986). *From practice to grounded theory: Qualitative research in nursing.* Menlo Park, CA: Addison-Wesley.

Dewey, J. (1939). The meanings of philosophy. In J. Ratner (Ed.). *Intelligence in the modern world.* New York: Modern Library.

Field, P., & Morse, J. (1985). *Nursing research: The application of qualitative approaches.* Rockville, MD: Aspen.

Glaser, B. (1978). *Theoretical sensitivity.* Mill Valley, CA: Sociology Press.

Goffman, E. (1959). *The presentation of self in everyday life.* Garden City, NY: Doubleday.

Goffman, E. (1961). *Asylums: Essays on the social situation of mental patients and other inmates.* Garden City, NY: Anchor.

Grieve, L. (1986). *Pretending: How intensive care nurses care for nonviable patients.* Unpublished master's thesis, University of Florida, College of Nursing, Gainesville.

Hume, D. (1777/1977). *An enquiry concerning human understanding: A letter from a gentleman to his friend in Edinburgh.* Indianapolis: Hackett.

Munhall, P., & Oiler, C. (1986). *Nursing research: A qualitative perspective.* Norwalk, CT: Appleton-Century-Crofts.

Sherman, R., & Webb, R. (1988). *Qualitative research in education: Focus and method.* London: Falmer Press.

Spradley, J. (1979). *The ethnographic interview.* New York: Holt, Rinehart & Winston.

Spradley, J. (1980). *Participant observation.* New York: Holt, Rinehart & Winston.

Strauss, A. (1987). *Qualitative analysis for social scientists.* New York: Cambridge University Press.

Strauss, A. (1988). Teaching qualitative research methods courses: A conversation with Anselm Strauss. *The International Journal of Qualitative Studies in Education, 1,* 91-99.

Wrigley, E., & Hutchinson, S. (1990). Long term breastfeeding: The secret bond. *Journal of Nurse-Midwifery, 35*(1), 35-41.

Dialogue

The Last Word

BRINK: If you could foresee 75 years from now and you knew that you were going to be alive and doing research—What kind of research would you like to be doing?

ANDERSON: Well, in terms of phenomenology, I don't think we have even scratched the surface! I think there is a lifetime of work there. And I am developing my skill and keep getting more insights. I go back to the data I gathered last year and I see a whole new range of things, totally new things! As I mature as a researcher, I gain new abilities to increase the richness of my analysis. So what I would like to do in the future is to increase my analytic skills and add more richness to my data, rather than to say this is to progress to a different level.

STERN: This has been so much fun, we must do it again. We could sell tickets!

Author Index

Subject Index

About the Authors

Agnes M. Aamodt, RN, MA, PhD, is Professor Emerita, the College of Nursing, University of Arizona. She is a nurse and anthropologist who writes, talks about, and conducts research on the generation of primitive conceptualizations on care using the field methods of ethnography. Her educational background consists of a Baccalaureate in Nursing, College of St. Scholastica; a Master of Arts in Child Development, the University of Minnesota; and a Doctor of Philosophy in Anthropology, the University of Washington. Her educational background prepared her to be a practicing nurse, clinical teacher, and clinical nurse researcher. She conducted her work in Chicago, the U.S. Army, Minneapolis, Denver, Tucson, and Seattle. The Tohono O'odhjam Reservation, Norwegian communities in western Wisconsin, and a pediatric oncology clinic served as field settings for her research on the child's view of health and healing, Norwegian women and care, and the child's view of care during chemotherapy. Recently, she was awarded the Distinguished Lectureship Award from the Western Institute of Nursing.

Joan M. Anderson, RN, PhD, is Professor at the University of British Columbia School of Nursing, and a Canada Health and Welfare National Health Research Scholar. She has done research in the areas of chronic illness, and migration and health, with a special focus on immigrant women, work, and health.

Vangie Bergum, RN, PhD, is Associate Professor, Faculty of Nursing and Associate in Ethics, Joint-Faculties Bioethics Project, University of Alberta. Recent publications include *Woman to Mother: A*

Transformation, a book resulting from her phenomenological research with women during and following pregnancy. Further research continues in this area with the additional focus on ethical questions in women's health care, especially in the area of new reproductive technologies. Her teaching focus is on ethics in health care and nursing, and health teaching, both at the graduate and undergraduate level. She serves as a reviewer for a number of nursing journals and is dissertation editor for *Phenomenology and Pedagogy: A Human Science Journal*.

Joyceen S. Boyle, RN, PhD, is Chair of the Department of Community Nursing at the Medical College of Georgia, Augusta. A graduate of Brigham Young School of Nursing, she holds a Master's degree in Public Health Nursing from the University of California at Berkeley and a PhD in Nursing from the University of Utah. As a certified Transcultural nurse, she has published numerous articles on culture, health, and nursing care. She is co-editor of a text entitled *Transcultural Nursing Concepts in Nursing Care*. Her clinical and teaching experiences include community health nursing with diverse cultures. She has completed numerous field studies in Guatemala, The People's Republic of China, and in Appalachia in the United States. Her current research focuses on health promotion in high-risk, low-income populations.

Bonnie J. Breitmayer, MS, PhD, is Assistant Professor of Psychiatric Nursing at the University of Illinois at Chicago. She received her MS in Psychiatric Nursing from the University of California at San Francisco and her PhD in Developmental Psychology from Cornell University. She is interested in children at developmental risk and has published research on risk and resilience factors among socioeconomically disadvantaged children. Currently she is studying children with chronic illness and their families.

Pamela J. Brink, RN, PhD, FAAN, received her BS (Nursing) from Mount St. Mary's College in Los Angeles; her MSN in Psychiatric Nursing from The Catholic University of America in Washington, DC; and her PhD in Cultural Anthropology from Boston University. She has conducted research among the Northern Paiute Indians of Nevada, mountaineers of southeastern Kentucky, and the Annang of

Nigeria. She has published articles describing this research, as well as on heroin addicts and the characteristics of successful students. Her current research involves the characteristics of successful dieters. She has published three books: *Transcultural Nursing* (1976/1990) and two on research with Marilynn J. Wood, titled *Basic Steps in Planning Nursing Research* and *Advanced Design in Nursing Research*. She is currently Professor and Associate Dean, Research, Faculty of Nursing, University of Alberta, Edmonton, Alberta, Canada.

Marlene Zichi Cohen, RN, PhD, is Assistant Professor at The University of Iowa, College of Nursing. She obtained an MS in Psychiatric-Mental Health Nursing and a PhD in Clinical Nursing Research from the University of Michigan. Her research focuses on the patient's experience of illness and hospitalization, using phenomenological methods.

Janet A. Deatrick, RN, PhD, received her PhD in Nursing from the University of Illinois in Chicago. She is currently Assistant Professor and Program Director, Nursing of Children Division, University of Pennsylvania School of Nursing in Philadelphia, Pennsylvania. Her work and interest in the family began as a staff nurse in pediatric nursing and was cultivated during her master's and doctoral studies. Her special interest is the day-to-day work involved in the care of children with chronic conditions and the contribution of qualitative research to an understanding of that phenomenon.

Sandra A. Faux, RN, PhD, is Associate Professor and Coordinator, Graduate Program, Faculty of Nursing, University of Western Ontario. She previously taught undergraduate and graduate students in pediatric nursing at the University of Illinois at Chicago and the University of Maryland, Baltimore. She obtained an MN in Pediatric Nursing at the University of Pittsburgh and a PhD in Nursing from the University of Illinois in Chicago. Her doctoral research involved a grounded theory study of siblings and mothers of children with craniofacial and cardiac defects. Her current research studies (using qualitative and quantitative methods) focus on how chronically ill children and their families (parents, siblings) manage the illness and the perceptions of siblings of children experiencing chronic pain.

Peggy Anne Field, RN, PhD, is Professor and Nurse-Midwife at the University of Alberta, Edmonton, Canada. She earned an MN from the University of Washington and a PhD from the University of Alberta. She has used qualitative methods to examine the birthing experience, breastfeeding, and public health nursing. Internationally acclaimed as a research consultant and lecturer, she has published extensively on women's health, and coauthored *Nursing Research: A Qualitative Approach* with Janice Morse.

Sally A. Hutchinson, RN, PhD, FAAN, is Professor at the University of Florida, College of Nursing, where she teaches master's and doctoral courses in research methods and cultural influences in nursing care. Her research interests lie in several diverse areas: nurses, their work, and family caregivers of Alzheimer's Dementia patients. In her research, she uses qualitative methods because they provide access to human experience. She is on the editorial boards of *Image, Nursing Research, Western Journal of Nursing Research,* and *Advances in Nursing Science.* She coauthored the book *Applying Nursing Research: A Resource Book* with Dr. Holly Wilson and has written numerous chapters in books and articles in research journals. She has been a co-leader of Professional Seminar Consultants trips to China, East Africa, Australia/New Zealand, and Scandinavia.

Kathleen A. Knafl, PhD, received her Doctorate of Philosophy in Sociology from the University of Illinois at Chicago. She is Professor in the Department of Psychiatric Nursing and Associate Dean for Research at the University of Illinois College of Nursing. Her research interests focus on family response to illness and disability. Currently, she is principal investigator on a study entitled "How Families Define and Manage a Child's Chronic Illness," which is funded by the National Center for Nursing Research.

Juliene G. Lipson, RN, PhD, FAAN, is Associate Professor in the Department of Mental Health, Community, and Administrative Nursing at the University of California, San Francisco. A nurse-anthropologist, she is coordinator of the International/Cross-cultural Master's specialty in nursing and is on the faculty of the doctoral program in Medical Anthropology. She is codirector of the Mid-East S.I.H.A. Project, a health resource center for Middle Eastern immigrants. Her ethnographic-style research has focused on birth-related women's self-help/support groups and the health of Iranian and Arab immigrants and Afghan refugees.

Katharyn Antle May, DNSc, RN, FAAN, is Associate Professor and Chair, Department of Family and Health Systems, Nursing at Vanderbilt University, Nashville, Tennessee. Prior to her current position, she was on the faculty at UCSF School of Nursing. Dr. May has focused her research on psychosocial adaptation in the childbearing family, beginning with her dissertation research on the social psychological experience of first-time expectant fatherhood. This and other studies related to fatherhood, including an exploratory study of fathers' responses to unexpected caesarean birth, have gained her media attention, including appearances on *PM Magazine* and *The Today Show* and in numerous newspaper and magazine articles. From 1984 to 1987, Dr. May was a coinvestigator in an NIH-funded study of the impact of antenatal stress on maternal, paternal, infant, and family outcomes in the first year after birth. At present, she is directing a three-year project funded by NIH to examine the impact of prescribed home-management of preterm labor on families. She is recognized as an expert in the grounded theory method, and she serves as a methodological consultant on several research projects. She has published a major textbook on maternity nursing and numerous original articles in journals within and outside nursing. She has served on the editorial boards of *Journal of Perinatal and Neonatal Nursing, JOGNN* and *Health Care for Women International,* and is an Associate Editor for *Qualitative Health Research.*

Janice M. Morse, RN, PhD, is Professor of Nursing and an Adjunct Professor in the Department of Family Studies and an NHRDP/MRC Research Scholar at the University of Alberta, and an Adjunct Professor at the University of Northern Arizona. With doctorates in both nursing and anthropology, her research interests focus on the experience of illness, in particular in the area of patient care and comfort. She has completed research on the topic of patient falls, infant feeding, childbirth, and cross-cultural health and has conducted fieldwork in Fiji. She has published more than 100 articles, has authored and coauthored several books, and is the editor of the journal, *Qualitative Health Research.*

Patricia L. Munhall, RN, EdD, FAAN, is Professor at Hunter College School of Nursing, New York. She is also an Adjunct Visiting Professor in the Doctoral Program at Teachers' College, Columbia University, New York. She has presented and published widely in the area of qualitative research methods, and coauthored a book titled *Nursing Research: A Qualitative Perspective.*

Phyllis Noerager Stern, DNS, RN, FAAN, holds an international reputation for research concerning family survival strategies in extreme situations. She has focused on stepfather families, immigrant families, and families who belong to other than mainstream culture. Other research concerns women, health, and culture, and how nurses do their work. She is widely known for her descriptions of the grounded theory method of research. Beginning in 1980 with her seminal article in *Image: The Journal of Nursing Scholarship,* her clearly written articles and chapters have made available to the researcher the nuances of the method. She is editor of the interdisciplinary journal, *Health Care for Women International,* and first Council General of the International Council on Women's Health Issues.

Judith A. Strasser, RN, MS, DNSc, received her BS in Nursing, Villanova University; MS in Community Health Nursing, University of Maryland; and DNSc in Nursing (minor in Anthropology), the Catholic University of America. She has conducted research in the area of women and homelessness, doctorally prepared academic nurses and quantitative-qualitative research issues, new-age nurses, and forgiveness and health. Current interests are in the area of conflict resolution and meditation, community studies and the use of "weasel words" in nursing documentation.

Toni Tripp-Reimer, RN, PhD, FAAN, is Professor and Director, Office for Nursing Research Development and Utilization, College of Nursing, The University of Iowa. She received her MS in Nursing and an MA and PhD in Anthropology from The Ohio State University. Her research interests lie in the area of culture and health, and she has conducted numerous research projects with urban Greek immigrants, Vietnamese refugees, the Appalachians, and the Iowa Old Order Amish. She has published numerous articles and books and serves on the editorial boards of several journals, including the *Western Journal of Nursing Research* and *Qualitative Health Research*.

Rodman B. Webb is Professor of Education at the University of Florida, where he teaches courses in qualitative research methods and the sociology of education. He and Robert Sherman are founding editors of the *International Journal of Qualitative Studies in Education*. His major publications include *The Presence of the Past, Making a Difference* (with Patricia Ashton), *Qualitative Research in Education* (edited with Robert Sherman), and *School and Society* (with Robert Sherman). He has published numerous articles, chapters, and book reviews in journals and books published in the United States and Great Britain. His research interests include professional careers, institutional change, and the education of at risk children.